A PORTRAIT OF SLINDON

Published in 2002 by

WOODFIELD PUBLISHING
Woodfield House, Babsham Lane, Bognor Regis
West Sussex PO21 5EL, England.

ISBN 1-903953-57-8

A Portrait of

SLINDON

JOSEPHINE DUGGAN REES

Woodfield Publishing

Slindon from the air, c.1960.

CONTENTS

INTRODUCTION .... *iii*

PREFACE .... *v*

Illustration acknowledgements .... *vi*

I.   Setting the Scene.. 1

II.   The Charter, Administration & Archbishops........... 10

III.   The Kempes at Slindon House 27

IV.   The Countess of Newburgh 33

V.   Jimmy Dean, Slindon Chronicler 45

VI.   After the Newburghs.................................... 62

VII.   Churches & Schools 82

VIII.   Properties.. 110

IX.   Shops, Industries, Businesses & Crafts.................. 129

X.   Transport, Water & Amenities 148

XI.   Slindon Cricketers.................................... 158

XII.   More Sports, Organisations & Occasions 169

XIII.   Writers & Personalities........................... 178

XIV.   Woods, Downs & Wildlife 202

XV.   Smugglers & Ghosts................................ 222

BIBLIOGRAPHY 229

INDEX 231

Books of Local Interest fom Woodfield Publishing............... 237

Jimmy Dean, the Slindon Chronichler
(see Chapter V, p.45.)

INTRODUCTION

This is a new and updated edition of Josephine Duggan Rees's much-appreciated book about Slindon, first published by the author herself in 1969, with revised editions in 1974 and 1988. This is the (somewhat belated) 'Millennium edition', revised and updated, which it has been my pleasure and privilege to publish.

Mrs Duggan Rees first came to Slindon with her husband in 1952, on his appointment as farm manager at Court Hill Farm, where they lived for over 27 years until his retirement, during which time they both made a significant contribution to the life of the village.

Mrs Duggan Rees developed a deep interest in the history of Slindon and over a period of many years gathered a wealth of information in whatever spare time her busy life as farmer's wife and mother to a growing family would allow. The resultant book was very well received by Slindonians, their friends and relations, and many others from further afield with an affection for the village. It is hoped that this new and revised edition will be similarly well received.

Modestly, Mrs Duggan Rees has left herself and her family out of her history of Slindon, but her contribution, both in writing the various editions of this book and in acting as Slindon's correspondent for the *Chichester Observer* and *West Sussex Gazette* for many years, should not go without mention. Like Jimmy Dean, whose writings from the Victorian and Edwardian eras form an integral part of this book, she has acted as village chronicler and thanks to her efforts the activities of many of her contemporary inhabitants of Slindon have become part of the historical record.

She should also be added to the list of Slindon's notable authors, for this is not her only book. *Corduroy Days*, a delightful account of her youthful days in the Women's Land Army during World War II was published in 1998, and *Boys & Other Animals*, an equally entertaining and humorous account of her life as a farmer's wife and mother in Slindon during the 1950s and 60s is to be published this year. I can heartily recommend these books, but then, as it has been my good fortune to publish both of them[1] perhaps this goes without saying!

As we move into a new century, the landscape of Sussex is under threat as never before, due to the decline in agriculture and ever-increasing government pressure to build thousands of new residential properties in our little corner of England. The last 25 years have seen many ancient farms turned into 'business parks' and barns, cowsheds and piggeries become 'character homes' for the well-to-do, sold for sums that would have bought a country estate just a few years ago. Vast new housing developments sprawl out from many towns and villages and there are plans for many more. At this rate, in 50 years time there will be little or nothing left of the Sussex that Jimmy Dean knew. We can only wonder what he would have made of it all...

While most other villages and towns in Sussex have changed beyond recognition, thanks to the benevolent influence of the National Trust, the heart of Slindon has remained relatively unaffected, making it an ever more precious jewel among Sussex villages. Long may it continue to be so.

Nick Shepperd, 2002.

---

[1] *Corduroy Days* and *Boys and Other Animals* are both published by Woodfield Publishing. Full details on page 237.

PREFACE

This book is called a portrait rather than a history because it is not the purely documentary work usually implied by the latter term. It is a collection of varied material intended for the pleasure and some enlightenment of those who enjoy Slindon today and are curious about its past and those who love to remember, nostalgically, some of that past.

There are many people to whom my thanks are due for help they have given me in compiling this history.

I am grateful to the late Martin Venables FRS and to Mr A.F. Oaten, Dr A.G. Woodcock and the staffs of the County Reference Library and the West Sussex Record Office, Chichester; to past Slindonians for their knowledge and memories and to those today who have given their time and assistance; to my late friend Arthur Russell for correcting the original text, to Dr John Vickers for the original indexing, and to Denis McQuoid for drawing the map.

I gratefully acknowledge permission from Lady Iddesleigh to use excerpts from the writings of her mother and grandmother, Madame Belloc Lowdes and Madame Bessie Parkes Belloc and the poem 'The Nameless Knight' by Hilaire Belloc; Mr Maurice Burn MA, LLB for the benefit of some of his research into the history of the Leslie family and extracts from Slindon in the Old Days; Mr John Apps for his article on the great storm of 1987 and the West Sussex Gazette and Chichester Observer for use of excerpts from their files. Also Mr Timothy McCann for excerpts from his article in the Journal of the Cricket Society Vol.10 (1981) and Mr Brian Bannister for information from his Post graduate study for Architectural Association 1991, The Restoration of St Marys 1866/7. JDR

Illustration acknowledgements

I am indebted to Miss Jane Reid for permission to reproduce her drawings of Elm Cottage and The Pottery; to Mr. Lou Friend for his drawing of the Post Office and to the following for the reproduction of photographs and lithographs:

St. Mary's Church (before restoration)	Mrs. Mary Izard
St. Mary's Church (interior, present day)	
Slindon C of E School 1874	
The Rev. Wm. Chantler Izard	
The Countess of Newburgh	Mrs. E. Wingate
Jimmy Dean	Southdown Observer Series
The Silver Queen	Mrs. A. Hilton
Slindon Beeches	Mr. C. Foster
The Mill on the Downs	Mr. A. Palmer
The Grange	Francois Barker
Madame Belloc	Madame S. Lowndes Marques
Beachlines, Slindon Park	J.J. O'Hea
Slindon Forge	Cherry Alexander

I. Setting the Scene

Outlined against the hillside, commanding splendid views of the coastal plain, Slindon, flint-walled and girdled by beech woods, has been described as "the most Sussex of Sussex villages". It is perhaps one of the most picturesque and historic of the many lovely and historic villages in the county. With 3,500 acres of beautiful farm and estate land, it is today the property of the National Trust.

The *Victoria History of the County of Sussex* describes Slindon as "a ring or loop of roads to the east of the Parish Church, with a tail at the south end." From Slindon's Top Road, running parallel with the Downs, is slung the loop consisting of Church Hill, Church Road and School Hill. Reynolds Lane forms the tail leading down to the A29. The area between the A29 and A27 comprises Slindon Common.

In 1984 the Parish boundary was extended southward to the A27 and eastward to include Shellbridge Road and a portion of woodland, absorbing approximately 90 hectares that was formerly in the Parish of Walberton and 9 hectares from the Parish of Tortington.

Mill Lane, leading from Top Road to the Downs, with Mill House on one corner and Mill Cottage on the other, has not for some two hundred years, led to a mill. Previously a post mill stood on the edge of the Downs, on the site of one that was rebuilt, according to the *Victoria History of Sussex*, in 1456. When it became overtopped by trees, it was removed with horses and wagon to Slindon Common, where there is still a Mill Farm and

a Mill Road, names that remain although the mill was dismantled in 1906.

The old post mill at Slindon Common, dismantled 1906.

The old flint-built cattle-pound at the end of Mill Lane, restored by the National Trust, is reminiscent of the days when
cattle were driven across the Downs from Portsmouth to Chichester and London and strays were impounded. Cattle grazing or

resting on the Downs were a familiar sight in the 19th century. The families of Fleets, Collins and Roberts of Slindon were drovers.

A rough track continues from Mill Lane over the Downs to Bignor. The lane curves right-handed and from here a fine view of the coastal plan can be enjoyed. From 130ft at the south edge of the village an elevation of 650ft is reached at this point, before declining steeply past Baycombe Woods to the A29, on the other side of which are Rewell Woods, part of the Duke of Norfolk's estate.

Because of its close proximity to woods and Downs, Slindon has always been a favourite area for horse riders. Single riders, strings of hacks from riding establishments and horses from racing stables are daily seen exercising through the village and along the bridle paths. There is always plenty of work for Slindon's farrier.

At the junction of Top Road and Church Hill stands an ancient lime tree encircled by a wooden seat. Inscriptions testify that the seat is in memory of Mr F. Wootton Isaacson (who bequeathed Slindon House and Estate to the National Trust in 1949) and of his sister Violet, Lady Beaumont. When the original became dilapidated, it was renewed by the Trust.

Here the cottages end, but the road continues, the line of its flint walls broken only by the entrances to the Roman Catholic Church of St Richard and St Richard's House on the right. Opposite, the lofty Tudor chimneys and green copper cupolas of Slindon House rise above the walls, overtopped here with fine old ilex trees while, beyond the church, the delicate tracery of beech branches overhangs the road. Adding to the charm of the old walls, clumps of fern sprout from between the flints, with trails of crimson ivy and cascades of dainty ivy-leaved toadflax.

By the driveway of Slindon House the road bends southward to Eartham and Chichester, while a track to the north leads across the Downs to meet with the one from Mill Lane, and a road bends steeply under tall beeches to Court Hill Farm, once the home of Hilaire Belloc.

Following the Slindon Park boundary as it turns left from the Eartham road, one comes into a delightful wooded lane called Slindon Bottom (although it is actually in the Parish of Aldingbourne). From earliest times, the contours of the village have changed little. The roads are virtually those trodden by medieval Archbishops and serfs; men in rough tunics watered their cattle at the same pond as exists today; goodwives in wimples roasted meat before open hearths where hearths still burn today, for as old cottages decayed, new ones were built on the same sites.

Saxons gathered by their tiny church to hear the news of the Danish raids which continued intermittently in Sussex for nearly two hundred years. They may have seen the sky lit up by many fires as the invaders burned and ravaged the countryside; some would have known of the onslaught repulsed from Chichester in 895, others heard the din of battle raging on Bury Hill in 1009, when the castles of Arundel and Amberley were destroyed. Men and women would have climbed those same streets to hear that Harold had set sail from Bosham and when Wiiliam the Conqueror landed at Hastings.

But long before these events took place the scene was set by a geological phenomenon. One hundred and twenty million years ago there began a thrusting up of the chalk seabed with its underlying sands and gravel, which resulted in an elongated dome, curving from what is now Hampshire in the west, to Calais, in France, in the east and forming the South Downs. The chalk, which along with flint is the geological characteristic of these

Downs and therefore of Slindon, was formed through the ages by the shells of minute organisms called *foraminifera*, which lived in the sea and as they died, sank to the bottom. Flint, formed at the same period, was the result of chemical segregation in the matrix and was closely related to the decay of sponges on the sea floor. There, contained siliceous spicules attracted more free silica to form a nodule of flint. The fact that sponges periodically died in large numbers accounts for the definite strata of flint in the chalk.

Many ages after the formation of the Downs, less than a million years ago, raised beaches were thrown up all along the foot of these downs, exactly resembling the Sussex beaches of today, from the shingle beds of beach-rolled pebbles to the lug-sand exposed at low tide. During this raised beach period, the sea washed against chalk cliffs at Slindon.

The old beach lines near the south boundary of Slindon Park can be clearly seen from the air, while parts of the shoreline can be traced in quarries and gravel pits at intervals between Arundel and Goodwood, the height above sea level varying from 70 ft. to 135 ft. This higher level is considered to be a storm beach. The beaches are now only visible where exposed in gravel-pits, owing to the deposit of 'Coombe rock', so called because it was formed in the dry valleys or coombes in the chalk, which buried them as it spread out from the Downs over the coastal plain.

The brickearth was deposited on the South Sussex plain after this period, toward the end of the ice age, about 8,000 BC. A final washing down of silts from the Downs (many so-called Brickearths were formed in this way) accounts for the occasional seams of good loam that break across the light chalky soil in the Slindon area.

At the lower end of the village the chalk gives way to sand and gravel. Underlying the gravel of Slindon Common and the chalk of the Downs is clay, at the lower levels no more than two feet down. In this clay subsoil, as in the chalk, are numerous flints, also many marine fossils, a legacy from the period when this area was under the sea. Most common are the 'shepherd's crowns' – sea urchins changed into flint millions of years ago that still show the dots where the spines of the living creatures once grew. These fossils had a superstitious value in the Neolithic Age and afterwards, when it was believed that their presence would protect persons and animals. Collections of them were buried with the dead and placed on windowsills to protect the homes.

Flints enclosing traces of fossilised sponge are also found. One sent to the British Museum in 1948 was identified as "a flint nodule enclosing traces of exceptionally large fossil sponge. The traces are preserved in a bluish silica called chalcedony."

In 1928, Mr E.M. Venables, Fellow of the Geological Society and palaeontologist, found a fossilised *Nautilus Atlanta* weighing 90 lbs on the Downs near Bignor. It was the only example of the species to have been found in Britain at that time and is now in the British Museum.

The earliest evidence of human habitation in the Slindon area belongs to the Palaeolithic (Old Stone Age) period and can be dated to some 300,000 years BC. A nomadic hunting people, their remains have been found in the NW of Slindon Park, associated with the raised beach, which bordered a small inlet (now a dry valley) when the sea level was some 100-130 feet higher than the present day.

In 1973, archaeologists under the direction of Mr A.G. Woodcock, then curator of Chichester City Museum, began excavating the site of the Palaeolithic camp. The flint implements found included hand-axes and scrapers, which now form part of the Museum collection. These nomadic people may have stayed only a few days in the camp. Their practice of making tools where and when they needed them rather than carrying them from place to place accounts for the number found on this and other sites.

An unexpected find resulting from the dig, in a higher stratum, was a flint sickle blade of the Bronze Age. The next people who left traces in the archaeological record belonged to the Mesolithic (Middle Stone Age) period, which lasted in this country from about 8,000 to 3,500 BC. It was during this time that the English Channel was formed and Britain became an island for the last time. These people were hunters and gatherers. They skilfully worked small tools out of carefully struck flat blades and used them to tip arrows and spears. They also invented the shape of the axe as we know it today, in the form of shaped flints which they sharpened with a transverse or 'tranchet' blow. The artefacts left behind by these people are quite common in the Slindon area.

The first traces of permanent settlement come with the arrival of the Neolithic (New Stone Age) groups from the continent. This later Stone Age man was the first to polish his flint implements, and some fine specimens of these have been found in the fields of Slindon.

From this time on, man left his decisive imprint on the land. The whole Slindon Estate, looked at from the air, is a palimpsest of earthworks, barrows and settlement sites of all periods. There is scarcely any part of the landscape which is untouched. Flint mines to reach the higher quality seams of flint within the chalk, long barrows over the graves of the dead, and an earthwork of the characteristic type known as a causewayed camp, witness the presence of the Neolithic peoples. This ten-acre settlement known as Barkhale Camp, is situated on a spur of Bignor Hill in the North East corner of the estate. Pottery found during an excavation of the site is in Barbican House Museum in Lewes.

The parish can also boast one of the sixteen examples of a Covered Way, (type of earthwork) to be found in Sussex.

Many round barrows mark the graves of the Bronze Age. The massive network of field systems and boundaries is testimony to the predominantly agricultural exploitation of the area for the past 5,000 years.

The Romans found the region particularly attractive and there is evidence of a villa of about 4 to 5 acres on the edge of the village. Stane Street, one of their principal trunk roads, passes through the north west corner of the parish. The road was the direct route from *Noviomagus* (Chichester) to *Londinium* (London). The three miles between Seabeach (Eartham) to Gumber Corner is the best preserved section of the whole road. It is constructed of seven layers of varying mixtures of turf and mould, chalk and flints, gravel and sand, all of which the Romans would have found near at hand. There were also secondary and third class roads, not laid out or engineered but merely native trails, which connected the hill farms. Roman coins and pottery have been found on the estate, a bronze thimble in one of the village gardens and a stone coffin containing bones in a glass jar with several objects which belonged to the deceased.

Romano-British farmsteads are common on the downland to the north of the village, where the medieval peasant settled.

In recent years, the examination of aerial photographs has led to a number of new discoveries of Iron Age settlements on the Slindon Estate, including the remains of an unrecorded Iron Age hill fort to the north of the village. The same photographs also revealed many first century military Roman sites, possibly from the invasion period of AD43. The Roman military sites consist of a number of marching camps two ludi,[2] a possible *gyrus* (lunge ring) and other sites as yet not fully identified, of which one may be the remains of a Roman fort.

There is a road running from the Iron Age hill fort to Havant, passing through Court Hill Farm, a few metres from the farmhouse front door. Another Roman road runs from Court Hill Farm to Walberton, about two miles south of Slindon to join an east-west Roman road.

There are several other Roman side roads and tracks, one of which runs from Slindon Park, through the village north of St Mary's Church, on towards Baycombe Lane.

When this evidence is coupled with the archaeological finds of the region, Slindon has an exceptionally rich and interesting foundation to its later history.

Slindon Foll as it was in 1819 by Nicholas Duggan Rees.

---

[2] *Ludus* = Roman amphitheatre.

II.   The Charter, Administration & Archbishops

After the Romans withdrew in 407 AD, the village probably lay deserted for a hundred years before the Saxons came. Although it was not their habit to settle on old Roman sites, they were perhaps attracted to this one, like other tribes before them, by the pond with a spring and the excellent position for seeing approaching animals and enemies.

They would have lived in a collection of one-roomed thatched huts made of mud and straw with a timber frame. These people did not acquire the art of building in brick and stone, like the Romans, until much later. They practised pagan rites, remaining aloof from the teaching of St Augustine (who brought the Gospel to Kent) and other apostles from the north and west, until St Wilfrid, formerly Bishop of York, was driven from his diocese and came southward to Selsey. There he established a monastery on land granted to him by Aethelwalh, King of the South Saxons, whence he travelled with his preachers to the villages of Sussex and possibly, although there is no record of this, to Slindon.

In 683, Caedwalla, of the West Saxons, conquered the South Saxons and Aethelwalh was killed. In the time of oppression that followed, Caedwalla, although a ruthless and barbaric pagan, did not impede the work of the Church and in 685 he made a pilgrimage to Rome and was baptised. At his death three days later he made three benefactions to Wilfrid, the first being the grant of a large estate in Pagham and the neighbouring villages which included Slindon.

In 686, Wilfrid donated Caedwalla's gift to the See of Canterbury in the person of Archbishop Theodore, who succeeded to the See in 668 and died in 690, and the estate, except for one brief interlude, belonged to the See until Archbishop Cranmer exchanged it with Henry VIII for other possessions. Although Pagham, at first, was the summer residence of the Archbishops, the manor at Slindon was afterwards chosen.

Caedwalla's charter is preserved in the British Museum. The document is of a later date than the original transaction of which the record, it is supposed, may have been burned during the ravages of the Danes, but the copy appears to have been written in Saxon times. A beautiful 16th century transcription is in the Bodleian Library at Oxford; this includes Slindon and the gift of St. Wilfrid, and there is another, of the 14th century, in the records of Chichester Cathedral.

Slindon, both in Saxon and Norman times, was assessed at 8 hides (a hide being approximately 120 acres or, in origin, the area ploughed in one year by one full team of eight oxen.) In Domesday, Slindon is recorded as being in the Hundred of Beneslede (probably Binsted) in the Rape of Arundel, but later, as a peculiar of the Archbishops of Canterbury, it was recorded in the Hundred of Pagham (later of Aldwick) in the Rape of Chichester.

Originally the hundred was an area containing a hundred heads of households, who formed a body responsible for maintaining order in their district and supporting the king in war. In due course this developed into an organ of local government.

The division of Sussex into Rapes came later with the Normans, who made six of these areas, each having a strip of coastline, a piece of downland for grazing, a river and a stretch of forest for hunting and the feeding of hogs.

It appears from a study of Lindsay Fleming's *History of Pagham* that:

> "The Hundred of Pagham, which became the Hundred of Aldwick in the 14th century, comprised from early times the districts of North and South Bersted, Shripney, Bognor, Aldwick, Charlton (now under the sea) Nyetimber, Crimshaw and North and South Mundham to which became added Slindon, Tangmere and the Pallant in Chichester. The latter three were only joined for administrative convenience."

Later the Bailiwick of Pagham arose, in the reign of Henry VI when the See of Canterbury was organised into such divisions for the purposes of collecting the revenues. It comprised Pagham, Nyetimber, Slindon, Shripney, Bersted, Aldwick, Bognor, Crimshaw, Charlton, Mundham, Lavant, Tangmere, and Tarring. These divisions were abolished in the reign of Elizabeth. Another organisation, now defunct, was the Deanery of Pagham, Bersted, Lavant, Tangmere, Slindon and All Saints in the Pallant, Chichester.

The Deanery possessed a seal. There is a note in Archbishop Simon Islep's (died 1366) Register that Sir John, Rector of Slindon, Dean of Pagham, relinquished his office and handed his seal of the Deanery to Master John de Carleton, Chancellor of the Archbishop.

At the Norman Conquest, Slindon Manor was granted to Earl Roger de Montgomery, nephew and favourite captain of the Conqueror, created Earl of Arundel, and he is recorded in Domesday Book as its lord. The name of the village was then Eslindon; eslin meaning 'chieftain of the tribe' and don meaning 'a hill'. By 1106, the name had become Slindune.

In *Place Names of Sussex*, Mawer and Stenton give the name Eslindon with occasionally 'y' replacing the 'i', also Slingdon from *slinu*, slope, hill or dun.

Another interpretation is derived from coupling the name Slindon with the similar Slinfold. The Saxon chieftain liked to establish his settlement along the coast, but the coastal districts did not offer sufficient 'pannage' to feed the herds of swine, which constituted his main wealth, and he was obliged to keep them further inland. So we get Slin*don*, which was the home or *don* of a chieftain named perhaps Slind or Sling, and Slin*fold*, which was the fold of Slind's herds of swine. Other examples in Sussex are Cowdown and Cowfold, and there are many more.

The following is the entry for Slindon in Domesday Book:

The same Hugh holds Eslindone of the Earl. A certain freeman Azor held it in the time of King Edward. Then and now it vouched for 8 hides. There is land for 8 ploughs. In demesne is one plough and a half and 23 villeins and 12 cottars with 7 ploughs. There is a church. In the time of King Edward it was worth £20 and afterwards, and now, £16.

In 1106 the Manor was restored to the See of Canterbury by Henry I at the request of Archbishop Anselm, to be held at two knights fees. (This meant that the cost of equipping two knights had to be met by the lord of the manor). The Charter of Henry I records the gift of Slindon by that king, stating that for some time it had been alienated from the Church. For the next 436 years, Slindon was associated with many eminent clerics.

St. Anselm, created Archbishop in 1903 by William Rufus, often stayed at Slindon and it is probable that Thomas a Becket did also. A path through the shrubbery from Slindon House to St Mary's Church is known to this day as 'St. Thomas a Becket's Walk'.

13

Archbishop Stephen Langton died at Slindon House in 1228 and his body was conveyed to Canterbury. His death is commemorated in St Mary's Church by a plaque, given in 1935 by a descendant of his family. He is credited with being the first to divide the Bible into chapters, but is chiefly remembered in connection with his efforts in obtaining the Magna Carta.

St Edmund Rich, who became Archbishop in 1234, defended the English Church against Henry III and died in 1240. Chichester's saint, St Richard of Wycke, continued St Edmund's work and was reduced to poverty. The two men, who were lifelong friends, are incorporated in the statuary under the High Altar in St Richard's Church, Slindon.

Archbishop John Peckham spent a lot of time at the manor and held ordinations in the House chapel in 1288 and 1291. Letters of John Peckham were dated from Slindon in 1281 and 1283. Peckham was unfortunate in succeeding to the archiepiscopal estates when they were just recovering from the effects of civil war and three years vacancy following Boniface's death (Archbishop Peckham, *Decima Doucie*). Although the accounts of Kilwardy, who preceded him, show that he undertook repairs to many manors, including Slindon, Peckham still found the residences in a dilapidated condition.

In 1421 in the chapel at Slindon, Archbishop Chicheley confirmed the election of Thomas Ludlowe as Abbott of Battle.

It is very probable that the great John Morton, Cardinal, Archbishop of Canterbury, also resided at the manor, as did Sir Thomas More when serving as a page in the Archbishop's household.

It is uncertain which of the Archbishops built a 'palace' at Slindon on which the present Slindon House now stands. Chichester Record Office gives the date 1108 for Slindon House, which suggests St Anselm as the builder. Elsewhere there is reference to 'Anselm's house'.

Archaeological Collections, Col. 23, p.211, says that Slindon House was one of the more important archiepiscopal residences, built in the early 13th century, supposedly by Stephen Langton.

Because Slindon belonged to the See of Canterbury, at no time was any part in the possession of the monks of Boxgrove, as were many Parishes in the vicinity of the Priory. The only reference to Slindon in the Boxgrove cartulary (in Lindsay Fleming's translation No. 27) is a deed of Stephen Langton dated 1223 4 and delivered at Slindon, confirming to the Monks at Boxgrove, the various churches, tithes etc. granted by Robert de la Haye to William and Roger St. John.

In a Parish survey compiled by the children of Slindon C of E Primary School in 1948 are the following extracts from the Canterbury Cathedral Archives:[3]

> *"Richard, by the Grace of God (etc.) Archbishop of Canterbury to all faithful sons of the Mother church, greetings.*
>
> *"We have heard (etc.) complaint of our beloved sons Godard, the Rector of the church at Slyndon and of Alexander, the chaplain, vicar of the same church saying that our ministers have unjustly denied the rights and privileges of the church in woods and pastures granted by Theobald to Godard aforesaid church, by Charter.*
>
> *"The terms of said Charter not being very clear, we had an investigation on the witness of faithful and honest men, both clerical and lay and discovered that, in the time of the knights who held the village (villam) before the aforesaid Theobold and*

---

[3] *Charta Antiqua* No. 5.354. This is a copy made late 13th or 14th century of a document drawn up in the time of Archbishop Richard, Becket's successor, Archbishop of Canterbury 1174-1184.

the glorious martyr Thomas that the said church had everything necessary from the wood of the said village and it had in the pasture (the common pasture of the village) 2 horses, 8 oxen, 60 sheep, lambs in the corn, pigs in the stubble and at the time of pannage it had 10 pigs in the village and 5 in the weald. (Slyndon in keeping with other villages had pig runs in the Weald).

"The rectors of the said church may erect houses etc on the ground belonging to the church."

There followed more about the rights of the church ending with:

"We grant an indulgence of 10 days each year to those who come to pray and make an offering to the said church if fully confessed."

From Cathedral Archives, Canterbury *Charta Antiqua* 5.39:

"To all whom these presents shall come etc. Thomas, Cardinal Archbishop of Canterbury, greeting, know ye that we have for his good service, granted to William Broke the Office of Keeper of our Manor of Slyndon in Sussex, and of our gardens there. He is to receive from us 2d per day together with the other profits and emoluments of his office given at Lambeth 20th November 1469."

Confirmed by John Prior of Christchurch Canterbury Thomas Bourchier, Archbishop of Canterbury (1454-1486).

"Grant by Archbishop Henry (Chichester) to Hugh, the arbalaster, of the office of Keeper of the part of the manor of Slyndon and of the manor, woods etc. 12th October 1441." [4]

Manumission of a nativus (villein) by the Archbishop of his demesne of Slyndon:

---

[4] Archives Folio F43:

"John, Archbishop of Canterbury etc. know ye that we have freed John Burre of Slyndon from all bondage and yoke of servitude and of villeinage and will that he shall be free. Lambeth, 12th November 1450."

The school children found further reference to Slindon in the Sussex Archaeological Collection.

One of the well known series of letters from Simon de Senlis, astute steward of Ralph Nevill, Bishop of Chichester and Chancellor of England informs his master that the Archbishop Richard Wethershed (1229-34) will be coming to Sussex in the following Lent and intends to journey from Slindon to Tarring.

"As long as the Archbishop stayed at Slindon he was well supplied from your manors of Aldingbourne and Amberley."[5]

In 1258 Pope Innocent IV gave additional benefice to Richarde de Clifforde, Rector of Slindon.[6]

Pope Gregory IV was unwilling to relinquish the hold on the English Church that Henry III and his father King John had given his predecessor and in 1240 sent an order to Archbishop Rich to provide 300 Italian clergy with the first vacant benefices. When twenty-four foreign priests came to his gate clamouring for livings, the old cleric fled and came to Slindon accompanied by Richard of Wyke, and thence to Chichester and sailed to France. A national party arose, "England for the English," Archbishop Rich at its head.

Elsewhere it is said that Chicheley confirmed the electing of Thomas Luden as Abbott of Battle in 1421 while at Slindon.

A volume issued by the Sussex Record Society[7] throws some light on the lives of the tenants of the Archbishops in the 13th

---

[5] Vol. 44, p 191.
[6] Vol. 44, p. 187 (The Life of St. Richard).

century, many of whom owed duties when the Archbishop visited his properties. Among the tasks of certain tenants were:

"He shall summon the lord's guests to food."

"He shall carry the lord's venison when he moves from Slyndon to the dwelling place at which he lodges."

Carrying services listed (1280) include "carting of two cartloads of hay to Slindon and one cartload of underwood from Slyndon to Nytimber" also "to fill the Archbishop's larder with venison from Slindon Park."

In Doucie's *Archbishop Peckham* are the following extracts:

"At Slindon 4 days work a week was done by the virgate holders. Cottars also did week work which in spite of the smallness of their holdings was often in excess of that done by the villeins."

"There was at Slindon an archiepiscopal charwoman, Emma atte Pette, who had her holding free of rent and a certain quantity of barley in return for cleaning the hall, chapel, bakery, kitchen and other rooms as well as collecting apples, shearing sheep and doing certain carrying services."

"The general impression was of a well established tradition of administration which worked both efficiently and benevolently. The Archbishop provided the seed for the sowing of his lands and the wood for the making of hurdles, enclosures and building and repair works; and although certain services were done free, the meals in return for others were on a generous scale. Moreover, the villeins at Slindon, besides the usual Christmas, Easter and Pentecost holidays were allowed one months sick leave in the year."

---

[7] *---ostumals of the Sussex Manors of the Archbishops of Canterbury.*

"In 1401 the King granted an extension of power to the Archbishops over his tenants. Nearly all of these Cranmer relinquished in 1542. It would seem from this that some Archbishops were hard Landlords: e.g. the strict provision that a tenant "cannot marry himself or marry his sons and daughters without leave, nor sell for himself a foal he has foaled, if male."

Nor according to Horsfield[8] was their integrity always infallible:

"In 1330 a Proctor of the Pope was confined for three days at the prison attached to the mansion of Petworth, having attempted to serve a writ on the Archbishop at Slindon. The Archbishop's retainers maltreated the Proctor and his men and pursued the former over the hills. The Archbishop was later excommunicated on the suspicion of having connived at these doings."

There was not always harmony, either, between the Archbishop's household and the villagers, according to a letter from Colonel C.S. Leslie of Slindon House (undated) to Revd William Chantler Izard, Rector of Slindon:

"Lives of the Archbishop of Canterbury gives an amusing account of a regular scrimmage between the Archbishop's servants and some of the country people. One poor wretch got an awful licking."

Because Slindon Park, which dates from the time of Henry I, adjoined the Forest of Arundel, disputes arose between the Earls and Archbishops over their respective hunting rights, until an agreement was reached whereby the Archbishop was allowed to take one deer a year from Arundel forest, with greyhounds, not with the bow, while the Earl agreed to pay yearly into the Archbishop's larder, thirteen bucks and thirteen does. The places called Overs and Baycombe in the woods were to be unenclosed

---

[8] *Churches and Manors of West Sussex.*

so that the deer could pass freely, and the Earl must not enclose any part of the forest adjoining the wood.

The arrangement was confirmed, in 1259, by Edward I, but later, in the time of Archbishop Langham 1366, the payment of deer was commuted to a money payment of £160 and 20 marks as annual rent.

The good Archbishops were well aware of the needs of the flesh and the episcopal larder lacked very little. In 1302, when Edward I halted at Slindon on one of his journeys through Sussex, he drew supplies which included many casks of wine, beef, mutton, several pigs, four swans and two peacocks. The swans would have come from Pagham Harbour, where they were reared and zealously guarded as the property of the Archbishops.

In 1344 Archbishop John appointed Roger de Spyney his huntsman and keeper of the park, warren and outwoods of Slindon, to receive weekly a bushel of wheat, half a bushel of barley for his groom, and 13s 4d yearly for his robe and shoe leather.

In 1451, the lands of the manor were farmed by Robert Huberden for an annual rent of £26.13.4d. In 1535 it was valued at £37.18.11d. Of this sum fixed rates accounted for £20.10.6d and the farm of the demesne was said to be worth £4.1.4d, the perquisites of court £4.11.4d and the Farm Mill £1.6.8d. The farm of the demesne was the home farm, the part of the manor, which was the property of the lord and the whole of whose produce was sent to him; whereas the term 'in demesne' meant that the Archbishop retained the lands as well as the lordship in his own hands.

There are earlier references to the farm mill than in the above valuation. In the account of the Keepers of the Archbishopric, in the king's hands on the death of Archbishop Winchelsey, for the period 13th May to 21st October 1313, is reference under the heading Bailiwick of Pagham to the mills of Slindon and Nytimber. The expenses include 4s.10½d in 'repairs of divers defects of the mills'. From other accounts during vacancies of the See (1313-1314) receipts of the Bailiwick of Pagham included £4.1.0d. from the Mill at Slindon. Further excerpts from these accounts appear in Mr Fleming's history of the Hundred. In 1453, when the farmer of Bersted was William Purdeux, liveries included 48s.0d to Robert Aylewyn, parker of Slindon.

1454 Bersted was relet to William Purdeux. The farmer was allowed 6s.8d for two cartloads of hay, with carriage to Slindon, for the horses of the auditor, and at other times on the Lord's business.

1457-1458   the accounts of Thomas Mutlow, chamberlain, include 2s, the price of a sword in the custody of the parker of Slindon.

1458-1459   Perquisites of Court returned by the chamberlain were £9.7.2d. Of this sum, 12s was allowed, the price of an ox as heriot because it was given to the parker at Slindon to be kept until sold. Also in this roll the Bersted farmer was allowed 9s for three cartloads of hay supplied to the parker at Slindon, Robert Aylewyn, two for the use of Aylewyn and the other for the lords and ministers on the same occasion.

From an earlier roll, period November 1327 to October 1328, is an account of the sale of grain and livestock from the manors of Lavant, Tangmere, Nytimber, Bersted, Shripney and Slindon amounting to £173.3.10½d.

From a detailed study of these accounts, from subsidy assessments and other records, a complete survey could be compiled

of all payments made to the Archbishops. The following is a list
of Contributors to Subsidy in Slindon in 1327:[9]

Stephano de Lucy	2s.0d.	Rico Alayn	4s.0d.
John atte Lanecude	4s.0d.	Thomas Maroyn	7d.
John le Wheghler	2s. 0d.	Rico de Mallyng	1s.0d.
Her Mazoun	6d.	Rico Sopere	1s.6d.
Willo Burton	1s.0d.	Johne Burry	7s.4d.
Willo Person	1s.0d.	Rico Stapeler	7s.4d.
Relicta Baron	6d.	Johne de Wode	9d.
Adam West	7s.4d.	Willo Plashudde	4s. 0d.
Thomas Wydesparre	2s.0d.	Ad' le Wogher	1s.6d.
Robto Crul	1s.0d.	John Rounifold	1s.0d.
Willo Mareschal	9d.	Rico Whithurst	1s.0d.
Walto Garlaund	2s.6d.	John Felip	2s.0d.
Rico ate Purie	1s.0d.	John Hundeshole	1s.6d.
		Total £2.0s.6½d	
	Ditto 1332: Total for Slindon £2.16s.11d.		

It appears that in the 13th century Slindon also contributed to
a National Tax known as the King's Tax. In the old Court Rolls of
Sussex are listed the names of those who paid this tax in each
parish. In the Sussex Archaeological Collection, Vol. 50 it is recorded that Slyndon paid £4.2.4d.

After 1333 the tax became a fixed amount, towns paying one
tenth of their value and villages one fifteenth and no further records were kept.

In 1310, Boniface of Slindon was appointed Collector of Sea-
ford Port as well as of Chichester and in all the ports between
this town and Portsmouth.

Local Government in the middle ages was comparable in effi-
ciency to that of today and in respect of the tithing system, even
had certain advantages.

---

[9] The Sussex Record Society, Vol. X.

Lindsay Fleming,[10] gives a detailed description of the local justice and the courts of these times. Briefly, there were the Manorial Courts, which recorded transfers of land, ascertained the lord's dues, affirmed the king's regulations, enforced the manorial customs, settled disputes and kept order. There were also the courts of the Hundred. These dealt with private pleas, such as the case of Thomas Stakyer and Jon Rayner. Thomas complained that Jon had detained 2 shillings for 4 bushels of barley malt bought of him in October 1485 at Slindon. The defendant acknowledged the dues and was ordered to pay, with 6d damages. There were three classes of courts, the View of Frankpledge, View with Hundred, and Hundred Courts. These dealt with three types of business: that of a hundred; of a Manorial Court; and of a Court Leet or Petty Criminal Court. 'Views' had special cognisance of royal rights. Associated with them was the whole tithing system, whereby the whole tithing was made responsible when the culprit could not be discovered.

In the 13th century, the judicial powers of the Archbishop were still unimpaired; but royal justices, owing to the constitutional reforms of Henry II, were enlarging their authority. Assizes were held at Chichester or Lewes. These were by no means the forerunners of the proceedings we know today, presided over by specially appointed judges. The phrase Chichester Assizes indicates a session of the royal justices itinerant, delegated from the royal court.

Courts were held in Nytimber and Barton Farm until transferred to Aldwick in the 14th century. Other courts were at All Saints Chichester and Wythering among other places, one of

---

[10] *History of Pagham*, Vol 2, Part V, Chapters II, XI, and Vol 1 Part 1 Chapters XI and XII.

which could have been Slindon estate according to an item in the chamberlains accounts of the estate 1455-1456:

> "*8s.3d. paid by Richard Aylewyn, collector of the court at Slindon.*"

If indeed there was a Hundred House at Slindon it could perhaps account for the origin of the name Court Hill, although *The Place Names of Sussex* only mentions Courthill (spelt as one word) in the 1587 Rental and offers no explanation of the name.

At these courts, twelve jurors represented the hundred. These jurors and the whole tithing could be punished by fine if the evildoer escaped, or if they in any way were considered slack in their public duties.

Such was the case at the Chichester Assizes in 1285 when Stephen Bygge of Tangmere and John de la Coudre "disputed one with the other" in the field of Tangmere. Stephen killed John. He fled and was outlawed at these pleas. The Hundred incurred the judgement of a murder fine. A further fine was imposed on Slindon and other townships in the Hundred for not attending the inquest.

Periods when the See was vacant and the Archbishopric in the King's hands, gave rise to disputes and disorder which were brought to the courts, especially if the king's representative was unscrupulous, as in the case of Richard de Clifford, who brought action against Nicholas le Bretun, Bailiff under him for the manors of Pagham, Nytimber, Lavant, Tangmere and Slindon. Richard accused Nicholas of having received the issues of these manors and not answering for them. Nicholas maintained that he had not received them. The case failed because a certain John de Middleton whom Richard cited as a witness that these monies had been delivered could not be found, but further court cases between 1279 and 1281, involving Richard and Nicholas, suggested that while he accused his bailiff of withholding monies, he himself was similarly guilty of defrauding the king.

In 1328 a commission was appointed, touching evildoers who entered parks and woods of the Manor of Slindon, possessed of the Hundred of Pagham in the See of Canterbury (in the King's hands during voidance) and felled trees and hunted, carrying away trees and deer.

As the king drew all the revenues during these voidances, a grasping monarch sometimes postponed the consecration of the new Archbishop. Such a period followed the death of Stephen Langton (1228) until the consecration of Richard Wethershed in 1229. He died in 1231 and his successor Edmund Rich was not consecrated until 1234.

Friction between kings and archbishops, which had existed for many centuries, reached culmination in the reign of Henry VIII, when Archbishop Cranmer was forced to yield up, under colour of an exchange (Lindsay Fleming affirms) "many territories and the ancient rights of the See in the Pagham Hundred." In 1542 Cranmer entered a deed of exchange and yielded up Pagham for property in Canterbury. Slindon featured in this exchange.

Only one matter out of the various clauses of the transaction gave rise to dispute. This regarded Slindon. The Archbishop claimed that Sir Garrett Kempe, father of Anthony Kempe who received the grant of Slindon from Philip of Spain and Queen Mary, had wrongfully encroached on Burton Wood, which was not included in the grant but was part of Eartham Parish. The case was heard by Francis Bacon in the High Court, but the Archbishop's claim was dismissed. [11]

---

[11] Pagham History, *ref* 'Reports decided by Francis Bacon in the High Court of Chancery 1617 –21'.

It would appear that Slindon's connection with the Hundred of Pagham (of Aldwick as it was then) continued until 1608, for the Parish is mentioned in the survey of the King's possessions, made by 'Thos Marshall, gent.' in September of that year. When the crown sold the Aldwick Hundred to the City of London in 1630 there is no mention of Slindon in this transaction.

The wooden effigy of Anthony St Ledger in St Mary's church, Slindon.

III.   The Kempes at Slindon House

Slindon now being the property of the Crown, Queen Mary in the first year of her reign, made Sir Anthony St Leger keeper of the park and manor in conjunction with Sir Geoffrey Poole. In 1540 St Leger had been appointed by Henry VIII as Lord Deputy of Ireland. He died in 1558.

There was an earlier connection between Slindon and the St Leger family. Anthony St Leger Esq, of the neighbouring parish of Binsted or Binstead, who died in 1539, requested in his will that he should be interred by the wall of Slindon Parish Church and he is remembered today by an interesting wooden effigy in the church.

The name St Leger is perpetuated in Binsted by a pond named Sellinger's Hole, attached to a farm that once belonged to the Slindon Estate. The pronunciation of St Leger as 'Sellinger' is common in England.

The tenure of Sir Anthony St Leger was brief. In 1552 the estate passed to Sir Thomas Palmer, returning again to the Crown when Sir Thomas was executed for supporting Lady Jane Grey's claim to the throne. At the end of her reign, Mary granted the manor to Anthony Kempe Esq, third son of Sir William Kempe, Knight, of Olantigh in the Parish of Wye, Kent, descendant of the great cleric, Cardinal John Kempe, founder of Wye College.

In 1603 the Kempe family bought Eartham Manor, uniting this property to the Slindon estate for nearly 200 years.

Anthony Kempe's only surviving son, Sir Garrett, rebuilt Slindon Manor in the time of Elizabeth I, constructing within it a secret chapel where mass was held continually for 300 years, even throughout the penal days. All through the Reformation the house remained the stronghold of Catholicism and the Blessed Sacrament was always kept in the chapel. Few details are known about the secret chapel. It is said to have been built in the roof and was not visible from inside or out. Narrow staircases and passages led from it and communicating with the chapel were 'priest's holes' into which someone could lower himself by leather straps and make off through an underground passage. Dr S.H. Arnold mentions three hiding places, one with leather straps, which were visible in 1872.

Sir Garrett was frequently under suspicion on account of his religion but at no time was there conclusive evidence of the indictments against him. In 1644 he was accused of having, during the Civil War, armed two servants and sent them with two horses to Chichester. He was said to have brought up his children as papists and to have absented himself from the county for two years. Although proved not to be a papist he was nevertheless fined £2,931.10.0. In June 1649 four physicians certified that as he was very aged and infirm, he should repair to a spa to take the waters. He went on a pass signed by Fairfax.

The Religious Census of Sussex, 1676, says that Elizabeth, daughter of Sir Edward Caryll and Philippa Gage of Framfield, married Sir Garrett Kempe and founded the Roman Catholic 'mission' at Slindon.

Sir Garrett was succeeded by his son Philip who left no heir, and the manor passed to his brother Garrett. In 1660,[12] it was asserted that the heir to Sir Garrett was Philip Eyre, son of Thomas Eyre and Katherine, daughter and heir of Philip, son of Anthony Kempe. Under the terms of the original grant the

---

[12] According to the *Victoria History of Sussex.*

manor should have reverted to the Crown. It was granted to Walter Fowler but the grant did not take effect and the manor descended to Garret Kempe's grandson, Anthony, who died in 1753.

His only surviving child, Barbara, married James Bartholomew Radcliffe, 4th Earl of Newburgh, born in France in 1725, the son of Charles Radcliffe, who with his brother, James, Earl of Derwentwater, was engaged in the unsuccessful attempts to place the descendants of James II on the throne. Both were executed and their estates forfeited.

James Bartholomew succeeded to the title, 4th Earl of Newburgh, in the right of his mother, Charlotte Maria, Countess of Newburgh, the only daughter and heir of Charles, 2nd Earl of Newburgh, who was the only son and heir of Viscount Kinnaird Garron Levingstone, who died in 1694. He was Sir James Levingstone, a staunch cavalier and one of the gentlemen of the bedchamber of Charles II. He was elevated to the peerage of Scotland as Viscount Newburgh in 1647 and later captained his majesty's bodyguard. He was created Earl of Newburgh, Viscount of Kinnaird, Lord Levingstone of Fracraig, to hold to him and his heirs whatever, by letters patent, dated 1660.[13]

"In the time of the 4th Earl of Newburgh," says James Dallaway, "Slindon House was considered among gentlemens' seats in this country of advantage most eligible, situated upon an eminence of considerable height commanding a maritime view ranging from the Isle of Wight to Brighthelmstone [Brighton]", but of this stately flint edifice, with its eighty-three rooms, 300 windows and 50 chimneys, very little of the early work remains. During repairs in 1870, says Horsfield,[14] an archway, probably of

---

[13] *Burke's Peerage.*
[14] *Churches and Manors of West Sussex.*

the 13th century house and either early English or decorated, was discovered on the west front of the house to the left of the entrance, half underground and only big enough for a man to creep through. The archway in the course of the repairs had to be built up. This may have been the old escape route of the Catholic priests; or it has been said (but the suggestion is improbable) that the passage led from Slindon House to the vaults of the parish church. Some 16th century work can still be seen in the porch of the house and there are some 18th century fireplaces. Before 1791 the turrets were circular; later they were rebuilt in angular style, but during extensive alterations in 1914, the circular turrets were restored.

There still remains today the large handsome hall; its distinctive feature is a minstrels' gallery at one end, with two apertures of Jacobean design, where travelling minstrels used to play.

During alterations in 1914, two ancient windows were discovered high up in the south end of the great hall. The style of construction shows that they were outer windows, not merely squint holes through which to view the hall from an upper storey. Their discovery suggests that the original hall was further south and that a tall, mullioned window beyond the entrance, belonged to this older hall. It is thought that the house, was once far larger (which is proved by what airmen see of the old foundations) and had a central court into which these windows looked. This is but one of the mysteries that surround this old house.

The house chapel, which replaced the secret one built by Sir Garrett, was situated over the great hall, and is described by T.G. Willis[15] as "arched over, having a rich altar over which is a fine picture of Christ taken down from the cross, and on either side a painting of St Peter and St Paul. Here also are all the decorations

---

[15] *Records of Chichester.*

proper for mass." The chapel was taken out during the 1914 alterations.

Among portraits described by Dallaway were those of Sir Garrett Kempe, aged 102; Lady Mary Tudor, given by Charles II to the Countess of Derwentwater (mother of the unfortunate Earl of Derwentwater); and the Beggar of Antwerp, exquisitely finished by Sneyer, a repetition of which was destroyed in the fire at Cowdray.

It is natural that such a house and such a village should have its ghosts, and many ghosts have been conjured up by the lively imagination and fluent pen of Madame Bessie Parkes Belloc, mother of Hilaire Belloc, in the preface of her book *In a Walled Garden*, published in 1895, written when she lived at The Grange, Slindon. She writes of:

> "...a young girl who grew up in the great house 150 years ago; her name was Barbara and so far as I know there exists of her no portrait. In the year 1749 she made a very great marriage. She wedded the son of a famous man who had been executed on Tower Hill three years before. Barbara, who survived what brothers and sisters she may have had, remade her husband's fortunes. I have seen the girl come in with her lover, James Bartholomew, a young man of five and twenty. She wears a sacque: he has a coat of coloured silk and a three-cornered hat. When they are married the bells of the parish church will ring, and so also for the birth of their one boy, Anthony James. Anthony James and his august widow carried on the history of the village for 110 years. Is it wonderful that Barbara and her descendants should inhabit for me the scenes where they were born and died?"

Barbara and her Earl were married in the House Chapel. A daughter born to them died at the age of twenty-seven, unmar-

ried, and is buried in the Kempe vault at Slindon. Barbara outlived her daughter and her husband and died, Dowager
Countess of Newburgh, in 1797.

In Archbishop's *Spectrum*, a manuscript record book at Lambeth Palace Library, mid 18th century, are several notes relevant
to these times:

> *"Slindon – 56 houses; Protestants 185, Papists 85 (including)*
> *the Earl of Newburgh, a young man who married Mr Kemp's*
> *daughter and thence hath a large estate here. Very charitable to*
> *the poor without distinction."*

> *"Captain Burtle, wounded at Culloden and rewarded with £500*
> *a year, never comes to church; intimate with the Dean of Chich-*
> *ester."*

> *"The Hogs Feast given on St. Stephen's Day by Rector to the*
> *whole parish; A Hog of 18 stone, 24 stone of beef, ½HHd of ale,*
> *Do of small beer, 1½ bushel of Meal in Bread etc."*

There are also letters of August 1761 about the dissoluteness of
the people and the negligence of the churchwardens!

IV. The Countess of Newburgh

In 1789, Anthony James, 5th Earl of Newburgh, married Anne, only daughter of Joseph Webb Esq of Northampton and sister to Sir Thomas Webb, Baronet. The marriage took place in London by special licence, but Slindon had its share of the festivities when the carriages from Slindon House brought home the Earl and his bride and the whole village turned out to welcome them.

The Countess took the Sussex village to her heart and appointed herself its guardian and benefactress. Every facet of village life became her concern, from the provision of an annual gift of bread to the poor (this was received on Maundy Thursday at the Parish Church in quantities according to the size of the family) to the trouble of an unknown servant girl.

This girl, journeying on foot to her home in Chichester, gave birth to a twin boy and girl in a barn that stood at the end of Park Lane. The Countess adopted the baby girl and she was brought up at Slindon House with a young kinswoman of the Countess, in every way as her own child, until she married. The mother, who came to Slindon House for occasional work, once passed her daughter in one of the many corridors of the mansion, each without knowing the other's identity.

This industriously-minded noblewoman could not see anyone unemployed and kept the estate workers constantly busy on some addition or improvement to the village. In 1814 she employed Samuel Refoy, a master flint-builder, to erect, from an old Italian print, a great flint archway on Nore Hill. Known as Slindon Folly it is used as a landmark by ships in the Channel to this day.

Behind the arch was a reed-thatched teahouse, of which nothing but the foundations remain. Here the Countess would take her friends to admire the view across the coastal plain. They drove there in a four-horse wagonette, having been preceded by the estate handyman with the requisites for a picnic.

The Countess of Newburgh's folly, drawn by E.M. Venables, 1986.

A popular story goes that the Countess gave this work to Samuel Refoy when he was destitute after the Napoleonic Wars, and tramping the country in search of work. She paid him liberally and gave him a furnished cottage where, united with his wife and children, he settled down. However, Samuel's present day descendants, who maintain that the first Refoys came over from Normandy with William the Conqueror and that members of the family were living in Slindon long before the Folly was built, have refuted this tale. They maintain that the Countess favoured them not only for their skills as master craftsmen but also because they were steadfast Roman Catholics, like herself.

There were Refoys working on the estate for over a hundred years after the building of the Folly. With the Saxbys, another of Slindon's oldest families, they built many of the cottages and flint walls in Slindon. The last Refoy to live in the village was Joseph Antony who died in 1956 and is buried in St Richard's churchyard. But in the 1960s, a Refoy from Bognor, a builder, though working with bricks and cement and nostalgic for the days of the old flint craftsmanship, built a modern milking parlour at Court Hill Farm, just below the Folly built by his great-grandfather 150 years before.

After a century-and-a-half, the flint edifice had fallen into disrepair and in 1973 was restored by the National Trust. The cracked and disintegrating towers were repaired, one with coping stones and final capping. The other was built up but un-topped so that the whole piece retained the romantic appearance of an ancient ruin but safe and in good repair. The rear towers, which were never capped, remain in their original state. The architect responsible for the restoration was Mr Francis Pym, and the builder, the late Mr Roy Ayling, who had almost a lifelong association with Slindon. Part of the funds for this repair work was donated by Mrs Ray of East Grinstead, who left in her will £500 for the "preservation of an historic building in the south-east."

To return to the time of the Countess, Slindon House then, as in other phases of its history, was renowned for entertaining; dinner and house-party guests included celebrities and aristocracy from all over the country and Europe.

In the summer of 1808, one youthful guest was the charming twelve-year-old daughter of George IV, Princess Charlotte. During her two-year stay at the Dome House, Bognor, as the guest of Sir Richard Hotham, she exchanged visits with all the neighbouring nobility. A leaflet dated 18th July 1808 bore an engraved portrait of the Princess and a verse, which included the lines:

> *On Newbury's sloping lawns[16] delighted smile*
> *and Norfolk's stately bowers her sight beguile.*

But never were festivities at such a peak as in the summer of 1814, for the Earl decreed that there should be six weeks of continuous rejoicing to celebrate a defeated Napoleon's exile to Elba, which brought a temporary peace to Europe. Balls and banquets were held in the great hall for the gentry of the neighbourhood, and feasts and dancing in the servants' hall for the staff, the estate workers and the trades people in turn, throughout that time. Not far away, at Petworth House, were assembled the Prince Regent, Alexander (Emperor of Russia), and many other crowned heads of Europe.

Many carriages rolled up the mile-long drive carrying guests who included officers of the Sussex Regiment (it did not become 'Royal' until 1832), their scarlet tunics and tall helmets already a familiar sight at Slindon's social functions. These elegant uniforms mingled with the rich empire-style gowns of the ladies in the white and gold rooms, whose long windows would have been un-shuttered, shedding light onto the sloping lawns.

---

[16] 'Newbury's lawns' refers to Slindon House (Newburgh's).

Carriages came through the village too, where children sat on doorsteps on summer evenings, gazing wide-eyed at this pageant of grandeur.

In November of that year, 1814, the Earl died. He left no heir but bequeathed a life interest in the estate to his widow. After her husband's death the Countess went to France, where she lived quietly for three years, accompanied by a few chosen servants from Slindon. At the end of this time she returned to administer her estate, proving a competent landowner for nearly fifty years. She endeared herself to all who worked for her and never parted with a servant.

The first of May each year was 'Garland Day' for the children of the village school, when they paraded before the Countess on the circle of lawn in front of Slindon House, carrying flowers picked from their gardens and the Downs; waving red, white and blue flags. Afterward they filed past her as she sat by the front door, her butler at her side, each receiving three pennies from her hand.

Slindon flourished under the administration of the Newburghs. By 1801 the number of houses had risen to 66 with a population of 374; in 1811 it was 437 with 76 houses. The acres of furze and heather that comprised Slindon Common were empty except for a small farm or two, the mill and mill house, and the poor cottages mentioned in the Tithe Book. These were places of free lodging, admission to which went by favour of the Churchwardens and Overseers. They were semi-derelict dwellings with bracken reaching the door.

Slindon's population today is 600 with 87 houses in the village and approximately the same on Slindon Common.

The Newburgh era saw many changes and events on both a national and local level including the introduction of the Penny

Post in 1840. Sad indeed was the Slindon child who, having proudly bought one of the first 'Penny Blacks' to be sold at the cottage Post Office that stood above the present No. 9 Church Hill, lost it on the way home.

The Countess of Newburgh, 1846.

At about that time the Newburgh Arms was built, to become a centre not only of social life but also for all kinds of meetings. Even inquests were held there. In 1864 an inquest was held into the death of Jack Peachy who was found dead beneath an over-turned cart after the horse he was driving had bolted and jumped over the hedge into Lees Lane at Court Hill.

When the vaccination Acts of 1861 and 1871 required every child to be vaccinated before the age of three months, the local pub was the venue for public vaccination. Walberton mothers had the choice of the Newburgh Arms or the Shoulder of Mutton and Cucumber at Yapton.

The pub sign bearing the arms of the Earls of Newburgh did not appear until after 1910 and was the work of Arundel artist Ralph Gordon Ellis.

In 1857 the first County Police Force in West Sussex was formed, which marked the beginning of the end for the previous keepers of law and order in Slindon and other villages, the Parish Constables, who were selected and sworn in by the neighbouring justices. Slindon's constable, in his long blue coat and trousers and tall hat and armed with his truncheon, would march off any disturbers of the peace to the nearest magistrate, having sometimes first allowed the miscreant to cool off in the lock-up, situated since 1808 in Dyer's Lane.

A previous lock-up stood at the junction of Top Road and Church Hill; an ugly little round house which offended the Countess of Newburgh's eye, so she had the building pulled down by William Bateman and gave him a plot in Dyer's Lane on which to build a cottage for his family and a new lock-up, using the flint and brick material from the one he had demolished.

The cottage still stands with the initials W.B. above the door as does the lock-up by the front gate. The flowers are level with the roof, for the garden is raised. As Slindonians were law-abiding folk, it was little used. The last prisoner, a drunken sailor, escaped through a hole in the roof; it is now kept in good repair by the National Trust. A later William Bateman, a blacksmith, used it to stable his horse.

A barred window at one end of Lime Tree House – often thought to have been a lock-up – was a room, once a separate building, used by the estate builders for storing lime.

During the latter part of her life the Countess was drawn about in a bath chair and her bedroom was the large white room on the ground floor of the house. Yet, her faculties were good to the end and she took pride in the fact that she was able to read without spectacles. Her life continued to be busy and eventful as the following excerpts from two of her diaries show.[17]

Heading the first page of the 1857 diary are the words:

> "*The gift of my dear nephew, Sir Henry Webb, Bart. This pocket book belongs to Mrs. Catherine Mellersh. Anne Newburgh. December 15th, 1857.*"

Both diaries contain many references to Mrs Mellersh, her sister and brother-in-law John and Lucy Mercer and their daughter Anne.

Feb 2nd 1857 *Sent Anne Mercer to Goodwood with a bouquet for the Duchess of Richmond.*

August 24th *Mercers took little Catherine to Chichester in my carriage. (Little Catherine was the daughter of John and Catherine Marshall nee Mercer, married in the House Chapel 1847. Most of the family marriages took place in the Chapel).*

The diaries contain sad little reminders of her widowhood:

November 28 1852 *My beloved husband's anniversary. Went to confession.*

June 20 1857 *My dear husband's birthday. R.I.P. No longer a day of joy.*

---

[17] Copies of these, for the years 1852 and 1857, are in the Chichester Record Office. The diaries were given by the Countess to her housekeeper, Mrs Catherine Mellersh (1783-1861) and have been handed down to a descendant of Mrs Mellersh, who agreed to copies being taken for record repositories.

November 28 1857   *My very painful anniversary. Went to Communion. Made ... prayer on this disconsolate day.*

Other anniversaries and events are recorded:

Mar 17th 1852   *Made my... jubilee. Fine day. My dear Mother's anniversary.*

Nov 18th 1852   *The Duke of Wellington's grand funeral.*

There are notes on that ever-fascinating subject to the English, the weather, which seemed to be as unpredictable in the 19th century as it is today:

June 14th 1852   *Wind, hail, rain. Stormy day. Mr. and Mrs. Mercer at Slindon.*

April 28th 1857   *Very cold.*

April 29th   *Extremely cold. Frost morning and evening.*

June 19th 1857   *A violent thunderstorm and pouring rain.*

The extent of her correspondence recorded in the diaries is remarkable for one of her years. One can imagine her at her escritoire each morning, in the little drawing room, her voluminous skirts spread about her, beribboned cap on her grey curls, writing in a rapid scrawling hand.

May 12th 1857   *A letter from Lady Kinnaird to inform me of the marriage next July of the Hon. Ashley Ponsonby.*

May 13th   *A long letter from the Duchess of Norfolk*

August 1st   *Wrote to Bishop Clifford...Bristol. A letter from Dower House.*

August 12th	...wrote to Lady Victoria Fitzalan Howard ... Charles Dickens Esq.
August 22nd	A letter from Dr Rock ... from Charles Dickens Esq.

There are many other references to her correspondence with the novelist and it is not improbable that he could have visited her at Slindon House.

The Countess also liked to paint. In the corners of some pages of the original diaries are small flower pictures each with a note of the time of day that she painted it.

Aug 11th 1857	*Painted a flower in the book at half-past seven in the evening, between dark and light for my amusement.*

The year 1852 began quietly:

January 17th	*Dined in my bedroom.*
February 5th	*Dined alone in the East Room.*
February 14th	*Luncheon party.*
March 1st	*Alone at home.*
March 12th	*Dined at home in the little drawing room.*

But from then onward, throughout the summer, crowded entries appear in the diary on most days of the week. There is a galaxy of titles but unfortunately the names are illegible. Later, the writing becomes clearer:

October 20th	*Went to communion. Sir H. Webb Bart. left after an early dinner.*
October 27th	*Sir H. Webb Bart. came...dined.*
October 28th	*A large luncheon party.*

November 1st   Rev. M. Sheehan came to dine in the dining
                 room.

December 14th   Mrs...and three children came to Slindon.
                 (They stayed three days).

In 1857, although Anne Newburgh was in her 95th year, her programme was no less busy, but she does admit to feeling tired on occasion.

Jan 11th 1857   Dined in my little drawing room.

February 13th   Very much fatigued. Several persons called on
                 me.

February 27th   The Duchess of Norfolk and her daughter
                 called on me...to Holy communion.

April 5th   Palm Sunday. The Rev. M. Sheehan called
                 upon me.

April 11th   Holy Saturday. Much fatigued with moving
                 from one room to another.

April 12th   Rev. John Sheehan dined with me.

May 4th   Lord and Lady Kinnaird and...Kinnaird to
                 luncheon and to stop one night.[18]

The whole of May is busy and eventful, in contrast to the last week of June which is quite blank, although there is no mention of indisposition. There are only two entries in the diaries which concern the writer's health.

June 24th 1852   Paid a small bill to Dr Short.

---

[18] Lord Kinnaird was the tenth Baron Kinnaird, a kinsman of the later Earl and in that year M.P. for Perth.

> *May 11th 1857   Mrs Mellersh was brought to the East Room…restless night with painful knee.*

The following month her nephew Sir Henry Webb paid her another visit.

> *July 3rd 1857   Sir Henry Webb reached Slindon at ten o'clock at night.*

> *August 1st   A party to eat fruit, twelve in number.*

August 2 was a full day. There were several callers in the morning; (of these Lady Georgiana Fullerton, of Dower House, Slindon is the only legible name. There were guests to lunch and others who called in the afternoon until after 5 o'clock).

> *August 6th   Lady Levingstone Gore called. Lady Georgiana Fullerton came to lunch.*

November 1857 has some interesting entries:

> *November 11th   …from Arundel Castle of…and the Duke of Norfolk calling at Slindon. The Duke's carriage came with His Grace and Cardinal Wiseman at 4 o'clock.*

> *November 12th   His Eminence Cardinal Wiseman came to Arundel Castle.*

> *November 13th   Sent my good chaplain to Arundel Castle at 3 o'clock in the afternoon to dine with his Eminence.*

> *November 14th   Sent my carriage to Arundel Castle for the Rev. John Sheehan.[19] His Eminence left Sussex.*

---

[19] Father Sheehan was the Roman Catholic priest at Slindon from 1845-1869. It was during this time that the church of St Richard's was built and opened.

V. Jimmy Dean, Slindon Chronicler

A vivid picture of life in Slindon from the latter days of the
Countess of Newburgh to the early 1930s is conjured up by another diarist, Jimmy Dean, ploughboy, estate handyman, and
chorister, who, for almost forty years wrote *Slindon Notes* for the
West Sussex Gazette. From 1918 to 1934 he recorded, in desk
diaries given him every Christmas by the Rector, not only personal and family notes, but local and national events and
descriptions of village customs recalled from his earliest days.
These diaries, carefully preserved by his family, have now been
deposited with the West Sussex Record Office at Chichester.

James 'Jimmy' Dean was born in 1853, the eldest of six children of Charles Dean, a gamekeeper to the Duke of Norfolk. He
was the fourth generation to live at the family cottage, 'Biddleside', on the lower boundary of Slindon. Jimmy attended the
little school at Rectory Cottage in Dyers Lane, where the master
had only one leg and walked with crutches. He tells the story of
Jack Purdy who, when reprimanded, rushed at the master and
seizing his crutches, threw them out of the window. The Rector,
the Revd Maurice Smelt, was summoned and arriving promptly,
administered his cane with memorable severity. Jack afterwards
ran away and joined a Guard's regiment.

Jimmy Dean's father went to Chichester school and was the
best scholar in the village in 1854, during the Crimean War.
Every Saturday night he read out the war news at the Newburgh
Arms from a small weekly newspaper, which was priced 6d.

"At the present time," Jimmy Dean writes in 1905, "the daily paper and the *West Sussex Gazette* can be bought for 1d and the latter is even delivered at the door. In 1854 three out of four men could not read the paper."

Many Slindon men fought in the Crimea. Several volunteers from the village were on the last ship to go out. They reached their destination just as peace was proclaimed. Those men who returned from the war were met and honoured by their village.

Jimmy's schooling came to an abrupt end when his father died in 1865. The eleven-year-old boy was sent to work at Court Hill Farm, assisting John Dean the carter for 2/6 a week. He never forgot that first March day, ploughing with three horses on Nore Hill, crying with cold in the bitter north wind that blew across the Downs. He stayed on at Rose Barn stables until he finally took charge of four fine young cart horses, the second team at Court Hill, where fourteen horses were kept. His wage was then 15/- a week.

In 1873 the first mechanical threshing tackle came to Slindon and Jimmy joined the threshing gang.

He married Harriet Chalk, second laundry maid at Slindon House. They lived at Biddleside where ten of their eleven children were born, until it was accidentally burned down in 1900 and they were put into No. 47 Park Lane, where they remained as tenants of the Slindon Estate.

Jimmy had a fine voice, particularly suited to sacred music. He was a member of Slindon Choral Society and a chorister at St Mary's for sixty years, at one time with five of his sons. He sang at over two hundred concerts in Slindon and other villages and towns as far away as Brighton.

He served for three years as Parish Constable and was once commended for bravery by the Arundel bench for his handling of a dangerously drunken butcher from Fittleworth, who had overturned his cart in a ditch. Jimmy was unscathed after the incident, but was more fortunate than Constable Smart before him, who, while arresting a vagrant, 'Pedlar Proudly', was viciously stabbed in the side by the pedlar's long knife. A doctor, hastily summoned, saved Smart's life, but the constable walked 'one-sided' for the remainder of his life. Proudly was caught and sent 'over the water' for three years.

Cricket was another facet of Jimmy Dean's busy life, both playing and organising matches with other villages. Descriptions of matches and cricket scores appear in his diaries, along with accounts of other sports including the meets of the local hunt.

Perhaps the most fascinating feature of his records is his portrayal of village life in the time of the Newburghs. Then, he writes, Slindon was full of reed-thatched cottages and thatched barns filled at harvest-time with corn ready for the flail.

These large barns were built with great uprights of solid oak. All of the rafters were chopped out with an axe, and the floors were boarded with oak to thresh the corn upon. Men worked at this task all the year round and as each wagonload of corn was threshed out, it was taken to Chichester market. The large yards were full of cattle in winter, fattened with hay and roots and oil-cake, with plenty of straw under them to make into manure for the fields. There were a great many orchards with apples of all kinds, and pears, plums, damsons, quince, walnuts and filbert nuts.

All food was home-produced and home-made. Villagers baked their own bread in the large brick ovens, which were usually situated in the centre of the cottage and must have kept the whole beautifully warm. The ideal oven went far back but was shallow, its small opening covered by a well fitting iron door. A wood fire was lit in the oven, and by the time the dough was ready the bricks were hot. The fire was then raked out and the bread baked perfectly in the diminishing heat.

There was home-killed pork in the tubs and plenty of home cured bacon; and a great many fat hogs hung – smoke dried – in the cottage chimneys.

Jimmy Dean was proud to possess his grandfather's pig-killing knife and chopper – the knife formerly wielded by his grandfather and great-grandfather, had stuck thousands of fat hogs in Slindon. These hardy men would get up early in frost and snow to kill hogs, having warned the owner overnight to have the copper boiling, the tub and pig-killing stool ready at an appointed time. Having killed and dressed the hog (or hogs) at one place, they would go on to the next, where the same preparations had been made.

When the pig-sticker had finished his round, he went home to breakfast, which was washed down with several pints of beer. Then he thatched cottages and farm buildings all day long in Slindon village. After dark he would cut up the fat hogs for the pork tubs and chimneys. Some families had as many as four hogs killed, all fed on the best Slindon barley. After supper he would sit for a while in his 'Saxon' chair, with his pipe of 'bacca' and mug of home-brewed beer; then to bed and to a sound sleep, "lying as warm," writes Jimmy Dean, "as a hot plum pudding, without blankets in the coldest weather."

Today, only the bricked-up pig-holes in the cottage garden walls – the exits for the foraging pigs – are a reminder of those days.

As essential to life as home-grown food was the good home-brewed beer of those days. Most cottagers brewed their own, besides making quantities of wine and cider. In the making of cider, the villagers pressed their apples at the cider press owned by Jimmy Dean's father. Jimmy recalls a New Year celebration in 1918 when some very mature home-made wine was consumed: Mangel Wurzel 1866, Hedgepick Wine 1865, Rhubarb 1882, Ginger 1887. "Come over the hill to Slindon" Jimmy Dean gave an open invitation, "and we will gladly give you a glass of hedgepick wine 1865, though the hands that made it are resting, alas, in the Parish churchyard!"

But it was the home-brewed beer that flowed copiously at all Fair Days and Feast Days and in the fields at haymaking and harvest time. Every heavy or arduous task on the estate carried with it a liberal allowance of free beer. Tea was too expensive in those days for the villagers to buy, and beer was drunk at breakfast, dinner, lunch and supper – in fact all day long.

Brewing for Slindon House took place twice a year, the beer being run through pipes into the cellars.

On Boxing Day 1870, Jimmy Dean was assisting builders to cart flints from the downs for the new village school. It being Christmas and a bitterly cold day, the landlord of the Newburgh Arms, Frank Fleet, plied them with quart tankards of hot gin until they were too drunk to unharness the horses!

But in 1884, when an infant classroom was being built on to the main building, it was a sweltering midsummer day. Building was thirsty work, and the drink was again beer.

"Never," said the foreman, "have we had to drink so much beer to build anything this size. It must be remembered!" With that, he filled his tankard with cement and worked it into the gable, where it can clearly be seen to this day.

Constant imbibing of home-brewed beer led to high spirits in Slindon, and on occasion, belligerency. Election days usually ended with a free fight.

Once, the bell-ringers quarrelled while ringing in the New Year, over who should pull the bells. George Shepherd, a chorister, tried to take the rope from James Walker, the schoolmaster, but Mr Walker would not give it up. In the altercation that followed, the schoolmaster was laid on his back and suffered two black eyes.

On another New Year's Eve, three bell-ringers: Frank Fleet, landlord; his son George and Tom Bateman, sheep-shearer and cricket umpire, all merry with the good home-brewed Christmas ale, "sent the bells ringing gaily into a beautiful moonlight night."

Earlier, Frank Fleet had overheard Lane, the carter, saying in the Tap Room of the Newburgh that he was going to Chichester the next day with three loads of wheat, and instead of going to bed, he intended to polish his harness and grease his wagon which stood in the cart-house in Dyers Lane. Carters were very proud of their four-horse teams. The bell-ringers, instead of going home, went to Mr Lane's cart shed, pulled out the wagon, and sent it rattling down Dyers Lane, down Church Hill and into the pond.

The carter had just got into bed when he heard the ringers' voices and the rattle of wheels. He dashed out and ran down to the pond in his underwear, to see his wagon well out in the middle.

"You've had the pleasure of pushing my wagon into the pond", he said, "now you can have the pleasure of pulling it out, or I'll have the law on you!" A very wet and sobered trio of bell-ringers pulled the wagon out of the pond and back up Dyers Lane!

The next day, Lane, with his wagon and four horses, red white and blue ribbons flying, went to Chichester market.

When Jimmy Dean was young, most of Slindon belonged to the copyholders, who held their properties for life at the will of the lord of the manor and had certain cherished rights. Other families were tenants who lived for many years in the same cottages, paying no rates, but 1/6 or 2/6 per year to the estate. Copyholders could turn out their sheep and cattle on Slindon Common, and in the autumn their pigs into North Wood to live on the beechnuts and acorns. When the time came to bring them in, some were fat enough for killing.

Early in spring the villagers earned money by stripping bark, and later by tending sheep, haymaking and hoeing.

Harry Jackson, who lived at the Dog and Partridge, collected ash from the Slindon cottages. This he sold to farmers at fourpence a bushel to put on the meadows laid up for hay. As all of the cottagers burnt wood on their fires and in their bread ovens, there were large quantities of ash gathered, and large hayricks in Slindon.

"If you want a good hay crop," wrote Jimmy Dean, "dress your meadows with grit and mole soot, then we will all go haymaking, pitchers, rankers, on a beautiful midsummer day!"

"Now," he wrote, many years later, "there are no wood fires on the dog-irons and no ash for the meadows."

In those days hay was cut by hand. Jimmy Dean recalls a heavy crop of broad-leaf clover in 1866:

The field was cut from end to end by four mowers with their scythes. The men would mow from morning until night, their blades made razor sharp with Devonshire bat rubbers and their thirst slaked with plenty of good beer.

At dinner and lunchtime all sat down amongst the hay. At the words 'Tip out', out came the home-brewed beer and home-made cider, the young onions, the lettuce, home killed bacon, bread and cheese.

St Swithin's Day was Slindon Fair Day, when all work was abandoned save the feeding and care of stock, and preparation for this was made overnight.

The day began at 11 a.m. with a cricket match that continued until 7 o'clock in the evening. Slindon Cricket Club challenged teams from Bognor or Chichester, Arundel, Petworth and many others, rarely losing a match.

Frank Fleet took a large booth and pitched it at Slindon Common for the match.

When the Slindon House Stable clock struck 11 a.m., sounding across the park to the cricket ground, out went two batsmen with the umpires in their high black bandbox hats. The booth was, by then, full of spectators. There were two innings for each side. At 1 o'clock the bell rang for lunch and an hour's break.

After the match, the Earl of Newburgh's head keeper would call out the names of the men and boys who had found pheasant and partridge nests on the estate. Each was given a shilling for the year's nesting.

Then scrapping began. When Slindonians fell out they would save their grievances until Fair Day, when they would fight it out, usually giving in after a black eye or a broken nose.

The highlight of the day was Slindon's brass band, clad in their gold-braided uniforms and peaked pillbox hats. No festive occasion in Slindon or the neighbouring villages was complete without them.

There were coconut shies, roundabouts, swings and other amusements at the Fair. Local people set out their stalls laden with various home-made brews. There was a whelk stall and a gingerbread stall. Old Mrs Farrington from Eastergate came each year with a large basketful of gooseberry tarts, sold at a penny each, sometimes walking back twice to her home to bake more pies, such was the demand for them.

Slindon's Brass Band, c. 1890.

When the heavy crops of corn began to ripen, the Slindonians would meet at the Newburgh Arms for the reapers to choose their mates. The carters and their boys helped cut the corn for two weeks, turning their horses out in the meadow to rest until the corn was ready to cart. Then carters, horses and wagons were in the fields, carting sheaves to the ricks and filling the many barns with corn. All the horses wore bells, and their pleasant jingle must have been a more musical accompaniment to the day's work than the modern roar of the tractor.

Harvesters came from Barnham, shutting up their houses for six weeks; afterwards they went hop-picking in Kent. In fine weather they slept in the shocks of corn in the fields; if wet, in the farm buildings, cooking their food in large iron pots over fires in Nore Lane.

The Slindon women would cook hot breakfasts with plenty of vegetables and take it to their men in the fields. They would cut corn all day with the hook, and go home to do the household chores and cook hot supper.

Whole families cut corn, earning enough money to pay their debts before the winter and buy new boots made by Slindon boot-makers. Harvest suppers were held at the Well House. They started at 7pm and continued until morning, with plenty of food, beer and songs.

After the corn had been carried, the villagers and their children went leasing, picking up the loose corn for home-made bread. They attended to their own gardens, storing their potatoes, apples and roots in clamps for the winter.

After the harvest, huge oat and barley ricks stood everywhere. As soon as the last head of corn was carted, the plough and presser was at work making ready for another harvest. Three labourers loaded dung from the yards where the cattle stood.

In 1868, 100 acres of wheat was sown in Nore Lane fields, Court Hill; it yielded a good crop, all cut by hand with the 'fag-hook' or sickle. After threshing it yielded 10 sacks to the acre, while the fields behind North Wood yielded 14 to the acre.

Wheat sowing was finished by October 20th, which was Sloe Fair Day at Chichester. Slindon's five bootmakers: Peter Sherlock and his two sons, John Fleet and Charles Jackson, went to the Sloe Fair to pay for their boot leather yearly. Other Slindonians would walk to the fair and back after their day's work – 16 miles. Families were measured for new boots, paying for them after the harvest.

In March, men, women and boys went cutting thistles out of the wheat and pulling docks; there was no rubbish to be seen in the corn. That month, too, wheat fields were well rolled with heavy rollers.

Other fields were sown with oats. 'You farmers, plough your ground well,' advised Jimmy Dean. 'Sow your oats early in fine dry dusty weather, if you want a good crop'.

There were fields full of fat sheep fed on oil cake, plenty of roots and good malt barley meal. One year there were 1,800 sheep on Folly Field. Fleeces were stored in the huge barn in Park Lane.

During the winter months other activities were afoot in the fields and woods.

Rat catcher 'Hookey' Howard (one of his arms ended in a hook) came to all farm hedges with his ferrets and four dogs to hunt for rats and rabbits, but he was not allowed in the pheasant coverts. At the threshing of corn ricks, too, Hookey was seen with his dogs and ferrets.

Rabbits were common and Slindonians would go tracking and killing rabbits in the snow.

Labourers cleaned out the ditches, putting their loads on to the land; they carried sand and stones for their own buildings. Many wagons came south to North Wood for faggots and cord-wood.

Then as now, there was an extensive shoot connected with the estate. Jimmy Dean makes little mention of this, except that at a partridge shoot in 1897, 200 birds were killed in Folly Fields; and earlier in the century an underkeeper was sentenced to three months hard labour for poisoning 500 pheasants with arsenic.

When recording gardening notes in his diaries, Jimmy Dean delighted in creating rivalry between the gardeners of Slindon and other villages. Graffham, near Petworth, was a particular target.

He would tramp miles over the Downs to a remote hamlet in search of an extra large cabbage or mammoth marrow. These things he described for "the paper".

In 1917 he wrote of apple-tree boughs being propped up against the weight of fruit – "a wondrous Slindon record".

That year a huge cabbage lettuce was cut in the school garden, 4½ feet in circumference. It weighed 4½ lbs.

"The largest ever in Slindon and the wonder of a room full of eyes at the Newburgh Arms."

There was an especially heavy lifting of potatoes that year, one root weighing 9½ lbs, having thirty potatoes, four of these weighing 1lb each and one weighing 1lb 3oz.

"How are *your* spuds, Graffham?" asked Jimmy Dean.

During the 1914-18 war, the *West Sussex Gazette* was sent to Arundel men serving abroad, but copies were sought after by others who had never before heard of this corner of Sussex – they wanted to know how Slindon and Graffham were getting on!

In 1897 James Dean beat all with his potatoes at the Arundel Flower Show and at the Arundel Park and District Show.

In 1923 he tells of green peas in full bloom in April.

Jimmy's habit of depicting everything in Slindon as larger than life led to some good-natured leg-pulling. One day he brought a very large and heavy wild rabbit into the West Sussex Gazette offices.

"Ever seen a rabbit to beat 'e? Feel the weight of 'im." said Jimmy, unaware that some practical joker had inserted a handful of shot inside the creature, carefully sewing up the small hole. While it was being passed round and admired, the jogging about to 'try the weight' broke the stitches and out fell the shot.

That story did not get into the paper, but another, concerning an errant pig, did. On his way home one evening, Jimmy bought a young pig, and having borrowed a sack to carry it in, set off with his wriggling, squealing burden. But the sack had contained potatoes and was rotten at the base. The pig soon made its escape and bolted into a field of wheat, which stood tall, ready for harvest. There had been a heavy rainfall that day and the corn was saturated, but neither this fact nor a large notice, which said 'Keep Out' deterred Jimmy from pursuing his quarry. For an hour he chased the elusive piglet until his corduroy trousers, new on that day, were in a sadly soggy state. At last, the pig was driven into a yard, caught and carried home in a stronger sack.

"The rain must have done a lot of good," was the Editor's comment. "Only last week Jimmy reported that the corn was so poor one could not lose a mouse in it, but this week he has lost a pig."

Jimmy Dean also recorded all phenomena of weather. In earlier times minor earthquakes were not uncommon in Sussex.

In 1638, earthquake shocks were felt in Chichester and great damage was done. In 1734 an earthquake shook Shoreham, Tarring, Goring and Arundel; beds were rocked and bells rung. In November 1811 there was a shock at Chichester and neighbouring villages; and again in September 1833, when bells were rung, blinds unrolled and chimneys thrown. On the downs, a great mass of chalk was dislodged, killing a man.

In January 1881 deep snow obliterated Slindon, except for the largest buildings. Heavy snowflakes fell all one day and the following night. The next day, James Dean walked on top of the hedges on frozen snow on his way to work. Returning at night, however, from Slindon House to Biddleside, he sank up to his shoulders in snow and was forced to seek an alternative route.

The village was entirely cut off and all work brought to a standstill. Villagers sat before their roaring log fires drinking homebrewed beer and smoking their clay pipes until men from Barnham and Arundel helped them to dig passages through the snow.

During that severe winter, James Dean worked hard at Slindon House, carrying wood and coal for fires all over the house. A shipload of coal, 90 tons, was got through to the mansion from Arundel.

In April 1892, heavy falls of snow on Easter Sunday and Monday bent the evergreens double.

The next year a shepherd making his way back to Gumber from Slindon at 10 o'clock one night, got stuck in a deep snow drift and was found dead the following morning.

In 1923, after eighteen hours of snow, the village was isolated and sheep and lambs buried.

Jimmy recalls many Christmases in his diary, especially a Christmas party in the servants hall at Slindon House in 1883:

> *"Jimmy Dean was at Slindon House all day helping with the preparations for the Christmas dinner. All the servants from the housekeeper and the butler down to the stable men filled the servants' hall. The long grand old oak table, which had belonged to the Earl of Newburgh, was loaded with turkey, pheasants, roast beef, roast legs of mutton, roast pork, ham, chicken, with all kinds of vegetables, plum pudding, mince pies and all kinds of fruit; and to drink, ale, port wine and sherry."*

Bottles of wine and spirits were raffled each Christmas at the Newburgh Arms and Spur Hotel. The Parish Church bells rang merrily and choirboys were out singing glees and carols. Slindon and Arundel brass bands played in Slindon village. Tipsters were round at Christmas and New Year.

In February 1920, at the age of sixty-nine, Jimmy Dean was admitted to the Royal West Sussex Hospital for the amputation of his right leg. He made a remarkable recovery and by May that year, neighbours were taking their turn at pushing him in a wheeled chair to flower shows and concerts and cricket matches in the district. After that he got about on crutches and then on a cork leg. He continued writing his diary and his articles for the *West Sussex Gazette* until almost the end of his life.

He died in 1935 at the age of eighty-three.

"His writings are still treasured in Slindon," said a local newspaper at the time, "and the tales told of him make him something of a legend. There is no one speaks ill of this kindly man." A tribute paid to him by the Cricket Club at Addington, Surrey, ends:

> *"Jimmy has been to Slindon in a modest and unlearned way, what Gilbert White was to Selborne."*

Others too had memories of Slindon's past. Alfred Booth of Croydon recalled the trips he made with his father on the Fisherman's Excursion train in 1894. The train ran on Sundays from London Bridge to Amberley Station. The fare was 2/6 return. Young Alfred and his father had not come, like their fellow passengers, to fish in the Arun at Houghton, but to walk via Whiteways Lodge to Slindon.

Later in his life, Alfred Booth spent many holidays at the Newburgh Arms. He recalled many personalities from those days, including Harry Sherlock, the local snob (shoemaker) and Clun Lewis, a Sussex character and his family who gave puppet shows in the barn behind the Newburgh. He remembered incidents such as being rewarded with coffee by the French cook when delivering crates of beer to Madame Belloc's house, Gaston Cottage. The Beer was very likely for her son Hilaire, who wrote:

> *"French is my heart and loyal and sincere,*
> *Is and shall be my love of British beer."*

He would have visited her there from Court Hill farmhouse, later from Kings Land, Shipley.

Mrs Minnie Forden, who afterwards lived in Derbyshire, remembers Chichester Lodge, Madehurst, where she and her four sisters were born. They attended Slindon C of E school where they were taught by Mr and Mrs Bowden and a pupil teacher Cissie Thorpe. Before school, they fetched milk from Bowley's Farm in School Hill. The price was a penny a pint for full cream and a penny a quart for skim. Most working families had skim.

She recalled the Garland Days, when children rose early to gather both wild and garden flowers to make posies or double circlets, which were tied to a stick. Sometimes hoops were decorated with a doll inside. These they carried to every house, receiving a halfpenny or farthing from the occupants. Promptly at 11 o'clock they presented themselves to Miss Sylvia Leslie at Slindon House who judged the garlands and awarded a shilling, a florin or half-crown according to merit. Then there was a rush to Bateman's sweet shop to spend their wealth, but some children spent only one penny, saving the rest towards a day at Bognor in the summer, when they would walk to catch the train at Barnham and have a picnic on the beach.

Mrs Forden remembered with pleasure the Christmas treats. First the 'petticoat' treat. Annually the Mothers Union made every girl a petticoat and every boy a shirt. A local resident recalls today with amusement that: "all the shirts were the same size, but all the boys were not." The garments were presented at a party held at the National School, where they also received buns and oranges, sang carols and were shown slides by the Revd Arthur Izard with his magic lantern.

The second treat was given by Colonel Leslie at the Catholic School. There was a lighted and decorated tree, a tea, and music supplied by a gramophone. Each child received a present, an orange and a bag of sweets from Miss Leslie.

Minnie Forden left school at thirteen to work as day girl for Miss Bateman, the blacksmith's sister. The hours were 8am to 6pm, the wage 6d a week.

There were happy memories of her courting days on the Downs at Court Hill. Her sweetheart, a Yorkshireman, was first journeyman at Dale Park gardens. They were married in Madehurst Church in 1913. There was sadness too, for the little girl of four who is buried in the churchyard.

Winnie and Linda Bowley, who lived the latter part of their lives in Bridle Lane remembered the frugal fare of their young days, when even an egg or an orange was shared. At Christmas the family were given a pig's head by the local butcher and ingredients for a pudding by the grocer, otherwise there would have been no festive meal.

Linda left school at thirteen and went to work in a doctor's house in Worthing, cycling to and from Slindon.

VI. After the Newburghs

In 1861 the Countess of Newburgh died. "The village of Slindon," said the *West Sussex Gazette*, "over which the late Countess watched with such maternal solicitude, has now the appearance of a deserted village, being bereft as it is of its chief prop and ornament."

The Countess was buried in Chichester at the little Roman Catholic Church she herself had built, which stood opposite the site of the former South Gate of the City. Later, her body was brought back to rest in the graveyard of St Richard's, Slindon. Her effigy was broken in transit and the grave is marked today by a plain curb and headstone.

Her funeral was reported in the WSG:

> "...conducted in a style commensurate with the rank of the late excellent lady, the remains being followed to the grave by the different tenantry. It is uncertain on whom the estate will devolve. There are several claimants in the field; and before the final settlement some work will be made for the gentlemen of the long robe."

The rightful heir was Vincent, 6th Prince Giustiniani of Rome, who was the grandson of Anne, daughter of Charlotte, a Levingstone of Kinnaird and Countess of Newburgh in her own right, by her first marriage. By her second marriage to Charles Ratcliffe she had a daughter, Mary, sister to James, 4th Earl of Newburgh.

The title went to the grandchild of Anne, but the Prince did not take proceedings to establish his claim, and Francis Eyre, in

Hassop, Derbyshire, son of Mary Ratcliffe, and his daughter Dorothy Eyre after him, assumed the title erroneously.

Dorothy married Colonel Charles Leslie of Balquhain, who was descended from the Counts Leslie of the Holy Roman Empire, the most colourful of whom was the first Count, who was granted the title by the Emperor after the assassination of Wallenstein in 1634.

According to Sir Bernard Burke·

1863, Charles Leslie Esq. of Balquin, J.P. and D.L. for the Cos. Aberdeen and Derby and Colonel in the army, K.H. late of the Grenadier Guards, married 1st Mary, daughter of Major-General Sir Charles Holloway and had by her one surviving son, Charles Stephen.

Colonel Leslie married 2nd, Dorothy, sister and heiress of Francis, 8th Earl of Newburgh, on whose death in 1852 she assumed the title Countess of Newburgh. Colonel Leslie, 26th Baron of Balquhain, served in the Peninsular war and was severely wounded at Talavera.

The founder of the Leslie family was Bartholomew, a noble Hungarian, who came to Scotland with Queen Margarite in 1067. He was much esteemed by King Malcolm Caenmore, who conferred upon him land in various parts of Scotland, particularly in the district of Aberdeen, where the ruins of the old castle of Leslie still remain, in the parish of Leslie, Bartholomew's son, Malcolm, was the father of Norman, whose grandson was Sir Norman de Lesley.

On Dorothy's death, without issue, Colonel Leslie inherited under her will, both the Hassop and the Slindon Estates. Colonel Leslie, who was stationed at Chichester Barracks was at

Slindon House at the time of the death of Anne, Countess of Newburgh, and was prompt in claiming his inheritance.

Prince Giustiniani did not prosecute his claim and appeared several times at Court to confirm that he wanted no part of the estates.

The present holder of the Newburgh title, according to Debrett, is: Prince Fillipo Jan Baptista Camillo Francesco Aldo Mans Rospigliosi (Born 4th July 1942) 12th Earl of Newburgh, Viscount Kynnaird and Baron Levingstone. His other titles include: 14th Prince of Castiglini, 11th Duke of Zagarolo, Marquis of Guillina, Count of Chiusa. He is the son of the 11th Earl who died in 1986. Married Baronessa Donne Luisa, daughter of Count Annibale Caccia Dominoni. Heir to the title is Principessa Benedetta Francesca Maria (English title, Mistress of Newburgh) Born 1974.

The family of Giustiniani reigned formerly in Chios, until 1346, and was finally expelled by the Turks from that island in 1566. The family of Bandini, originally from Umbria established itself in Rome in the 16th century.[20] This ancient lineage is represented in the splendid and colourful arms of the Earls of Newburgh. The shield is divided into six segments;

1st   *bendy of six argent and gules, on a chief of the last, a cross of the first, for* BANDINI;

2nd   *gules, a tower, ppr., on a chief or, an eagle displayed sa., for* GIUSTINIANI;

3rd   *or a lion rampant, sa., for* MAHONY;

4th   *chequy or and az., a fesse, gules, for* CLIFFORD;

---

[20] Burke's Peerage.

5th   *arg. on a bend gu., between three gilliflowers slipped ppr.,*
two and one, an anchor, of the field, all within a tressure
flory-counterflory, vert, for LEVINGSTONE; gu. on a bend
arg., a grasshopper ppr., for GRILLO, DUKE of
MONDRAGONE.

Supporters: Dexter, a wild man, wreathed about the temples
and loins with oak, ppr., sinister, a dapple pony, bridled and
saddled, gu.

The crest is a moor's head, ppr., banded with chequy arg. and
gu. and ear ringed arg. Motto: Si je puis.

There was no contestant to the Leslies' claim to the Newburgh title and estates until May 1887, when there was a three-day hearing in the Chancery Division of the High Court of Justice of the action Leslie v. Cave.

Colonel Charles Leslie was the plaintiff and claimed an injunction to restrain the defendant, Mr Gladwin Cloves Cave, from trespassing on the Hassop Estate, interfering with the collection of rents from that estate and from slandering the title.

The defendant counter-claimed to recover all the estates, to which he alleged he was entitled through his maternal ancestress Elizabeth Gladwin, a sister of the Countess and the 6th Earl of Newburgh. The defendant claimed that the settlement of 1812 gave to Thomas, the 7th Earl, a general power of appointment, which he exercised in favour of one John Gladwin, and that the descendants of Elizabeth Gladwin (afterward Clowes) his eldest daughter, became ultimately entitled to the estates of both Hassop and Slindon.

The plaintiffs alleged that no such appointment was ever made. The Slindon estate was settled by Anthony the 5th earl by his will in 1812. By this will a life estate was given to his wife Anne, Countess of Newburgh. Other limitations having failed,

Slindon estate descended to Thomas 7th earl in fee and afterward to Francis 8th earl, and on his death to Lady Dorothy, who made settlements under which Colonel Charles Leslie claimed in fee.

The plaintiff further alleged that in 1884 the defendant made claims to the Hassop and Slindon estates claiming to be the lawful heir to the Earls of Newburgh.

All these accusations Mr Cave denied. The defendant insisted on conducting the case himself and produced one witness, who said that in 1849 he had procured certain documents, which he had taken from behind a sliding panel in the Earl of Newburgh's bedroom at Hassop.

The judge did not find this story very credible. Mr Cave had not, said His Lordship, conducted the case the best way to his own benefit. The defendant failed to establish his claim and an injunction was granted to restrain him from slandering the title.

Yet, neither the breakdown of his case nor the fact that he had exhausted all his own resources, and much of his relatives, in meeting the expenses incurred (in 1890 he appeared at the London bankruptcy Court with heavy liabilities) deterred Mr Cave from pressing his claim.

In a further attempt, appearing this time as plaintiff, he claimed evidence that the Countess Dorothy had died long before 7 o'clock on the morning of November 22nd 1853, the hour on the codicil by which she bequeathed away the Hassop estate. But again he failed in action to establish his claim and the case was dismissed with costs.

Finally, in 1891 Mr Cave brought a further action on yet another ground that, under the settlement which Lady Dorothy took, she took only an estate for life, in which case she had no right to dispose of it in favour of her husband and son.

The action was dismissed as 'frivolous and vexatious' in the legal sense and it was to be regretted, said His Lordship, that the claimant had not heeded the warnings of Lord Justices in the former suits.

Despite the efforts of Mr Gladwin Cave, the Leslie family remained in undisputed possession of the estates for three generations.

On the death of Colonel Charles Leslie on 13th January 1870, the following passage appeared in the *West Sussex Gazette*.

"Death of Col. Leslie. Our obituary records the death of Colonel Leslie, at Slindon House at the ripe old age of 85. Col. Leslie was in the Peninsular War and was recalled from that service to proceed to Canada just previous to the Battle of Waterloo. He was severely wounded in the leg, the effect of which was felt to the day of his death."

"The gallant colonel succeeded to the Slindon estates on the death of the Countess of Newburgh in 1861. It will be remembered that Lady Newburgh lived to the age of 98. On the accession of Col. Leslie to the property his title was disputed and after some considerable litigation his claims were allowed and he has resided at Slindon at times since this period. The Leslie family are Roman Catholics, and since the accession of the colonel to the Slindon Estate a new Roman Catholic chapel has been erected in the village."

"He leaves behind a son who is married and has six children."

Colonel Charles Leslie was succeeded by his son, Charles Stephen Leslie, who, a few years later, left Slindon for his Scottish residence, leaving his wife Mrs Jane Leslie to administer the Slindon estate. This she did with the help of her eldest son Charles Radcliffe Aloysius Leslie, until he left Slindon for

France with his wife Katharine, whom he married in 1880. Eventually Jane went to live in Bordeaux, where she died. Her body was brought back to Slindon and she is buried in St Richard's churchyard.

The ever-informative Jimmy Dean records that after Mrs Leslie's departure, Slindon House was shut up for one year, during which time he lived there as caretaker. When C.R.A. Leslie returned, Jimmy was made valet and then butler.

The Leslie claim to the Slindon estate had not been popular with the village people, who declared that the inheritance would do no good for either the family or the estate. By the time C.R.A. Leslie took over the property the family fortune was on the wane. A handsome, pleasure-loving man, he proceeded to squander what was left; the estate fell into disrepair and some of it was broken up into small plots and sold.

It would seem that his insolvency dated from sometime earlier. On the front page of the first issue of the *Chichester Observer*, dated 15th June 1887, there appeared a column headed *'A Local Gent and his Creditors'*, concerning the Public Examination at Brighton County Court of Mr C.R.A. Leslie. It stated that he was 28 years of age and had received £500 a year since the age of 21. He was in debt to the amount of £300 when he came of age. The farm at Slindon yielded no profit, which perhaps accounted for his indebtedness. His father did not allow him anything. Since he came of age his income was £3,500 a year. His debts amounted to £18,000. He kept racehorses and his household expenses were £500 a year. The feature ends with saying that his debts were bought up by friends. Some creditors accepted 8 shillings in the pound.

There were two children of the marriage of C.R.A. Leslie and Katharine Georgina Drummond, a son, Allan Charles Malcolm and a daughter, Sylvia Mary. When C.R.A. Leslie finally left Slindon House, suddenly and quietly in the middle of the night, Sylvia accompanied him.

Allan Leslie never succeeded to the estate. In 1908 he was a Captain in the 3rd. Gordon Highlanders and residing at Slindon House. In that year he married Florence Lillian Morris. In 1909 their son Alistair was born, who was later to live in New Zealand; but shortly afterward the couple parted, Allan moving to the Dower House, formerly Slindon Cottage, and Florence to the house Newlands (now Woodlands Farm House) in Park Lane. Apparently a divorce followed for Allan remarried. Florence died in 1947 and is buried in St. Mary's churchyard. Florence's mother, Alice Morris, when widowed, came to live with her daughter whom she outlived, celebrating her 100th birthday on 1st June 1948.

The most dramatic change brought about in the Leslie era in Slindon was the enclosure of the common land. The areas of Slindon Bottom, Slindon Common and North Wood, where copyholders had held the rights of grazing for their pigs and cattle, were all enclosed.

Many were the stormy meetings held at the Newburgh Arms by the indignant copyholders, who declared that the act was the greatest legalized robbery of all time.

Slindon MSS Quit Rent Book of 1745-1807 states:

The privileges and conditions of Copyholders.

"Best living creature upon every Copyholders death except some stinted cottages."

"Liberty to let copyholds without licence.

All timbers belong to tenants.

*Liberty to put their hoggs in North Wood at 2d. per head when
the Lord shall think fit to make a lain, which is but for 7 weeks
and no more.*

*Liberty to digg chalk or marle in ancient chalk pits and marle
pits without leave of the Lord to spend on copyholds and not
elsewhere, denyied by the Lord; and liberty to digg stanes and
cut buss and fern upon the commons without leave, but this is
also denyied by the Lord."*

Copyholders paid no rent, but paid stipulated dues to the Lord of
the Manor in accordance with the long established custom of
Slindon Manor.

Now, however, many copyholders' properties were taken into
the estate, including Jimmy Dean's Biddleside Cottage, for
which he afterward had to pay £12 a year rent. Footpaths were
changed; a wall was built from St Richard's Church to the top of
Court Hill, and a gate put at the south end of Slindon Down.
Three more gates were put across the old London to Portsmouth
highway.

Eventually, the protesting copyholders were compensated under the Slindon Enclosure Award with plots of land on Slindon
Common, each proportionate to the size of their property in the
parish.

Mr Bernard Keeling, a former resident of Slindon and author
of *Slindon Parish Council 1894-1984* has done extensive research
into this allotment of land. The result appeared in an article in
the Slindon Parish Magazine in 1983. He writes:

*"This basis of distribution meant that the lion's share, 618 acres,
mainly Slindon Bottom and from Nore Hill up to Stane Street,
went to the executors of Colonel Leslie, the late owner of Slindon House and Lord of the Manor. 103 acres went to another
large landowner, Mr T.C. Williams, a Lincoln's Inn Solicitor.*

Seven acres on the west side of Mill Road were awarded to the Churchwardens and Overseers of the Poor and later passed to the Parish Council; of these, four were to enable them to provide facilities to the villages for exercise and recreation, and three to provide allotments for the Labouring Poor. The Rector, the Revd William Chantler Izard, was awarded five acres to the south of the new recreation ground, due to his occupancy of the old Rectory (now Mulberry House) and of other church land. A few other copyholders received two or three acres, but some only half an acre. In most cases about one acre was awarded. The total number of beneficiaries was 36. The majority of the new holdings were eventually sold, mainly as building plots, which means that many properties in the village are 'twinned' with Properties on Slindon Common, although no tangible link remains."

In a table accompanying the article Mr Keeling has listed every house in Slindon Common to the east of Mill road where most of the building has occurred, and shown to which property in the village the land on which it is built was allocated, e.g.

Houses in old village	Houses in Bridle Lane
Dairy Cottage	Barn at crossroads
	Pine Trees
	The Vineries
Biddleside cottage	Bridle Cottage
The Presbytery (now St. Richard's House)	Linden Lea
	Foulis Croft (now Dove Cottage)
	The Heys
	Fairbourne

Although the copyholders had been indignant at the loss of their grazing rights, Slindon was, in fact, behind most of the country in the enclosure of common land, due probably to the Countess Newburgh's preference for leaving things as they were. For almost a hundred years before the General Enclosure Act of 1845, most landowners and farmers had found it necessary to have all their land together, enclosed by fences to facilitate the improved methods of cultivation.

The enclosure map at the Record Office, Chichester, dated 1870, states:

"Good and sufficient fences for enclosing the several allotments described (i.e. North Wood, Baycombe Green and Court Hill, situate in the County of Sussex which have been duly authorised under the Provision of the Acts for the Enclosure, Exchange and Improvement of Land) if not already set up and made, shall be made within twelve months from the confirmation of the said Enclosure Commission."

In spite of the traumas of the Leslie era, many happier times are remembered, such as the occasion in 1901, when the whole village was invited to the grounds of Slindon House to see Charles Radcliff Leslie, who had been present at the coronation of Edward VII, in his robes.

In January 1888 the *West Sussex Gazette* reported:

"...a most successful entertainment in the great hall at Slindon House, admission being by invitation. The production was organised by Miss T. Leslie and Mr. J.C. Leslie assisted by Messrs. Bunbury and Belloc and Mrs. C. Fletcher from Dale Park. The chief residents of the village and neighbourhood were invited; also many of the working and artisan classes and the elder school children.

After the final departure of the Leslie family, Slindon House was let by the trustees for three years to Mrs Van Davies, who brought with her all her own servants and furnishings.

In 1913 the estate was purchased by Mr F. Wootton Isaacson. A barrister and the son of an MP, he maintained many interests and held the office of High Sheriff of Sussex, in spite of being disabled in his later life. Then he made his way about his estate in a motorised bath-chair he named 'Pegasus'.

He lived at Slindon House with his sister Violet, Lady Beaumont, widow of the 9th Lord Beaumont. With his sister he had travelled extensively in his younger days, and Slindon House contained many souvenirs of his journeys. In the great hall hung a long canoe and in the smaller or stone hall a cannibal's feeding bowl, both of which he brought from the Solomon Isles. They are now in the museum at Cambridge, where in his college days Mr Isaacson was a fine oarsman.

Preserving a link with history, in the same hall was a framed deed dated 1679, in which Anthony Kempe is mentioned as patron of the Rectory.

Mr Isaacson was a keen photographer, and pictures taken on his travels were warmly received by the Royal Geographical Society. An album of his snapshots is in Arundel Museum.

At the time of Wootton Isaacson's arrival at Slindon, the following passage appeared in a local newspaper:

The Wootton Isaacsons

Queen Victoria's dressmaker was Madame Elise, whose establishment was in Regent Street. This name, Madame Elise, covered the activities of Mr. Wootton Isaacson and his wife who, out of making the dresses of mid-Victorian society as well as royal dresses amassed a large fortune. They gave up business; Mr. Isaacson went into Parliament and their daughter Violet became the wife of a former Lord Beaumont.

Mrs. Isaacson presided over a house in Upper Grovenor Street and when a widow continued to give dinners and parties at which she had the good sense to make merry over her business experiences.

Her son bought Slindon House, a fine old Sussex mansion, and there he and his sister Violet, Lady Beaumont have been notable hosts for Goodwood parties.

Extensive alterations and an addition were made to the house in 1914. Thirteen indoor servants were kept and the gardens and woods were tended by a large outside staff.

Jimmy Dean, again employed as estate handyman, describes the gardens and park at that time and before, from the stately flint built house on its chalky hilltop, to the high flint archway with iron gates at the end of the mile-long carriage drive, which it was his duty to keep immaculate.

Immediately before the house was a circle of lawn, surrounded by driveway. A feature of this lawn was the 18th century 'blackamoor' figure of a life-size kneeling figure holding a platter, with a sundial on top. For its protection, it was boarded up during the war, before being moved to the Dower House when she and Mr Wooton Isaacson returned to Slindon to live there in 1946.

When it stood in front of Slindon House, the children used to parade round 'the black boy' with their garlands before the Countess of Newburgh. Many noble households in the 18th century had a small black servant, who was often richly dressed and a favourite with his mistress.

In 1983 the National Trust had the statue removed to another of their properties, West Dean House Garden in Hampshire, where it received necessary restoration.

Beyond the lawns and flower gardens, shrubbery and clumps of trees, was the kitchen garden of three acres, enclosed by high walls, then the fine stables and coach houses with a large ballroom above. Adjoining the stable yard was the carpenters' shop, the bricklayers' shop and the kennels.[21] There was a saw bench by the stream with an engine standing in the nearby shed.

Proudly over the stable buildings rose the clock tower; the clock, Slindon's 'Big Ben', had two faces and a peal of bells by which the villagers set their watches. A chauffeur at Slindon House, who lived in the coach house from 1908 to 1940, could recall an Arundel clockmaker coming out to Slindon every week to wind the clock, which many Slindonians claimed had not stopped in 150 years.

It was a sad day when the clock and tower, with the stables and coach house, were destroyed by fire in 1960. The tower crashed through the stable roof when the blaze, which could be seen for miles, was at its height.

That was the first serious fire in Slindon for many years; but when all the dwellings and buildings were thatched, fires were frequent and, if the sparks were carried before a strong wind, often widespread. The Slindon Estate fire engine and sometimes one from Arundel, with horses in full gallop, were a common sight in the village.

Concealed from the drive by trees was the keeper's cottage, with a large pond for the cattle that roamed the park. Both remain today. Behind another screen of trees were the cowyard, cowpens, pig-pens and a 228ft deep well which supplied the house with water and was enclosed with a substantial wellhouse in which a horse walked round and round, winding up a huge bucket on an iron chain, whilst at the same time letting down a second bucket. The buckets emptied into a large tank in the roof of the wellhouse. The operation of filling this took two hours. The well-house was pulled down in 1901, together with the old

---

[21] The 5th Earl of Newburgh kept a pack of foxhounds at Slindon.

dairy, which was built of flint with roof of reeds once thatched by Jimmy Dean's grandfather.

A deep 'ice well' was built underground with bricks in the time of the Countess. During periods of frost, ice was taken from the pond, with five or six carts working for two days. The estate bricklayers, wood-cutters and four gardeners worked at the well. Plenty of good beer was supplied and double wages were paid.

In the 100 acres of beautiful parkland, the beeches, believed to be the finest in England, bore their 275 years with imposing grace. One, known as the Beauty Tree (the word Beauty was carved on its bark), was so exceptionally tall and straight that Mr Isaacson forbade that it should ever be cut down – and there it stood, until felled by nature's hand, along with hundreds of its companions, in the Great Storm of October 1987.

One beech tree, thus slain, showed 335 rings in its massive trunk. With each ring signifying one year of growth, its year of planting would have been 1632.

Jimmy Dean tells of another terrible gale in 1893 when many beeches were blown down. One, where the root held in the earth, was brought 'twisted like a corkscrew' to the ground.

Oak trees grow in other parts of the park and many birches. It is recorded that Charles II, on his escape ride from Racton to Shoreham in October 1651, after the battle of Worcester, greatly admired an avenue of these birches and would have lingered to appraise them further had not the occasion been of some ur- gency. (The King narrowly escaped detection later that day at Whiteways Lodge, by the Cromwellian Governor of Arundel castle, who fortunately for the King, had been more intent on hunting.)

Beneath the trees, great clumps of emerald moss add colour to the russet slopes, while in spring the primroses and bluebells bloom in profusion, although the daffodils that once lined the driveway have given place to encroaching shrub and crimson bramble.

Three features of the park have their origin much earlier in history. One is the deer pale, part of a medieval deer pound to retain the deer within the park. It consisted of a nine-foot dyke, which was probably topped with a fence of upright pales. The remaining dyke runs parallel with the ride left of the park entrance from Park Lane and continues to the right where paths cross about a mile further on. The National Trust cleared the dyke in 1986.

In the middle of what is now a farm field near the Keeper's cottage is an ancient ruin, surrounded by scrub and fenced. Its origin is uncertain; it could perhaps be the remains of a medieval shrine or chapel. According to *Sussex Notes and Queries. Vol 26,* there is herringbone brickwork in the foundation at the east end with medieval stonework above. An iron end for a pole or spear was found (circa 1866?) in ground close by. It was 82 inches long and would contain a staff 2 inches in diameter. The iron was massive and much corroded.

Thirdly, the square tower behind the north lodge is believed to have been built as a prison at the time of the 13th century palace. The lower portion is of sandstone and ashlar; the upper, probably added later, is flint faced with castellated parapet. There are pointed casement windows on the south side, all of which are barred, and the only door is of strong oak. There are three floors, the upper two reached by flights of wooden steps, with a fireplace on the ground floor.

To the north an 18th century flint wall joins it to the lodge, a two storey dwelling which bears the date 1922 and the initials F.W.I.

The south gateway, of flint courses with galletting and stone crenellation, and the original south lodge are dated early 19th century. The lodge was rebuilt in 1927.

Mr Wootton Isaacson and his considerable fortune brought new prosperity to the Slindon estate. Lady Beaumont was a prominent figure in local and county affairs and was also a proficient horsewoman and enthusiastic rider to hounds. She was out hunting when Queen Mary telephoned Slindon House expressing a wish to visit her (at the time King George V was convalescing at Craigweil House, Aldwick). The butler who took the message was in such a flummox that he dropped the telephone, breaking the receiver, and the call had to be put through from the Post Office.

In due course, her Majesty arrived and after tea, at her own suggestion, walked along Thomas a Becket's Walk, through the churchyard and into the village so that the people might see her.

During the First World War, Slindon House became an auxiliary Military Hospital with Lady Beaumont as Commandant. An inscription above the hearth in the Great Hall commemorates this. Many houses in the village organised socials and entertainments for the wounded soldiers.

In 1940, Slindon House received eighteen children from the Princess Elizabeth of York's Hospital for Children at Shadwell, London. Seven nurses came with them, and part of the house was converted to hospital accommodation. The Princess Elizabeth Hospital expressed its gratitude by making Mr Isaacson and Lady Beaumont life governors.

Unfortunately, bombing in the area made the site unsafe for a hospital. The children were moved to other quarters and the house was taken over by the army. Signatures carved on the cellar walls with place names from all over Canada testify to its occupation by Canadians.

In 1942 paratroopers were trained at Slindon for the raids on Dieppe before D-Day. General Eisenhower visited Slindon House at that time. The soldiers were well known at the White House Stable Cottage (now Timbers), which was turned into a canteen and run by members of the local W.I. and Mothers' Union.

James Lees-Milne, conservationist, author, architectural historian and the first secretary of the National Trust's Country House Scheme, in his published diary *Prophesying Peace* tells of a visit to Slindon in May 1944:

"This property belongs to Mr Isaacson, an old man of 88, who offers it with 4,000 acres. We motored all round the estate. The part with a semicircle of beech trees and carpet of bluebells was a dream of beauty. We drove to the Downs at the north extremity of the estate, with a view towards Bignor.

Then to the house which is a travesty. Originally Elizabethan brick with flint courses, it underwent extensive Georgian alterations outside and in. The present owner mistakenly removed nearly all of these after the last war, inserting bogus ceilings with plasterine ribs. The main facade is practically rebuilt with 'Jacobean' bays where none existed before, and windows of plate glass in lieu of sash.

The only good features left are the seventeenth century screen in the hall, and the overdoors, the pretty eighteenth century wrought-iron balustrade of the staircase and the rococo plaster ceiling above it. The other main staircase was partially boarded up, but I think the framework is modern with Charles II panels inserted. Of their genuineness I am not sure. There is a little Regency temple with Trafalgar balcony round it, which the soldiery have burnt out. The big house has troops in it and is sadly knocked about. The dirt and the dreariness of the surroundings are what one has come to expect in these circumstances."

Mr Wootton Isaacson and Lady Beaumont, who had moved to Somerset when the army took over their home, did not return to Slindon House, but in 1946 took up residence at the Dower House, where Mr Isaacson died in 1948, aged 90. Among the chief mourners at his funeral, held at Slindon Parish Church, were relatives, the Earl and Countess of Ypres, Viscount and Viscountess French, Mr and Lady Patricia Kingsbury, Lord Howard of Glossop and Baroness Beaumont. The Duke of Norfolk was among the congregation. The coffin was borne from the Dower House on a horse-drawn estate wagon led by an estate employee.

Mr Isaacson bequeathed the estate of 3,600 acres to the National Trust, together with a substantial endowment. It was described as 'one of the most important bequests in the south, made to the National Trust.'

Lady Beaumont died the following year. The peerage descended to her niece, Baroness Beaumont, wife of Lord Howard of Glossop. The house remained empty for ten years, the hall and reception rooms being used to store corn and fertilizer from Court Hill Farm, while the fine stables made comfortable quarters for fifty breeding sows and their litters.

The house came to life again in 1956, when it was taken by Lindfield School for Boys until 1972, when it became Slindon College. From 1980 to 1987 the College was unique in having a racing stables attached to the establishment, and it sponsored two races at Fontwell each year at the Spring meeting. Additions to the grounds at this time were the ornamental pond, the gazebo and Italian garden.

Today this independent boarding and day school for boys, aged 11 to 18 years, has about a hundred pupils, a third of which are remedial cases and twenty-five staff. The college has strong links with the village. The congregation of St Mary's welcomes the sight of rows of boys at their monthly family service St Mary's church at the start of each day.

Music is part of a wide and varied curriculum and 1996 saw a new building area developed to house the increase in instruments and interested pupils. It included studio, performance and recording rooms. Among the many facets of rural studies is the keeping of a variety of livestock, including several Vietnamese pot-bellied pigs. In 1997 work began on a tropical butterfly house in the restored Edwardian conservatory. Heating, blinds, water features and plants were installed and lastly, butterflies and pupae. Naturalist, broadcaster and writer Dr David Bellamy opened the house in June 1998.

In company with many old mansions, Slindon House has suffered the vicissitudes of fortune, restorations and alterations and many years of school desks and dormitories, yet retains much of its pristine atmosphere and beauty.

Since the mid-1970s the Camping Club of Great Britain has had a site at the north end of Slindon Park. During early negotiations over the siting of the camp, a village committee stipulated that there should be tents but no caravans and that access should be at the park entrance in the Eartham road.

In May 1985, a National Trust Base Camp, converted from the former Trust Estate Office in the park, was officially opened by Mr Michael Marshall, MP. The premises accommodate 17 volunteers working on conservation projects. Slindon became a Conservation Area in 1975.

VII. Churches & Schools

The focal point of village life has always been its church. A study of Slindon's Parish Church of St Mary takes us back again to the Middle Ages and to the time of the Archbishops at Slindon Manor.

There is no record of the first church in Slindon; one is mentioned in Domesday about 1087 and there may have been one earlier, a very small, humble village church, attached to the Archiepiscopal Manor, but of insufficient importance to warrant remark; built perhaps by the Saxons who were converted to Christianity by the monks of Selsey.

The present church has its origin in a small building, consisting of chancel and nave, built in 1106, possibly by Archbishop Anselm at the recovery of the estate.

In 1154, it is recorded that Archbishop Theodore, dedicated, rebuilt and enlarged the "Church of Blessed Mary" and made a grant of land for its endowment.

According to the *Victoria History of Sussex* Theodore granted the Church to Lewes Priory; and in a charter confirming to Lewes Priory a large number of Churches which had been granted to it, Bishop Seffrid (1180-1204) included the Church of Slindon. (Possibly Theodore's gift did not take effect, probably because it had not been ratified by Canterbury, for there is no trace in the cartulary of the Priory of such a gift, or of the monks having taken any interest in the Church which seems always to have been attached to the Manor).

In 1160-70, the South wall of St Anselm's nave was taken down, an arcade of two arches was built and the south aisle added. A few years later a transceptal chapel was built out to the North and dedicated to St Thomas à Becket. The arch by the pulpit, once the entrance to the chapel, is all that remains.

The church of St Mary, Slindon

Of the fresco work executed at this time, only a small portion on the south wall by the lectern is still faintly visible.

The font is early 11th century, probably Norman or late Saxon.

Early in the 13th century the chancel was rebuilt, with alterations, and extended eastward.

In the fifteenth century an arch was made in the wall of the nave and the north aisle added; a further addition of one bay to the length brought the church to its present size, and a small tower was built.

The church is built of flint rubble with ashlar dressings. The material used in the interior during the early transition period was Caen stone and chalk; two pillars of solid chalk still remain. The 13th century work was of Isle of Wight stone and that of the 15th century was of Pulborough stone, also used in the little Norman window, which is the only feature left of the original nave. (Traces of another Norman window can be seen in the north wall. Both were splayed and had no glass). During the 19th century alterations, Bath stone was used.

The church was restored in 1866 by the Revd William Chantler Izard, Rector from 1865 to 1896.

The work included the rebuilding of the aisle walls and the construction of a new chancel arch, the old one being narrow and rounded and flanked by arched recesses. The east window of five lancets was installed together with the mosaic tile reredos, the centre panel depicting Matthew, Mark, Luke and John and the Star of David. The left side panel is inscribed with the ten commandments, the right with the Lords Prayer and the Nicene Creed. The floor was laid with encaustic tiling, the entire roof renewed and the old wooden tower replaced with one with a stone belfry. This work revealed the inner jamb and sill of a perpendicular west window where the present tower now stands. It also disclosed the blocked outline of a doorway into the 15th.century tower. Pre-16th century this door was the main west entrance to the church. A south door was built and a new south window. In the present north doorway is the original medieval door.

The £2,484, cost of this work was subscribed by the parish, the most generous benefactors being the Izards and the Newlands. The architect responsible was T.G. Jackson.

In October 1966, St Mary's celebrated the centenary of the restoration with a week of special services and music. On Sunday October 12th, the sermon at Matins was preached by the Revd Robin Izard, of St John's Church, Bognor, great-grandson of the Revd William Chantler Izard.

The church's most notable possession is the effigy, carved in oak, of Anthony St Leger, testator of the will in which he stated his wish to be buried in Slindon Church before the picture of Our Lady. This picture, no longer existent, may have been in stained glass or a mural in the chancel. The effigy is without date or dedication. The figure, though in armour, wears neither sword nor spurs, nor is there any heraldic beast or emblem at his feet. His head, resting on his helmet, is turned slightly to where light slants onto him from the south and east windows.

The armour, identified by an expert, is the type worn in the latter Wars of the Roses, or at the latest, during the early Tudor period. H.R. Mosse[22] considers the effigy to be that of St Leger and refers to Dr Fryer,[23] who is of the same opinion. Says Mosse:

> *"It is a sole example of wooden effigy in Sussex, and only 96 re-main in England and Wales. The figure of 5ft 2in is recumbent, the head bare and rests on the helmet; the hair is long and the*

---

[22] *The Monumental Effigies of Sussex 1250-1650.*
[23] *Wooden Monumental Effigies.*

hands in prayer. The plate armour exhibited is a good example of the period: the vambraces are fluted, the tuilles are chan-nelled; the coudes and geouilliers show Renaissance laminated, left is plain, gorget and left passé-garde, taces, fork protuber-ances. No gauntlets, sword or dagger."

Although his effigy is often referred to colloquially as 'the knight', Anthony St Leger Esq would actually have been a squire or shield-bearer, attendant on a knight.

The figure was removed from its resting place in the chancel (when the organ chamber was installed there) and placed in the corner of the nave, where it is of great interest to visitors to the church. It so fascinated Hilaire Belloc, when a boy of nine years, that he wrote the following poem:

> *There is no name upon his grave*
> *If his grave it haps to be*
> *And his face doth look towards the plain*
> *And towards the calm blue sea*
>
> *He lies in a quiet church aisle*
> *With the small churchyard in view*
> *By a little Gothic window*
> *And 'neath a shadowy yew.*
>
> *He may have been carved for ages*
> *And oft heard the tolling bell*
> *And he may lie for ages more there*
> *In that church aisle – who can tell?*
>
> *There is no name upon his grave*
> *If his grave it haps to be*
> *And his face doth look towards the plain*
> *And towards the calm blue sea.*

Among the many memorials in the church is one that reads:

Stephen Langton
Archbishop of Canterbury 1206-1228
Upholder of English Liberties in Magna Carta
June 15th A.D. 1215
Died in this Parish at Slindon Manor
July 9th A.D. 1228

This tablet was given in 1939 by Rhoda M. Muriello Langton

The first of the three bells is inscribed: *W.R.W.P.1616 T.W.*
The second: *Bryanus Eldridge me fecit 1651*
The third: *Bryanus Eldridge me fecit 1657.*

It is interesting to note that the latter two were cast during the Commonwealth, when Cromwell's stringent administration restricted the casting of bells. A fourth bell was installed by the Revd William Chantler Izard.

A Victorian chair in the style of Queen Anne, with needlework back was stolen from the sanctuary in 1998. A carved chair made of oak from a tree blown down less than two miles from the church, now stands in its place. It was made by Andrew Cossar, son of the Revd John Cossar, incumbent from 1981 to 1993.

The prayer desk came from the chapel in Slindon House when this was removed during alterations in 1914. The bible rest is inscribed underneath with the words '*Donat A. Izard me fecit un usum ecclesiae*'.

The piscina in the south wall is 13th century.

A tablet on the west wall of the north aisle bears the names of the Rectors of Slindon from 1203 to the present day.

At the west end of the south aisle are some 15th century 'poppy-head' benches; in the vestry a table of the 17th century and over the door, a representation of the Royal Arms of George III. It bears the letters 'G III' and the date 1783.

Until about two hundred years ago, red crosses on the two inside bays, on the north side, marked the places where the Bishop placed his hands at the original consecration.

A feature of which all trace is now obliterated is the Lady Chapel, which stood inside the churchyard, close by the gate. There seems to be no record of when this was built, but in 1524 John Hyllys of Slindon left money for the restoration of the Lady Chapel and a request that his body should be buried in Slindon Parish Church.

The chapel, a one-roomed square building with a single lancet window, was later used as a cottage belonging to the parish, the last occupant being Mary Martin, a pauper. In 1803 she was removed to the Parish poor house where she died a week later and was buried in St Mary's Churchyard. The Chapel was pulled down the following year.

In 1936 a new South porch was given by Mr Wootton Isaacson to replace the existing dilapidated one. Built of stone and flint, it harmonized with the abutting ancient structure. The lovely old weathered tiles were fortunately sufficient for the new roof.

In 1979-80 a chapel for the purpose of private meditation and prayer, special services, and various church activities was created in the east end of the north aisle on the site of the early Thomas à Becket chapel. Donations and gifts of furnishing came from many individual donors. The new chapel, known as St Mary's Chapel, was dedicated on Trinity Sunday, 1st June 1980, by the then Archdeacon of Chichester, the Venerable R.M.S. Eyre, later Dean of Exeter.

The Church registers go back to 1558, the first year in the reign of Elizabeth I, when the queen decreed that records should be kept of all births, deaths and marriages in each parish and written on parchment. These church records hold some interesting information about the lives of the early parishioners.

During the plague of London in 1665, not one person in Slindon died of this scourge, although a traveller brought the epidemic to Chichester, where it raged throughout the hot dry summer, taking a heavy toll on the population. Yet, sixteen people in Slindon had died of the plague in 1582.

The earliest marriage in the Register is 1588; the bridegroom's surname was Morley.

The death of a William Saxbie is recorded in 1666.

Another entry in the Register records:

"Elinor Booker, ye daughter of Thomas and Mary Booker, was buried in Woollen only (according ye Act of Parliament)[24] this 6th day October Anno Domini 1683".

The name Booker is not uncommon in the area today.

'A traveller unknown', 'a son of a travelling woman', 'Mr White, a stranger', and 'a child of a beggar unknown', are all recorded as having been buried at Slindon.

According to the registers, many village children (some years as many as six) died at an early age.

A number of benefactions made to the poor of the parish are duly recorded.

A charity derived from a lugger was given for the use of the poor. There was money given by one, Mr Allen, deceased, "to be rymployed as a stocke for the poore of ye parish of Slindon, which stocke is likewise rymployed accordinge to the intention of the giver."

---

[24] In 1678 an Act of Parliament decreed that to assist the wool trade, people should be buried in wool.

Later, by certificate is a similar return: "that the stocks given to the Borough of Midhurst and Parish of Slindon for the relief of the poor had been employed according to the donor's intention."

Early in the 18th century, an old man, a beggar, was found dying on Slindon Common. He gave the considerable amount of money on his person to Mr Newland, churchwarden, for the poor of the Parish. The fund created is still in existence and is called colloquially, 'the beggar's money'. No one knows where the beggar lies; by 1741 his name was forgotten (although there is a possibility it could have been Polycarpus Golcot, a beggar recorded as having been buried in Slindon in 1704).

Johannes Mellie, a Rector who conformed at the Reformation, died in 1682 and was buried at Slindon; his widow, Elizabeth, at her death in 1708, left to the poor of the Parish £2 a year, payable out of certain lands at Eartham.

In 1781 the Reverend John Smelt, when he succeeded to the Rectory, agreed to pay the sum of £5 a year 'for bread for the poor in lieu of a feast won't to be given at the Parsonage'.

Clara Toogood, by her will dated 30th July 1890, bequeathed £25 to the Rector and Churchwardens of Slindon, the income to be applied for such charitable purposes as they may see fit. The annual income amounted to 9s. 8d.

The Jane Izard Memorial: By a declaration of Trust dated 10th March, 1893, made by Ellen Shand, a sum of £200 was settled upon trust, the income to be applied in gifts of clothing to be distributed annually among the deserving poor just before Christmas. Annual income amounted to £5.

When, in modern times such gifts of clothing were no longer acceptable, this money was distributed in conjunction with Lady Beaumont's gift, which is commemorated by a plaque in the church.

According to this plaque, the gift of £520, invested by Violet, Lady Beaumont OBE for the benefit of the poor of the parish is in thanksgiving for our victory of the Great War, January 28th 1919. From this bequest £1 per annum is given, at the discretion of the Rector, to the sick and poor of the parish.

In 1866 the church, its Rector and Churchwardens had duties and responsibilities now in the care of the Parish Council.

In 1896 the Parish Council decided to distribute annually the interest on the Poor Man's (beggar's) charity capital which then amounted to £30, between eight, later four, deserving poor.

In 1972, the Charity Commissioners, under the Charities Act 1960, made an order for the regulating of the charities known as Lady Beaumont, Jane Izard, Poor Money and Sarah Toogood, whereby an investment now stands in the name of the official custodian for Charities and the income, under the title of the Lady Beaumont Trust, is administered by local trustees, comprising the Rector, two Parish Council representatives and two co-opted members.

Another bequest was made by Miss Ann Newland. An extract of her will (undated) states:

To the Rector of Slindon, for the time being, the sum of £200 upon trust to place the same out at interest etc. etc. and upon trust to pay the interest etc. etc. unto the schoolmaster for the time being of the Protestant School at Slindon in augmentation of the salary of such schoolmaster.

A list of Patrons of the Church goes back to 1297, beginning at that time with the Archbishop of Canterbury, followed in 1568, by Anthony Kempe Esq.

A list of incumbents dates from 1243, when Richard de Clifford was Rector, preceded by one undated – Godard Rector and Alexander chaplain, or curate.

In 1243[25] Henry III presented a living (during voidance of the See) and a vicarage was ordained at this time. In 1291 the rectory was worth £10, the vicarage £4.13.4d. During the 14th century the vicarage was reunited to the rectory, valued at £14.13.4d.

The Kempes, being Roman Catholics, sold the right of presentation which was exercised by Laurence Allcock 1683 – Thomas Carle 1708 – Thomas Groome 1738 – John Pannell 1764 – John Smelt 1781. In 1863 Charles Leslie sold the advowson to William Catt who later took the name of Willett; he sold it in 1865 to William Joshua Tilley at whose death it passed to his son-in-law John Shane who sold it to the Revd William Chantler Izard. It then passed from his son and successor to Miss Jane Izard. Since her death in 1970 the advowson is shared between the late Miss Izard's lawyers and the Dean and Chapter of Chichester Cathedral.

The Revd William Chantler Izard, who was remembered for his restoration of the church, was also well known as a missioner on Goodwood Racecourse, where he was very popular and held services for the gypsies and vagrants who gathered there. He was also a strong temperance advocate and started a Temperance Society at the Rectory.

The Rector's wife, the first Jane Izard, was also well-loved and remembered in the village. Amongst other works for the Parish she opened a night school for the men of the village, and all who attended it learned to write most beautifully. Jimmy Dean, whose handwriting was extremely good in spite of the brevity of his schooling, may have been one of her pupils.

While the work of restoring the church was in progress, services were held on the Rectory lawn, when fine, and inside when the weather was wet.

---

[25] *Victoria History of Sussex.*

The new Rector also made changes to the church. Jimmy Dean writes:

"When the Revd Chantler Izard came to Slindon, there was no choir and the organ was in the large oak gullery with long stairs close the bells. Copyholders of Slindon all had their own enclosed pews. After the restoration, the church choir was formed by the Rector and all pews were open. The new organ, gift of the Misses Newland, was installed in the chancel."

Jimmy Dean was one of the boys in the new choir, which sang at the first service in the newly-restored church. After a time, the choristers were put into surplices and Mr John St Clare from Chichester Cathedral came fortnightly to teach them, being conveyed to Barnham Station to catch the last train back to Chichester.

The present organ was built in 1895 by Forster and Andrews of Hull, organ builders from 1843 to 1956. It was hand-blown and mechanical throughout. Today the pedal action is pneumatic and the organ has an electric blower. The stencilled decoration on the front pipes is common in organs of this period.

Of the four bells, only one was rung for usual church services, but all were rung at Christmas and New Year.

The older of the two fine lectern bibles was printed by Eyre and Spottiswoode in 1865 and is a good example of the large family or lectern bibles of the period. In 1913 Mr Wootton Isaacson had a set of large, pierced and embossed corner plates made in silver or silver plate, and attached, together with a matching centre plaque. These unfortunately were stolen in 1986.

After the death of the Revd William Chantler Izard, his second son Arthur came from Wisbech in Cambridgeshire to take over the parish.

A wing was added to the old flint-built rectory during the Revd Arthur Izard's time to accommodate his family of four girls and three boys. The family kept their own cows on the piece of glebe land opposite the forge, and they were milked in a building that stood by the road. A track runs from this point through the wood known as "Parson's Copse", for the Rector was entitled to collect stakes, firing and brushwood from this property.

The glebe land today is distributed in small plots of land in the village, amounting to about twenty-four acres and farmed by local farmers. In the time of the Revd Maurice Smelt the glebe amounted to forty-three acres and was farmed by the Rector himself.

The Tithe book in Chichester says:

> "*The Glebe lands of the said Rectory which are exempt from the payment of all tithes when in the manurance or occupation of the Rector himself contain by measurement (outside content) forty-three acres, one rood and eight sq. perches statute measurement.*"

But later, it seems, some of the glebe was let, for there appears in the Title book the following:

> "*...and it is hereby agreed that the annual sum of £270 by way of rent charge shall be paid to Maurice Smelt as Rector of said Parish and owner of tithes thereof and to his successors.*"

The following excerpts containing the Parish were recorded in 1839, giving details of the rent charge in lieu of tithes in the Parish of Slindon:

> "*Whereas an agreement for the Commutation of Tithes in the Parish of Slindon was this 16th day of November 1839 confirmed by the Tithe Commission in England and Wales.*"

There follows a lengthy copy of the agreement, including:

All planted ground and underwoods are exempt from tithes.

A modus of £6 per annum is payable in lieu of all.

All manner of tithes great and small rising from the park and grounds belongs to the mansion called Slindon House, which contains by measurement, outside contents of 218 acres 1 rod 21 perches statute measurement."

Slindon Parish then contained '2,504 acres, 2 roods and six perches'. Among Church papers is a record of the glebe in the time of Charles I.

The Revd Arthur Izard and his four daughters were extremely musical, the Rector himself possessing a fine tenor voice and his daughters playing at least one stringed instrument. The Rector formed and led the Slindon Choral Society, and James Dean was one of its first members. The first performance, held in the church, was of Dr Stainer's sacred cantata *The Daughter of Jairus*, on December 19th 1897. The organ was supplemented by stringed instruments played by the Misses Izard.

The Choral Society was discontinued after the death of the Revd Izard in 1919. The following is taken from his obituary in the *West Sussex Gazette* of January 9th:

"We deeply regret to announce the sudden death, on Friday last, of the Rev. Arthur Izard, who has been Rector here since 1896 and has built himself a monument in the history of the parish and in the memories of all who knew him. He was single-minded, unpretentious, genial, careful, attentive to his clerical duties and most faithful in their discharge. In addition Mr. Izard was a source of village co-partnership and civilization such as all Sussex parishes do not find. He lived for and with his people. A good musician, he trained a gifted family or saw that they were trained in the most divine of arts; and though much of his daughters' remarkable skill was manifested in other spheres,

Slindon knew more of this than any other place. In the church and in the village music came into its own through this family, and its head was never happier than when he was operating with his lantern and slides. For his parish and for his friends he laboured tirelessly to make life happier and richer, and he succeeded so highly that his death leaves many mourning, not only for the friend and clergyman, but for the very spring of life in the parish. Mr. Izard had not been well lately and it seems clear that over-exertion while assisting with his car accelerated his end which came with extreme suddenness on Friday morning as he was helping to move the car into its quarters.

"Mr. Izard was educated at Trinity College, Oxford. He was made Deacon in 1876 and priest in 1877 at Winchester. He was attached to the Wilberforce Mission, Newington, S.E. from 1878 to 1883 and was Vicar of Wisbech, Cambridgeshire from 1883 to 1896, since which he has been Rector of Slindon. The latter is a family living and was previously held by Mr. Izard's father. The Rev. A. Izard, who was 66 years of age, leaves a widow, four daughters and three sons.

"The interment on Tuesday found the village in mourning for its treasured friend. Six members of H.M. Forces bore the coffin to the church from the hillside Rectory, to a service conducted by the Bishop of Lewes and Archdean Izard (a cousin of the deceased). The church was full to overflowing; officers, non-commissioned officers and men from the airship station and Canadian Forestry Camp mingling with friends and school children, the latter dropping bunches of flowers into the grave as they filed past later. There were very many wreaths."

In 1922 the Izard family made their home at Church House; the last surviving member, Miss Jane Izard, died there in 1970, at the age of 87.

In the 1920s a team of eight hand-bell ringers was formed, possibly by the Misses Izard, consisting mainly of young men from the village; they held practices in an outhouse at the Rectory and performed at church festivals.

A branch of the Mothers' Union, formed in the time of the Izard family, continued in the village until 1971.

Much local history and interest can be gleaned from the parish churchyard. A study of the gravestones at St Mary's evokes a picture of the past. Many bear the names of old Slindon families, Deans, Hersees, Carvers, Bowleys, Izards. There are the graves of Henry Mosse Oliver, who may have been Slindon's first baker and of George Hotston, perhaps the first Slindon carrier, and of Charles Hotston who carried on the business. On the left of the gate lie Alfred James Day, founder of Fontwell Racecourse, who died in 1935 aged 76; Nellie Pink, lady's maid to Lady Beaumont; Charlotte Daisy Hersee, personal maid and companion to Madame Belloc; and Sarah Mew, much loved nurse of Hilaire Belloc. Sarah's epitaph, composed by Madame Belloc reads:

In Sacred Remembrance of Sarah Mew,
who departed this life March 3rd 1896 aged 72 years.
Nurse and dear friend of the family of Madame Belloc.
Her children shall rise and call her blessed.

She had been brought up a strict non-conformist, embraced by a Roman Catholic family, and buried in an Anglican church.

There are the graves of the famous cricketer, Richard Newland, his young wife and child and other members of his family, and many who played cricket for Slindon when the team was equally famous.

A plain memorial, one of only two on the exterior wall of the church, has an aura of mystery. The wording is as cold and stark as the stone it is engraved upon.

To the memory of John Smelt, who died at Chichester
February 12th 1817
also to the memory of Caroline Smelt, sister of the above
who died June 9th 1817
Reader, Set thine house in order, for thou shalt die and not live.

What is the story of this brother and sister who died within four months of each other (at what age the stone does not say) and are remembered with such a sparcity of words on an outside wall, when other early memorials to the Smelt family are inside the church? Why the ominous epitaph, indicative of some grave misdoing that had incurred an apparent estrangement from their family, and which leaves the reader with a sense of sadness and foreboding?

Above it on the south wall is a memorial, the wording of which is almost obliterated, to Fanny Elizabeth Smelt, beloved daughter of the Revd Maurice Smelt and Mary Smelt, who died in infancy.

A John Smelt, LLB was Rector of Slindon from 1781 to 1815; he was followed by Maurice Smelt, MA, who preceded Revd Chantler Izard. The last members of the Smelt family to be buried at Slindon were William Anthony Casterton Smelt, who died in 1972 and his wife Margaret Jessy Hertzel Smelt, who died in 1982.

The plaque on the wooden seat by the gate is inscribed :

In grateful remembrance of
Dorothy Frances Marriott M.B.E.
for many years of devotion and generosity
to this church and Parish.
Died 31.3.65.[26]

---

[26] see chapter 13 'Writers and Personalities'.

The War Memorial, according to the inscription, was erected by members and friends of the village club.

On the right of the north path will be noticed a wooden cross between the graves of Mr and Mrs Charles White and this has a story. The cross commemorates the death in action of their son George, one of their family of four boys and a girl, raised in Slindon in the late 1800s to early 1900s. He was killed in France in 1918, a fortnight before the armistice. After the war, when the wooden crosses on overseas graves were replaced by more permanent memorials, the Commanding Officer sent George's cross to his parents. On their death, the cross passed to his sister, the late Mrs Florence Gammons of Arundel, who before her death asked if it might be given a place by his parents' graves.

In 1995 a memorial garden was created in the area of the War Memorial. Two seats, as well as trees and plants were donated by Parishioners; there is also a plaque in the church commemorating those who died in both World Wars. The rose bushes by the churchyard gate were all donated by parishioners in memory of deceased relatives, whose names are commemorated on a small tablet in the north porch.

Bay trees and hollies flourish in the churchyard, dominated by several large yews. A beautiful Magnolia Bean tree was lost in the 1987 gale, but a sapling has sprung from the root. A handsome cork tree stands by the south wall.

Since 1930 the Parish of Slindon has been joined with the Parish of Eartham. The tiny church of St Margaret's is of Saxon or Norman origin, the dominant feature being the fine Norman Chancel arch. Among several interesting monuments are two by Flaxman, one to William Hayley, the poet, who lived at Eartham House, and the other to a son of Hayley. There is also a memorial to the Rt Hon William Huskisson, MP for Chichester, who was knocked down and killed by Stephenson's Rocket at the opening of the Liverpool and Manchester Railway in 1820 and so goes down in history as the first ever railway fatality; there is also a large memorial to him by Carew in Chichester Cathedral.

From 1700 to 1854 the Slindon Parish shared an incumbent with the Parish of Binsted, the last rector to serve both parishes being the Revd Maurice Smelt.

Inlaid in the floor of the south aisle of St Mary's is a memorial to:

Rev Robert Stiles Launce
late Rector of this Parish and Binfted
objit auguft the 10ᵗʰ 1764

The little Norman Church of St Mary's, Binsted was built by monks of Tortington Priory in 1140 A.D. Several features of the original Norman Church remain. On the splays of the north window of the chancel is a painting of St Margaret of Scotland, immediately after the canonization; believed to be the only painting of the saintly Queen in existence. The Queen Anne prayer table came from the private chapel in Slindon House.

Up to the 16ᵗʰ century, these and other parishes were visited by the Bishops of Selsey and later of Chichester, when they were in residence at Amberley Castle.

In 1981 the Parish of Madehurst was combined with Slindon and Eartham. The tiny downland church of St Mary Magdalene was founded as a shepherds' chapel by the monks of Tortington Abbey, near Arundel in the 13ᵗʰ century. The tower, the oldest remaining section, contains two bells, which were hung to commemorate the centenary of the Magna Carta in 1315. The church was restored and enlarged in 1864 and an organ chamber and organ added in 1890.

The entrance to Slindon Park, off London Road (A29) Fontwell, as it was in 1985.

Postcard from the 1920s showing various views of Slindon.

Some Slindon Park's 300-year old beech trees, many of which were lost in the 'Great Storm' of 1987.

The beech woods of Slindon Park c.1900 and below after the 'Great Storm' of 1987.

Court Hill Farm, Nore Hill, the Folly and the Downs beyond c.1960.

Horses and men at Court Hill Farm in the 1890s.

Court Hill Farm c.1980 (above).
Court Hill Farmhouse c.1960 (below).

The old Victorian school house.

Architect's impression of the new school, founded by Rev W.C. Izard in 1871.

A hand-coloured postcard of School Hill c.1900.

School Hill in the 1980s.

Mme Bessie Parkes Belloc.

Gaston Cottage, in which she lived c.1900.

Miss Daisy Hersee, companion
to Mme Belloc, c.1900.

The Grange, for three centuries the home
of the cricketing Newland family.

Dairy Cottage, pre-renovations in 1921.
Note the Union Jack flags flying, possibly to mark the Armistice in 1918.

Signpost at the Mill Road/Reynolds Lane crossroads with London Road (A29) as it was c.1900.

Flint Cottage and Nurse's Cottage on School Hill as they were c.1900.

St Richard's Roman Catholic Church c.1980.

No.33 School Hill c.1890.

Village children playing in the street c.1900.

Wellnap Corner showing Manchester House and the village shop
as it was in 1900 (above) and in 1969 (below).

No.2 Slindon, showing the Tudor beams previously hidden beneath concrete rendering (the property has since been re-rendered).

Slindon's village pond, frozen in the winter of 1985.

Slindon Bakery, 1927.

A postcard showing Top Road as it was in 1959.

St Richard's House.

The White House.

The Well House, before and after alterations.

The Author and friend outside Slindon Post Office, c.1955.

Hope Cottage c.1900.

The Lime Tree in the 1960s (above) and in the snowy winter of 1985 (below).

Mill House and its occupants in the 1890s.

The Nore Folly as it was in 1980, prior to restoration.

St Mary's Church as it was before restoration by Rev Izard (above) and afterwards (below).

The interior of St Mary's church, 1980s.

Miss Bryant (with bicycle), church organist at St Mary's for many years, pictured in 1960 with the Author and her son Nicholas.

Wellnap Corner looking towards Pump Cottage, c.1900.

Lime Tree shop and beer house, as it was in the 1920s.

Two vintage postcard views of Slindon Pond – circa 1890 (above) and some years later (below).

Note how much the trees have grown in the second picture.

An etching of Slindon House as it was in 1780.

And below, an early photograph of its staff in 1885.

Slindon House after refurbishment in 1904.

And Slindon College, as it looked in 2002.

The horse-drawn Slindon Bus c.1900.

The first Silver Queen charabanc c.1920.

The village carriers with their horse and cart c.1900.

Charles Bowley giving funfair rides with his steam engine c.1900.

The Rev William Chantler Izard, vicar of St Mary's, Slindon in the 1890s.

David Voller (1850-1928), miller in Slindon from 1870-90, and his wife Sarah.

Hedley Clarke and Jim Carver,
Slindon Bakery's delivery boys, 1927.

Lady Belloc and Rev Arthur Izard at a
church fete c.1900.

Slindon Blacksmiths
The Old Forge in Dyers Lane (above).
The Forge at School Hill c.1960 (below).
Mr J.E. Janes, village blacksmith 1958-71 (inset opposite).
Peter Fenton at work in the Forge in the 1970s (opposite).

Colourful display of pumpkins grown by Ralph & Barbara Upton at their nursery (1980s).

Railway carriage outbuilding at Church House.

Macrocarpa struck by lightning 15/9/1973.

Jimmy Dean and his young family c.1890.

Slindon cricket team in the 1930s (note an elderly Jimmy Dean on crutches with only one leg).
Mr Wooton Isaacson of Slindon House is seated with walking stick.

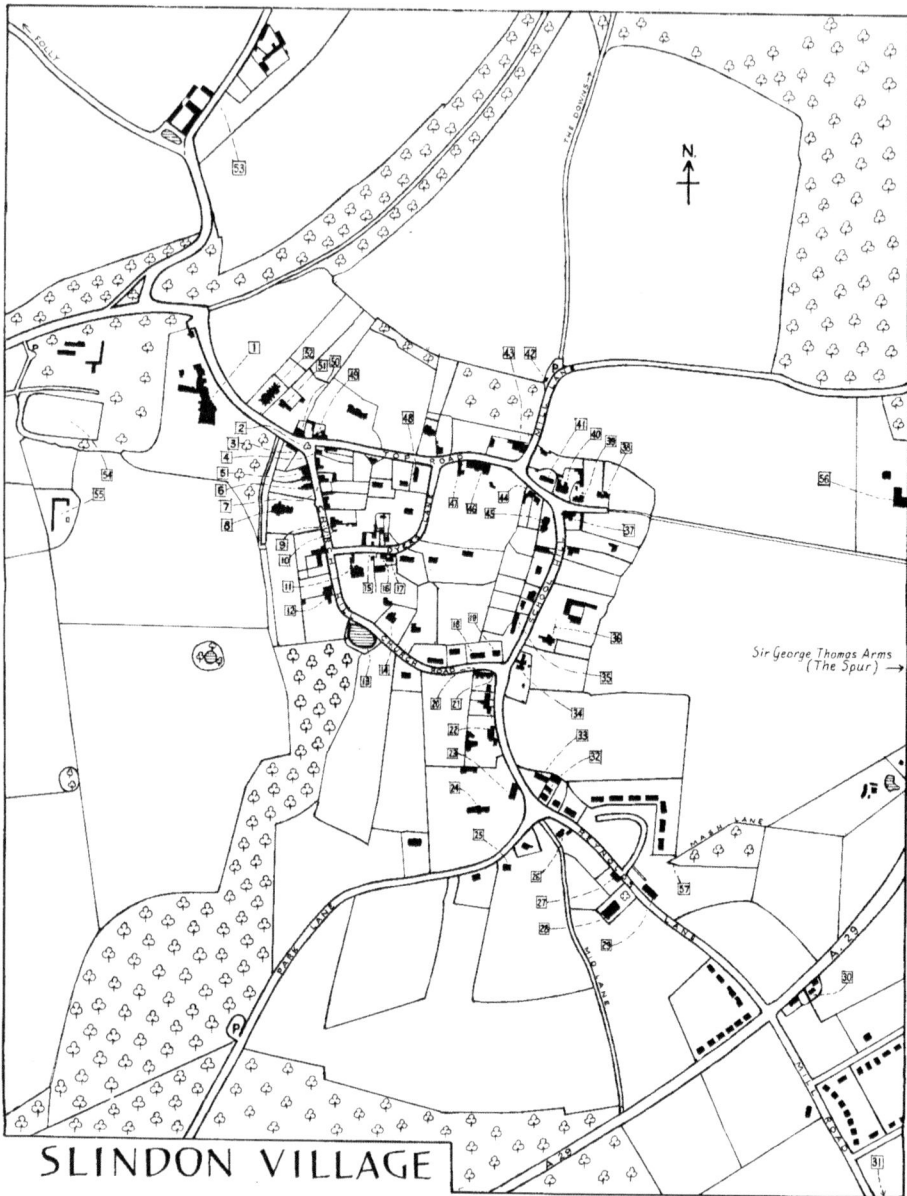

SLINDON VILLAGE

N.

Sir George Thomas Arms
(The Spur) →

1 Slindon House	16 Rectory Cottage	30 Site of Dog & Partridge	45 Old School
2 Lime Tree	17 Site of Old Forge	31 Site of Old Mill	46 Bleak House
3 No.2 Slindon	18 Watkins Cottage	32 Flint Cottage	47 Slindon Pottery
4 No.7 Slindon	19 Pump Cottage	33 Wades Cottage	48 St.Richards Cottage
5 The Hermitage	20 Village Stores	34 Elm Cottage	49 Lime Tree Cottage
6 The Old Post. No.11	21 Wellnap Cottage	35 Well House	50 Club House
7 Old Inn House	22 Timbers	36 Gaston Farm	51 St.Richards House
8 St. Mary's Church	23 Hope Cottage	37 Newburgh Arms	52 St.Richards Church
9 Church House	24 Millstones	38 No.33 Slindon	53 Court Hill Farm
10 Railway Carriage	25 No.45 Slindon	39 Vine Cottage	54 Camping Club
11 Mulberry House	26 Dairy Cottage	40 Gassons	55 Ice Well
12 The Grange	27 The Forge	41 Post Office	56 Highfields
13 Village Pond	28 Coronation Hall	42 Cattle Pound	57 Pond with Spring
14 Pond House	29 Slindon C of E	43 Mill Lane House	
15 Lock-Up	Primary School	44 The Old Bakery	

© Denis McQuoid 1988

There are several interesting monuments, including one erected in 1789 to Roque Ferdinand, a coloured servant of Sir George Thomas of Dale Park, who had been Governor of the Leeward Isles. The Victorian stained glass of Edward Burne-Jones, which filled the east and south windows, was largely blown out by a landmine in 1944.

Although the Roman Catholic Church of St Richard is little more than one hundred years old, the Catholic Mission in Slindon dates from the Reformation and its story is as dramatic and courageous as any in the long history of religious persecution.

With the change in religion under Henry VIII, Slindon's connexion with the See of Canterbury ceased and it passed into the hands of laymen.

The faith of Sir Garrett Kempe and his wife, who started the mission, and the building of the new mansion with the secret chapel have been mentioned in Chapter III. Mary Tudor's reign brought a respite in the persecution of the Catholics. Then Father Richard Wyatt said Mass again and the previous liturgy returned. But this ceased when Elizabeth came to the throne.

Priests came to Slindon House from far and wide; from Norfolk, Cheshire, Lancashire, and London, and from Lisbon, Valladolid, Paris, Douai and Rome.

Marriages and baptisms took place in the secret chapel and were recorded on the blank pages of a missal. One, printed in 1673 now in St Richard's Church contains the following entry:

"Miss Barbara Kempe, now Lady Kennard was married to Lord James Bartholomew Kennard on ye 26 Fbr 1749 it being then a Sunday evening."

There is also the addition "Since ye change of title (from Kennard to Newburgh) ye wedding day is commemorated on ye 7 day of December."

Also among the papers of St Richard's is a copy of a letter written by the unfortunate Earl of Derwentwater to his wife's parents, "The night before the execution".

Slindon House never ceased to harbour priests within its walls, nor, at any period to shelter the little band of worshippers who remained true to the ancient faith. The small chapel under the roof reached by narrow staircases and passages was for three hundred years the sacred sanctuary where generations of pious Catholics approached the Sacraments and heard mass, when to do so was a matter of life and death. This secrecy had to be observed far beyond the middle of the last century.

The Rev. Joseph Silveira buried a man (James Louch ob.1839 aetatis 85) who remembered when he was a boy, Pursuivants coming to Slindon House with a warrant for the apprehension of the Popish priest Father Molyneux, who escaped through the secret passage and eluded their search.[27]

During the course of his visitation, which began in June 1741 and lasted almost two years, Bishop Richard Challoner visited the Kempes at Slindon when the number of Catholics was ninety.

Today the church of St Richard, built to the design of the architect C.A. Butler by Robert Bushby of Littlehampton, stands in its prominent position on Slindon Hill. The Rt Revd Bishop of Southwark laid the foundation stone on 7th September 1864. Catholics and Protestants assembled to witness the ceremony.

"It is seldom," wrote Father Sheehan, priest in charge of the mission at that time, "that so beautiful a Catholic church as is now rising in Slindon is to be found in a quiet English village."

---

[27] According to *The History of St Richard's* by Father M.G. Costello, Priest at St. Richard's from 1946 to 1957.

The building was completed in November 1865 and thus were carried out the terms of the Earl of Newburgh's will which bequeathed:

> *"a farm and lands, a dwelling house and appurtenances, and five hundred pounds in money to establish a Roman Catholic chapel at Slindon and to maintain a priest to officiate in the same."*

Because the Countess of Newburgh preferred that worship should continue in the house chapel, work on the new building did not commence until after her death, when Colonel Leslie built St Richard's Church. The money invested by the Earl had by this time substantially increased, nevertheless it was supplemented by Colonel Leslie and, in recognition of this he was given the privilege of weekly mass in the House Chapel for five years, a period which lasted exactly until his death.

Among certain documents concerning the Leslie family is the following:

1906. Payment Schedule. High Court of Justices. Abstract of a mortgage executed in 1864 by Colonel Leslie etc. etc...

> *"Concerning grant by Chas. Leslie of messuage and garden and field estimated 112 acres ... also a piece of land adjoining etc... to permit a church to be built for use of Roman Catholic Religion with a Sacristy and for a burial ground and to permit the said messuage to be used by the official priest as a residence or for a school..."*

There is a stained glass window to the memory of the Countess of Newburgh above the high altar. The Earl (d.1814) is commemorated by his widow with a small monument by the great Danish sculptor Bertel Thorwaldsen, one of only three in Britain. The grieving figures of a woman and an angel "have great sculptural force" and their "detailed execution… is brilliant."[28]

On 28th November, 1865, the last public mass was attended by the whole congregation in the old chapel to celebrate the anniversary of the founder. That same evening, the Bishop, Dr Grant, sealed up the relics of the saints and placed them on the altar of the new church.

Together with the missal previously referred to, the church of St Richard possesses the Altar Stone, a white vestment, two ciboria, Holy oil bottles and a large relic of the True Cross, all of which were used in the secret chapel in Slindon House.

In Father Costello's history there is a list of priests from the Penal Times to the present day.

The second, Father Henry Kempe, born in 1672, the son of Anthony Kempe, served Slindon for several years. A kinsman of his, Francis Boniface Kempe O.S.B. never reached there, but spent many years in prison and exile until he finally died from exhaustion behind the parliamentary troopers' horses in 1643.

On March 5th 1953, 700 years after the death of St Richard of Chichester and to mark the anniversary, his Lordship, the Bishop of Southwark, consecrated the church dedicated to his honour.

The quiet graveyard behind the church, overlooking the Downs and watched over by the tall crucifix, has an atmosphere of tranquillity. Gravestones bear many names well known in the annals of Slindon. The Countess of Newburgh lies there and her friend and contemporary Lady Georgiana Fullerton. To the right of the steps, marked by a stone cross, is the grave of Madame Bessie Parkes Belloc and nearby that of Rowland Wedgwood and his wife Agnes. The Lourdes grotto on the left of the church

---

[28] Ian Nairn in *The Buildings of England*. Sussex series.

path, of local flint with its Mother of God hewn from Sussex stone, was built in the 1950s in the time of Canon Wake.

According to the tithe map of 1839, there was a school at No. 33 Slindon. An entry in the Tithe Apportionment book describes the property as: "house, school and garden, measuring 1 rod, 14 perch." The tithe was 1s 3d per annum. It was a Roman Catholic school where the priest of St Richard's assisted in the teaching. The schoolteacher occupied No.32; both properties belonged to the Countess of Newburgh.

In her *Social Study of Roman Catholicism in West Sussex*, Mary Kinoulty notes an entry concerning a Roman Catholic School in Slindon. 'At Slindon in 1785 there was a Popish School very lately erected where Catholic children can be educated separately, since there was another little school kept by a Protestant mistress.' According to Moore's visitation in 1788 return of the Revd J. Smelt, the number of Catholics in Slindon were, 16 in 1676, 100 in 1707 and 96+ in 1780.

A new Catholic school was built in 1883 on the site of an old farmhouse on the corner of Top Road and Dyer's Lane. It was closed in the 1940s and stood empty for several years before being bought for conversion into a private house, now St. Richard's Cottage. A plaque in the east wall, comprising an unidentified coat of arms and the date 1870, is puzzling and could have been added at a later date. Gothic Cottage, next door, was the schoolhouse.

The first Anglican school was probably in the cottage in the Rectory grounds in Dyers Lane, where the fee was threepence a week for the first child and tuppence for subsequent ones of the same family.

The school, which Anglican children from Slindon and often neighbouring villages attended for over a hundred years, stood with adjoining school house, opposite the Newburgh Arms at the junction of Top Road and School Hill. It was built mainly at the instigation of the Rector, the Rev. William Chantler Izard, on land that was formerly a paddock belonging to him.

After the opening in 1871, the following passage appeared in the *West Sussex Gazette*.

> *"On Tuesday, September 12, the new National Schools at Slindon were opened by the Lord Bishop of the Diocese. The service at the church was at three in the afternoon and the Bishop preached. He congratulated the parishioners on the completion of the work and he rejoiced at the unanimity and hearty co-operation it had called forth. It was impossible to overvalue education both secular and religious; the germs of useful and practical knowledge were sown in the mind which ripened in after life. The collection amounted to £53.14s.9d.*

After the service, the Bishop proceeded to the schools. The Slindon Band led the way playing the National Anthem. Then came the children, followed by the choir and congregation, with the Bishop and twenty of his clergy. Mr Henry Halstead, treasurer of the building fund, said the cost of the Slindon National Schools was about £930. Including the Government grant and those from the Diocesan and National Societies and collections at the service, he had received £773 4s 5d, leaving a balance of about £150 to be made up.

> *"We may say in conclusion that the schools are very prettily designed, the architect being Mr. Arthur Smith of Bognor and the builder Mr. Robert Bushby, Littlehampton. All the building materials were carted by the farmers of the parish, free of expense, each one assessing himself of his own free will according to the amount of his rating."*

One of the men working at Court Hill Farm in recent years tells how his grandfather, as his first job of work, drew flints by horse and cart from Gumber Farm for the school building and his great-grandfather helped to pick them from the field.

Jimmy Dean recounts that Mr Holston, living at Court Hill Farm, sent his men, horses and carts to draw flints for the National School.

The new school was placed under Government inspection according to the new Education Act, but the Rector, in his opening speech, strongly advocated the addition of diocesan inspection. Richard Holmes Esq, a solicitor from Arundel, read the trust deed conveying the site to the trustees forever for the purpose of education. The constituary board of managers included the Rector and Churchwardens, Sir Peniston Milbanke, Bart, JP of Eartham House; J.C. Fletcher Esq, Dale Park; W. Hudson, Court Hill Farm and W. Darlett, Madehurst.

There were 93 children in the school after its opening, with an average attendance of 50. By 1878 the number had risen to 100. All the children were taught in one classroom.

"A great many children have heavy coughs this morning," reads one headmaster's entry in the log book, "so that the master has great trouble to maintain discipline."

Other entries in the log book show that:
- a number of boys were absent for 'beating at shooting parties' or for 'gleaning';
- the school played cricket with neighbouring village schools as far away as Lavant;
- in 1874 the school choir attended a Choral Festival at Chichester;
- in 1895 the gallery was moved from one end of the school to the other.

An infant's classroom was added in 1884.

In 1970 the school still had fittings for three types of lighting; the old rings for oil lamps, the gas brackets and the electric lights installed in 1946.

In its early years, children from Walberton attended the school, walking back and forth.

Soon after its opening the school received a visit from Lady Victoria Wellesley, a descendant of the Duke of Wellington.

In 1924, Miss Ellen Terry visited the school while staying in Slindon. The log book says: "she spoke kindly to the children, heard a boy recite few lines from "Hubert and Arthur" and listened to the singing of a verse of "Ye Banks and Braes." She said to the headmaster, "Teach them prettily, it will be a comfort to them in their old age. Teach them Wordsworth."

In 1947, in the time of the school's only headmistress, Mrs Ward (except on two occasions when a brother and sister jointly ran the school) the children formed a branch of the Young Farmer's Club and entered a Village Survey Competition (junior section) promoted by the Federation, winning second prize in the Country.

On 4th October 1971 to celebrate the school centenary, a service was held in St Mary's Church, which was decorated for Harvest Festival as it had been for the original opening. Immediately after the service a short ceremony took place in the school when a commemorative plaque was unveiled by Mrs Mary Izard, whose late husband was a grandson of the Revd William Chantler Izard. She also presented to the school a lithograph of the building as it was in 1871.

Eventually, when more spacious premises became essential, the present Church of England (controlled) Primary School was built in Reynold's Lane. On 8th October 1975 it was officially opened by E.J.F. Green Esq, DL, Chairman of West Sussex County Council, with the Chairman of the School Managers, the Revd H.R. Gray in the chair.

The new school was built of brick, with a tile roof to harmonise with its surroundings, by J.G. Snelling Ltd of Chichester, under the supervision of the County Architect. It provides three home bases for infants and juniors with adjoining wet area facilities and a large central area for communal activity, which is also used for dining. Off this is a large quiet room, etc. Spacious kitchen and staff accommodation is also provided. The building has capacity for 90 pupils and four teachers.

In the interest of continuity, the old school bell, which had, from its stone belfry, summoned children to school for over a century, was taken down during a little ceremony in which it was rung by each child in turn. In due course it was rehung from a wrought iron frame made by Mr Jock Taylor on the north wall of the new school. This event was attended by parents and friends of the school. The brass bell is inscribed '*Meares and Stainbank, London 1871. 12m*'.

VIII. Properties

The National Trust owns two-thirds of the village, which includes fifty cottages, eleven houses and other buildings.

The majority of the cottages are 18th Century, although some date from the 16th and 17th centuries. In the construction of the walls of these properties, the flint is divided vertically by red brick, in contrast to the more usual practice of horizontal string-courses, of which there are only very few examples in the village.

The only examples of tile-hanging as a method of wall cladding, introduced in the 17th century, are at No.33 Slindon, and a small section at the east end of Lime Tree House, where the upper storeys are faced with red hung tiles.

Several cottages have 'hip tiles' or 'bonnets' (specially shaped tiles having the appearance of sun bonnets, used to cover the hip of a roof where two adjoining roof slopes meet). A feature of the 16th and 17th centuries, they were made in the same way as plain tiles, but bent into shape after being moulded. The Old Bakery and No.2 Slindon are examples of this.

A study of Slindon's chimney-pots is also worthwhile. Of various shapes and sizes, some are decorated with rings, dogtooth designs and other embellishments.

Following the general trend of the late 18th and early 19th centuries, the occupants of the larger Slindon houses sought to make them more imposing by the addition of a Georgian facade of stone or brick, or a cement-rendered facing, which was colour washed.

Many cottages have been altered and enlarged. All the houses in Top Road with the exception of Bleak House and St Richard's Cottage, were originally four-roomed flint cottages.

It is interesting to note the different types of flintwork in the village. In the building of the old C-of-E school, flints of all shapes and sizes give the appearance of a patchwork quilt. This contrasts with the accurate rows of square knapped flints at 'Gassons' opposite. Elsewhere, rounded beach flints or pebbles are arranged in rows. The Gothic shaped doorways and windows of 'Old Post', Church Hill, are examples of knapping so precise that no brick or stone dressing is necessary. Here too is an instance of 'galletting', a practice of filling in the mortar joints with slivers of knapped flint.

Possibly the oldest cottage in the village is No.2 Church Hill. It was originally an open hall house with arch braces and evidence of a cross wing at the northwest end; No.1 (adjoining) being the cross wing. The remaining doorpost of an arched doorway dates it as early to mid 15th century. The southeast end of the front could have been jettied. The house was most likely a yeoman's dwelling, built when the Archbishops of Canterbury owned the estate.

No. 2 has an original hip to the roof with a smokehole. The existing front door is possibly late 18th or early 19th century.

During the 16th century, a serious fire destroyed most of the roof and the NE end of the house. During the rebuilding the first floor at the northeast end was inserted, built with joists and support beams that extend to the end of No.1. The jutting end of the cross wing was removed and the front of No.1 was brought into line with No.2. Sometime in the early 19th century the rear wall of No.1 was rebuilt and a date stone,1671, was reset. Sometime later the back and end walls were raised to their present height and the first floor room, which was the whole of No.1 and possibly the northwest bedroom of No.2 was divided up. In the 1890s No.1 and No.2 were separated completely.

During alterations in 1974, a wattle and daub wall (early 16th century) was discovered beneath layers of plaster and some rush and daub (18th century) of which the ceiling was also constructed. A deep inglenook fireplace was uncovered at this time, complete with cubbyholes and wooden poles across the chimney from which pork and bacon were once hung. There is an adjacent bread oven, Some sewing needles found in a cubbyhole may have been used by Mr Penicott the village tailor, who lived and worked at the cottage in the 19th century. Kellys Directory mentions 'Penicott, George, tailor 1845-1887'.

In 1992, during redecoration of the exterior, the rendering of the front wall was found to be loose and was removed. This exposed the original timber framework, and a Medieval durn, the top of a curved door frame, dated about 1475. The rotten framework was replaced with new oak and the nogging panels of brick and flint were repaired. It was then covered with another coat of render.

Pottery from the 13th and 14th centuries have been found in the rear garden and nearby, two Meseolithic flint tools, evidence that the site was occupied seven or nine thousand years ago.

Behind the lime tree, the house of that name has undergone many changes since the 16th century, when it was supposedly a coaching inn, although it retains most of its ancient timbers. As a dwelling, with a beerhouse at one end, it was in the Apps family for 150 years. After the Beerhouse Act of 1830, most villages had a small house that was licensed to sell beer but not spirits. At the other end of the dwelling was a small general store until the

1970s, when the whole premises were sold and became a private house.

A small extension, once a separate building, with a barred window, was used by the estate builders to store lime. On the other side of a cobbled yard with stabling for horses (dated 18thc) was the ostler's house, now named 'Club Cottage'. The ground floor with the exception of the kitchen which was added in the 18th century, is thought to be a Medieval grain store circa 11th c. The cottage consists of three stories, the upper floor having been a long room divided into two at a later date. Half the building is of chalk blocks.

Here too, an inglenook fireplace was discovered during alterations, but differing from others found in Slindon by being shallow, and oval rather than rectangular. It is dated 1506. A double-sided inglenook, it has a bread-oven at the rear. Finds when the fireplace was opened included a 16th century silver piece, some pieces of clay pipe. pigs' teeth and pieces of 16th or 17th Century pottery. Among more recent treasures were a 1923 newspaper, a pack of cards, dice and some old money (sixpences, farthings, etc). All this, the occupants sealed up again, with some records and examples of present-day life, and buried them in concrete below the fireplace.

The Club House was built in the 1920s for the Farm Workers' Union as a club for local farm workers. Later it became the club room for the village and the headquarters for the Slindon Cricket Club and Football Club until they were temporarily disbanded in 1940. It has been the headquarters of the 1st Walberton and Slindon Scout Troop since 1961. Since 1997 the Scout group has been in recess, awaiting the emergence of a new Scoutmaster.

To the east of the church stands St Richard's House, formerly the Presbytery, which has a long and interesting history. Originally a cottage and croft, dating possibly from the 17th century, it was enlarged in 1814–1817 by the addition of a small Georgian house in front of the earlier dwelling. This new section housed the priest, while the rear premises became the first Catholic school in Slindon, the former farmyard, today a delightful walled garden, providing the playground.

The former tenant, Mrs Ann Salvin, was obliged to vacate the croft in 1814. She died in 1827 and is remembered by a plaque in the Anglican church of St Mary's. Although unmarried she is entitled to 'Mrs', a not uncommon form of address for spinsters of a certain age and status.

The Presbytery was sold by the church in 1983, when other accommodation was provided for the priest at Barnham. During extensive restoration carried out by the present owners, evidence of farm buildings has been found on the east wall of the garden and within the older part of the house; also evidence of the old Presbytery well, of a bread oven and of original thatch. For many years the front windows had outside shutters with the Papal Motif cut out in the wood, but these do not appear in Victorian photographs of the house. Replacement oak timbering in the older part came from demolished buildings of Fencote Abbey, near Leominster, Herefordshire.

It would appear from the Slindon Court Rolls that the 18thc section of the house was built about 1787 by George Lane, Merchant and Attorney of Arundel, who sold the property to the Earl of Newburgh in 1791. The property was clearly intended for occupation by the Catholic priest although they did not start living there until 1817.

No.7, by the lime tree, housed the village constable for about fifty years before 1931, when the police house was built at Fontwell and Slindon ceased to have a resident policeman.

The Hermitage, opposite, has a Queen Anne facade in the attractive brickwork of the period, built on to the original flint, an elegant door casing in the period style and a charming walled garden.

Below it, The Old Post, as the name suggests, once housed the village Post Office, when steep stones steps led down into the dim interior. It was originally three cottages facing south. The neogothic windows, which give the street side exterior its ecclesiastical appearance, were popular in the 19th century.

The village bootmaker once used the little square workshop to the right of the gate. The first built-up doorway formerly opened into it, while the one above led into what is part of the Hermitage.

On the other side of the road, Old Inn House, formerly The Little House, was built in 1716 as an inn. The cobbled yard and part of the stables are original and rings remain in the flint wall where horses were tied, as do the steps leading up to the original front door, now bricked up. A deep well by the present front door has been cobbled over. The room on the right of the house, formerly the bar, has a large inglenook fireplace, while under the entire premises runs a capacious cellar retaining the sump holes where the beer was sluiced away. A deed relating to the house, dated 1841, records that on 9th January 1841 Thomas Grout, or Grote, one of the tenants of Slindon Manor, for the sum of £208, surrendered to the Lord and Lady of the Manor a tenement in Slindon "late called Lord Newburgh's Arms, with the garden, hereditaments and premises thereto belonging, and the several buildings now standing" to which he was admitted on 6th April 1802. These premises with appurtenances were granted to Francis Mellersh and his heirs "for a fine on such his Admission the sum of £12"

It seems that Thomas Grout was the last landlord of Lord Newburgh's Arms, which became a private house when the present Newburgh Arms was built in 1840. Yew Tree Cottage below the house was once a barn belonging to the premises. In recent years, a large room has been added to the rear of the house.

To prove that dates on buildings are not always to be relied on, 1693, on Church Cottage opposite the church, is the date of the dwelling that stood there previously. Bricks bearing the date AD 1411 in the wall of the inglenook fireplace in the drawing room of Church House below, and another in the outside wall, were most probably taken from an earlier building or an older part of the house. Here again it would seem that a Georgian house, dated 1780, was built on in front of a 15th century cottage.

The thatched railway carriage at the entrance to the drive of Church House is always of great interest to visitors to the village. It is a Stroudley third-class smoking carriage and guard's van, one of the six-door fourwheelers that were built about 1874 to run on trains between Victoria and London Bridge for the London, Brighton and South Coast Railway. They became obsolete about 1906 and it is thought that this one was drawn by traction-engine from Barnham in that year. Originally painted white, the colour was later changed to maroon. In 1987 it received a new thatch of combed wheat reed. It was used by the Izards as an extra bedroom, when a passageway connected it to the house and a telephone was installed so that the host could talk to his young guests in the carriage. It was afterwards used as a summerhouse and toolshed.

Mulberry House on the corner of Dyer's Lane was formerly the Rectory. In the corner of the front garden is the stump of a 70ft Cupressus Macrocarpa, planted by the Revd William Chantler Izard in 1865. It was struck by lightning in 1973. The

Mulberry tree from which the house derives its present name just survived the 1987 storm.

In 1985, the present owner discovered in the garden a clue to the name Dyer's in the form of a memorial plaque to Charlotte Dyer who, according to the inscription was the relict of the Revd Kilgour and only daughter of John and Charlotte Dyer, born 18th June 1789 and died 25th April 1849. It is presumed that the plaque was originally in St Mary's Church and was taken to the Rectory garden, perhaps during the restoration of the church

Search made at the Record Office in Chichester revealed that between 1558 and 1877 the following were the only baptisms recorded in relation to Dyer's Lane, Slindon.

Andrew Dyer on 2nd May 1558
John Dyers on 16th March 1560
Mary Dyar on 29th Sept. 1590
Mary Dyer on 3rd Oct. 1591

So it appears that Dyer's Lane acquired its name in very ancient times, although whether Charlotte and her parents lived in the lane is open to speculation.

The new Rectory was built in 1961/2 behind the earlier one on land formerly part of the old Rectory grounds.

Returning to Church Hill, The Grange, immediately above the pond, was for three centuries the home of the cricketing Newlands (see Chapter XI). The rear or kitchen quarters would appear to be the remains of an Elizabethan cottage. The stucco facing at the front and sides of the house (at the rear the flint is still uncovered) was probably added in the early 19th century. Over the years there have been additions and many alterations to the original house.

During the stripping of a bedroom wallpaper in 1980, the following writing was revealed:

In the year 1826 this room was papered by
Robert White from Chichester and John Hartwell from Arundel.
White aged 15, Hartwell aged 20.

Beyond the pond and the grocer's shop and opposite Wellnap Corner, Elm Cottage has stood since 1649. Built of flint, vertically divided by brick, with brick dressing, it was originally thatched and had a kitchen under a "skeeling" or catslide roof at the back. One of three buttresses on the south side covers the former site of the front door. What appears to be a filled in window above this is more likely a decoration.

Elm Cottage.

Circa 1776, the lean-to kitchen was pulled down and a dining-room with adjoining new kitchen and rooms above were built. Later, servants' quarters were built further out to the north, joining the house to the harness room, coach house and stables, now a coal cellar and garages.

Another extension to the west is of knapped flint with galletting. Two small round headed windows of Queen Anne style at the east end are an attractive feature, as are the two curved and decorated portions of the eaves above them and over the blocked window in the front. Also of interest is the WC, entered by a door at the turn of the front staircase; an entirely separate building of weather boarding, poised on wooden stilts, it is one of very few examples of its kind in Sussex.

Following the road down the hill, one can rest for a moment on the wooden seat by the grass verge, placed there in memory of Daisy and Anne Walmsley. Daisy died in 1977, at the age of 100 years. Her sister was a talented painter, her charming water-colours depicting many scenes and dwellings in the village.

The grass bank by the path was planted with daffodils in 1985 by the Parish Council, the work being carried out by a local farmer, assisted by members of the 1st Walberton and Slindon Boy Scouts.

Picturesque 'Timbers', its white walls clad with climbing roses, was originally two cottages. An inscription over the bricked-up doorway of the lower half bears the initials T.N. (which can be for none other than Thomas Newland) and the date 1759.

Just below Timbers is the entrance to Adam's Field House, which was attractively converted from the fine stables and coach house of Millstones. The name Adam's Field is often mistakenly thought to be derived from the adjacent piece of land, supposedly once the property of Adam Newland. This distinction, however, belongs to a horse named Adam, the last mount of Miss Simpson of Millstones; it was his field.

Millstones House, formerly Millstones, which stands back from its imposing wrought iron gates, flanked by two large millstones, was built in 1909 on one of the plots of land sold by C.R.A. Leslie. The beautiful sunken garden in the grounds was transformed from a former brickyard.

Here at the junction of School Hill, Reynolds Lane[29] and Park Lane is another nucleus of very old cottages.

In Park Lane, the older of two detached cottages, No.45, bears the date 1647 in Arabic and Roman numerals. Some wattle-and-daub wall has been uncovered, while cereal grain (from old thatch) proved, when examined by an expert, that the ceiling was the original. It has a large inglenook fireplace, as has the next cottage, now named Cosy Cottage, formerly two semi-detached. The old skeeling roof has been removed from this cottage and the building extended at the back.

Flint Cottage and Wades Cottage on the left-hand bend of the road were, until 1910, one copyholder's property, known as Wades Garden. This can be traced through the quit Rent Roll Book to 1745.

Hope Cottage on the right is probably of the same date. Like Flint Cottage and Wades Cottage, it has a large inglenook fireplace. There are at least ten of these inglenooks to be found in the village, some of them uncovered in recent years.

In 1851, Charles Palmer, a horse-trader, purchased Wades Garden and the present Flint Cottage where he lived, became Reliance Mews and Wades Cottage, then four small tenements with stabling area, known as Jockeys' Row. The properties remained in the Palmer family, who continued in the horse trade, until 1910 when Frederick Palmer sold Jockeys' Row to Mr Wootton Isaacson for £326.

In 1912 the Palmers sold Reliance Mews, which was afterward rented to cobbler Jackson, then to Hardwick the postman, one of whom changed the name to Park View.

In 1930, Mr Sidney J. Challen, who had operated a cycle repair business on Slindon Common, became tenant and under

---

[29] Named after a resident 1185-1290.

the name Reliance Garage (the name can still be seen faintly on the side of Flint Cottage). Mr. Challen and his son, Eric, ran a cycle and taxi service and later an ambulance service until 1944.

Mr Eric Challen recalls that before the Post Office telephone kiosk was installed on School Hill, the telephone at Reliance Garage served the whole village. For a few pence, Slindonians could hold a long conversation with their relatives or sweethearts.

In 1916, under another ownership, the property became Flint Cottage. Behind the cottage was a large water tank with small trough above, built under the old cooking quarters and hayloft. These premises have now been converted into living accommodation.

Dairy Cottage, built of squared knapped flint with a horizontal course of brickwork, bears the date 1749. It derives its name from the small separate building behind the cottage, which was a two-storey dairy with thatched roof, where cream and butter was made for Slindon House in the time of the Leslies. The last dairyman, a Mr. Hill, kept pigs in the garden, which then extended to the forge. In 1923 the cottage became the home of the village carrier, who stabled his horse in what is now the garage.

There can be no prettier setting to a row of council houses than Slindon's at Meadsway, built in 1948, with a broad green, planted with a tall, graceful willow and flowering trees, sloping down to the forge. The council houses in Mill Road were built soon after World War I.

The Coronation Hall was built by Mr Wootton Isaacson in 1937/1938 to commemorate the coronation of George VI. A plaque to this effect is on the north inside wall. Below it a second tablet reads:

In memory and appreciation of Vincent Brown who served as Chairman, Secretary and Treasurer of this Hall 1938 – 1969

The hall was opened by Violet, Lady Beaumont on 10th January 1938. The Revd Barton, Rector of St Mary's and Father Peel, Roman Catholic Priest of St Richard's, participated.

Previously, an old army hut from World War 1, located behind Watkins Cottages, had served as a village hall. The last meeting held there was on 6th January 1938.

In 1939, a cinema projection box was installed and a travelling company gave weekly film shows. These were continued throughout the war and afterwards.

During World War II, a London County Council School was evacuated to the village and the hall was used as a schoolroom.

The post-mounted wrought iron sign, made by Mr Jack James, which stands in front of the great oak tree, was a gift to the Coronation Hall Committee from the Slindon W.I., to mark the 50th anniversary of the founding of the first Womens' Institute.

In 1988, to mark the 50th anniversary of the opening of the hall, a week of celebration was held from 22nd to 28th May. Starting with a special service in St Mary's Church, it included talks and slide shows on Slindon history; a traditional Sussex supper; a programme of recorded music in St Mary's (which was festively decorated with floral arrangements in green and white and gold) exhibitions of old Slindon photographs and many crafts. The grand finale was two performances of *Slindon Saga*, a dramatised Slindon history, written, produced and acted by Slindon folk, who also made the scenery and costumes. This memorable week raised £2000 for the Coronation Hall building fund.

The flagstaff and the semi-circular wall sheltering a wooden seat near the Primary School were erected in 1977 to commemorate the Silver Jubilee of Queen Elizabeth II.

The hall is let for regular local functions and entertainments. Throughout the year Brownie Packs, members numbering twelve to twenty-four, camp in the hall for a week, a weekend or during half-term holidays. At one time packs came from London but now they are mainly from local towns.

Returning to Wellnap Corner and continuing up School Hill, we come to the Well House. Originally two cottages and later a farmhouse, the earlier part is dated 1654. The interior is oak-panelled and many of the beams and rafters are re-used timbers. Reflooring in 1968 disclosed great posts that extended from kitchen to roof, and rafters of whole tree trunks were discovered. The back has a catslide roof, as have most of the 17th century cottages. In the front garden the outline of the original well can be seen. The old flint and brick wellhouse, long ago bereft of its machinery but used as a log store, was pulled down in 1977 when it became unsafe.

On the other side of the road is Gaston Farm, which is the farm referred to in the Earl of Newburgh's bequest. It remained the property of the priests of St Richard's until Charles Stephen Leslie took it over in exchange for a monetary sum. When the farmhouse was extended in recent years, evidence of an altar was found in an outer room. Under the house is a large cellar, part of which was a wine cellar, and a water cystern, which has now been filled in. At the east end of the building was a timber section, part of which was a chapel with a stained glass window. This was demolished during alterations.

Gassons, facing down School Hill, was originally two cottages attached to Gaston Farm and known as Gassons and Gaston Cottage. Formerly a glass veranda ran along the front of both cottages. A magnificent Judas tree in the front garden was yet another victim of the 1987 hurricane, although a shoot from the root of the fallen tree has since grown almost as tall as its parent.

The conversion of the cottages into one house took place in 1972, when bow windows were put in.

Mill Lane House, on the corner of Mill Lane, was the home of Rowland Wedgwood, grandson of Josiah Wedgwood (of pottery fame) and his wife Agnes. At the time of his marriage, Mr Wedgwood enlarged the house, formerly a four-roomed flint cottage, adding rooms at the front and a cement-rendered facing.

Bleak House, opposite, possibly has its origins in an early Tudor building. During alterations in 1955, a portion of wattle-and-daub was discovered in the drawing room wall and traces of Elizabethan windows in the bedroom above. A find of a later date between the broad oak floorboards of the bedroom was a George III penny, dated 1735. Whether the house was built as a farmhouse is not known, but it must have served as such for most of the 18th and 19th centuries, and the farm buildings were in use until the late 1940s. Formerly called 'Billingshurst', there is a theory that the present name derives from the "little steps up and down from every room," as in Dicken's novel *Bleak House*. The floors were levelled in 1955. John Newland, who was tenant in 1791, according to the initials over the north door, put in Georgian windows on that side, which have since been bricked up, and others on the south side.

The house is built of local materials, the east side of flint with horizontal courses of brick, and the front of brick over flint. It is said that a tunnel used by smugglers ran from the cellar to the grocer's shop. Evidence of a brick archway on the south side substantiates this story. There were also tunnels from the cellar to the Well House.

On the outskirts of the parish, at the end of Baycombe Lane, is an imposing house designed by Lutyens. Building was discontinued in 1914 because of the owner's German nationality; a firm of market gardeners, who cultivated the large garden while using the house for storage purposes, then took the unfinished property. It was sold to Colonel Francis J. Stratton CBE[30] in 1948 and completed in 1958. During the digging of the house foundations, remains of old flint walls were discovered, also a number of 17th century Nuremberg tokens, used for gaming. An even more exciting find was a bronze Roman thimble, one of very few to be discovered in England.

Another house of interest in Top Road is the Dower House, concealed from the road by a high flint wall. The earliest part, a small, stuccoed cottage at the west end, was later extensively added to in knapped flint. At one time, two stone vases bearing the date 1716 stood atop the gateposts. Until the turn of the century the property, then known as Slindon Cottage, included a large garden and the lodge on the other side of the road, now a nursery and nurseryman's cottage.

According to a Mrs Lloyd, who visited Slindon in the 1980s, her family, one member of which was a Major-General, came to Slindon in the mid-18th century and built the Dower House, which they called Mount Royal. They remained there until going to live in Italy in the mid-19th century, passing the balance of their lease to Lady Fullerton, who presumably renamed it Slindon Cottage (see Lady Fullerton Pgs.177-8)

Court Hill Farmhouse, which stands in a valley to the north of the village, is dated mid-18th century, with older outbuildings. The Georgian frontage, stuccoed and colour washed, dates from

---

[30] Colonel Francis J. Stratton CBE served in the Royal Artillery from 1939-47 with the rank of Major. He was married to a member of the Bowes-Lyon family. Among a formidable list of his appointments in *Who's Who* is Fellow of the Royal Society of Arts. He also won the American medal of Freedom, with palm. The present owner of Highfield is Anita Roddick, founder of The Body Shop.

about 1830, but the rear of the house would appear to very much earlier.

The tracing of a plan of Court Hill farm, dated 1805, shows the layout of house, stables, outbuildings and garden to be the same as today. During pipe-laying in 1960, old foundations were discovered which suggested that the house had not always been attached to the stables.

In 1978, the front face of the roof was tiled to match existing tiles on the other three sides. This had at some time been re-placed with slates. During recent repairs to the stucco, mathematical tiles (a type of tile-hanging which imitated brick-work used at the beginning of the 19th century) were uncovered.

By far the oldest building on the south side of the A29 is the Spur Hotel, formerly the Sir George Thomas Arms, on Spur Hill. Sir George Thomas, Bart, gave his name to the inn circa 1784, although the earliest part was probably built two centuries before. The name and sign were changed to the Greyhound early in the 1980s and a restaurant was added at this time.

In the early 1900s, Mr George Hotston was landlord (also at that time of the Newburgh Arms) following his father, Charles, who kept the inn for fifty-two years.

The first house to be built on Slindon Common, in 1912, was Pine View, at the Shellbridge Road end of Sunnybox Lane. It was some years after houses were built on the common that the two lanes were named.

Sunnybox Lane derives from an old railway guard's van and luggage compartment, named Sunnybox, which stood on the edge of the wood. Like the railway carriage at Church House, it is a Stroudley, probably built about 1880-90 to run on coastal lines for the London, Brighton and South Coast Railway. It was withdrawn from service in the 1920s or early 1930s.

The first occupant of Sunnybox was Miss Mabel, who held religious services for children in the caravan. It was removed in 1987 to the Brighton Railway Museum at Preston Park, when a house was built on the site.

Bridle Lane was probably a bridle path from Mill Lane to Shellbridge Road, which was so named because a bridge crossed the road halfway between the present A29 and A27.

A house within the Slindon Parish boundary since the extension is Firgrove, formerly The Firs, a large Grade II listed dwelling, dating from the early 18th century. Situated on the corner of Mill Road and the A27, it was built onto an earlier cottage (dated as Jacobean, by some lath and plaster walls, by Commander John S.L. Long, RN, in 1720. His family owned the house for the next two hundred years). The corner became known as Long's Corner. In those days, Mill Road was a lane.

Originally a four square building, John Long, to accommodate his large family, built on a ten foot extension at the back of the house and put in the dining room and main hall. A large cellar runs under these two rooms.

The estate was seven acres with three walled gardens, coachhouse, stables and wellhouse. Water was pumped from a deep well to supply the house, a workshop housing a forge, which provided heat for the greenhouses. These have now all been converted into private residences. The stables, which were mahogany-lined, were in use until 1990. Tall beech trees lined the garden, but all but one of them was blown down in the great storm of October 1987.

John Long was a scion of the Wraxall Longs of Wilshire, who originated in the time of Henry VIII. His eldest son Victor was an inventor. In 1910 he built an aeroplane, the 'Long' monoplane, which made its trials at Acton Flying Field in 1911. It was of the type in which the French aviator, Louis Bleriot, flew the channel in 1909. Another product of his brilliant mind was a waterwheel for pumping water to the house before mains water was brought to the district in 1900; the Firs being the first house to receive it. He also built a sandyacht, in which he took his friends sailing at West Wittering.

Victor Long ended his days in Devon, where he is buried, but he is commemorated with his younger brother Robert by a headstone in St Mary's churchyard, Walberton, beside the graves of his parents and an earlier member of his family.

An older sister, Miss Dora Long, remained at the house until about 1933. It was then bought by the chief Constable of Sussex, Mr Ronald Patterson Wilson. After his death, his widow moved into the cottage area. Part of Mrs Wilson's garden was created by German prisoners of war. During World War II, evacuees from London slept each night in the big hall of the house.

Although strictly in the Aldingbourne Parish, 'Pine Trees' in Little Heath Road, Fontwell, 'a cottage on Slindon Common' is the description given in the list of works of C.F.A. Voysey. He is currently being re-appraised because of his contribution to the 'Arts and Crafts' style of architecture, particularly cottage-style. 'Millstones' in Slindon village is the nearest in spirit, although he 'inspired' thousands of suburban homes with their 'Tudor bits and pieces'. Pine Trees has been sympathetically extended in recent years, but still retains the original Voysey ambiance.

IX. Shops, Industries, Businesses & Crafts

At the turn of the century, the village had at least eight shops. Until recently there was a grocery store and a Post Office/stationers.

The grocer's double fronted shop, built originally in 1654, with a flight of stone steps to the door, has probably changed little externally since it was rebuilt in 1791, at the same time as Manchester House, adjoining, and Wellnap Cottage. The date 1791 can be seen over the door of Manchester House and there is a brick bearing the date 1654 by Wellnap Cottage in the wall by the postbox. At one time there was a small butcher's shop on the east side of the grocers, afterwards used as a storeroom until demolished in 1972. To the west, at the corner of the road, was the slaughterhouse, formerly a malthouse, where Slindon beer was brewed (now Wellnap Cottage).

One of the first owners of the joint properties was George Knight, who lived at Elm Cottage. It would appear that the shop was rented during his time by two generations of Willshears and perhaps subsequently bought by a member of that family, for Jimmy Dean writes that, "John Willshear owned his own house at Wellnap Corner and shops, stable, cart house, walled garden and Rose Cottage."

Later the owner was John Watkins, a farmer, who built the pair of cottages opposite the shop for his farm workers. Today, much altered and enlarged, then divided, they are Watkins, Macauley Cottage, and Spinaway Cottage.

John Watkins started the slaughtering at Wellnap and Joseph Foreshew, who rented 'Ye Olde Butcher's Shop', continued this; he was followed by his son, Walter. Slaughtering ceased at the beginning of World War II and after the war Wellnap was rebuilt as a private house. Mr. Walter Foreshew moved to fresh butcher's premises in Top Road (now the Post Office).

The grocer's shop was rented from John Watkins by Frederick Grevett. Mr R.W.G. Rowland of Acton, who spent boyhood holidays at Rose Cottage, a flint-built, double-fronted dwelling, which was actually two cottages, on the site of which Pond House now stands, recalls "Grevett's shop" as it was then, "with its cooked meats, straw hats, bread, fly papers, ginger beer and 10,000 other items in glorious and cluttered profusion."

Pigot's Directory gives the dates of shopkeepers as:

John Willshear	1839-1882
John Willshear Jn.	1882-1887
John Watkins baker, grocer, dairyman and draper	1895
Frederick Grevett	1927

In 1927, John Channer came from London and took over the shop, joined the following year by his family. They lived at Manchester House, a rather imposing residence with its Georgian frontage, Doric pilaster, podium and handsome front door of six moulded panels. The name derives from the time when the shop sold drapery and Manchester goods, mainly haberdashery. Mrs Grevett also undertook dressmaking. The small room at the back of the shop, later an office, was used as her fitting room.

When John Channer arrived, the shop retained one of the few remaining candle-racks in Sussex, consisting of a long wooden rack, hanging from the ceiling over the counter. A row of wooden pegs, secured by short iron clips that went into the joists, held the tallow candles, which were made by the shopkeeper. As this form of lighting had been replaced by oil lamps, Mr Channer had the candle racks taken out and installed gas.

One of his sons recalls today the fascination of coming from London to the village store, and particularly his amazement at the contents of the warehouse over the shop. He remembered "piles of newspaper for wrapping, boxes of lamp glasses of various shapes and sizes, lamp wicks both long and round, hobnail boots of all sizes in heavy leather, rolls of cloth, pins, needles and boxes of cottons."

There was a bakery behind the shop with two large ovens, which supplied an extensive bread round.

John Channer's elder son, also John, took over the business when his father retired in the 1950s until his own retirement in 1972.

Mr Hugh McCorquodale, known to all in the village as 'Mr Mac', the proprietor until November 2001, extensively altered and modernised the premises, taking out the long, high counters with a narrow aisle between and introducing self-service, but still retaining that friendly "forum of democracy" – the village shop.

In the wall at Wellnap Corner is a Victorian postbox, the letters 'VR' picked out in gilt paint.

If Slindon children had a sweet tooth, there were plenty of little sweet shops to satisfy their craving, although pennies and half-pennies may have been scarce. The favourite was Dame Rout's, who was long remembered for her homemade humbugs. Children would watch her make them from a mixture that hung from a hook in the ceiling. It is uncertain just where her shop was, but according to the Tithe Apportionment Book of 1839, an Edward Rout lived at Vine Cottage, by The Newburgh Arms, and it is possible she was a descendent of his. There is a small single storey extension, with what could have been a shop window at the east end of the cottage.

There was another sweet shop at No.23 in Top Road, and one in an extension to the west of Telegraph Cottages in Church Road, which at one time was kept by a Mr. White.

A strange little shop described as, "a sort of glasshouse attached to a cottage, on the right-hand side of the road from Wellnap Corner to the Newburgh Arms" and kept by a Miss Bateman, sold the humbler sort of sweetmeats along with fish hooks and floats and a variety of oddments. Sweets were also sold at the general store by the Lime Tree and at the grocer's shop.

At a later date there were two small shops on Slindon Common. Sometime between the two wars a Mr Knight kept a general store in a cottage on the site of the old Dog and Partridge Inn. This was taken over by Miss Pauline Davidson when she left the army at the end of World War II. It was closed when she retired in the mid-1980s.

The other, which sold cottons, ices and confectionery, was housed in a wooden shed in the front garden of Ray Cottage, in Bridle Lane. It was started by the owner of the cottage for his son after World War II and was later kept by Miss Davis until the late 1950s.

A small rectangular flint building in School Hill bore a sign over the tiny window which read: *R. Sherlock, Bootmaker and Repairer.* Jimmy Dean records in 1903:

"There is a bootmaker living in Slindon who has eaten eighty Christmas dinners in the place and has never been out of the place a single month during his life. He may always be seen working from 8am to 8pm in a shop he has occupied for fifty years."

This was John Fleet, who also sang in St Mary's church choir for twenty years. In 1860 there were five bootmakers in Slindon.

Over the years the Post Office has had several homes in the village, the first probably being at a cottage which stood above No.9 Church Hill. Ann Bircher, daughter of the postmaster at this time, walked to Arundel and back twice daily to take and collect the mail. The cottage was pulled down when Colonel Leslie came to the estate and the Post Office moved to one of two tenant cottages above the Hermitage. When these were demolished it took up its quarters in the little room behind the stained glass window in what is now 'Old Post'.

After the death of the postmaster, Mr Cole, in 1969, the Post Office moved to its present home in the picturesque thatched cottage, once a butcher's shop, later a greengrocers, near the Newburgh Arms. In 1970 it was taken over by Mr & Mrs H.M. Dymock, who made extensive alterations to the interior, increasing the space without detracting from its character.

Built originally as two cottages, the oldest part probably dates from the 16th century. When work was carried out in 1972 on a new thatch, Mr Stapley, a thatcher from Littlehampton, found on stripping off the old straw to replace with more durable Norfolk reed, some very early layers that were tied together with the rope-like stems of pethwine (the Sussex name for Old Man's Beard). Later tarred string was used and today, hooks that fasten into the rafters.

Like the premises, the working hours of the village Post Office have altered during the century. According to Bernard Keeling's *Slindon Parish Council 1894-1984*, the council was consulted from time to time on Post Office matters:

"In 1909 the P.C. concurred with a proposal that the Post Office should open at 8am instead of 7am as previously; closing time

remained at 8pm. The Council took no decision as to whether Sunday opening should be from 8am to 9am or 9.30am."

About this time, the village postman had a hut on the common, in the corner of what is now the cricket ground. Here he would brew tea and sleep between deliveries. The village youths apparently took a delight in bombarding the hut and disturbing the poor man's rest! During World War II, Slindon's postwoman was Mrs Ann Poland, who often walked to and from Gumber, a distance of four miles each way, to deliver the mail.

Opposite the Post Office is The Old Bakery, where, in February 1986, Andrew and Anne Turner-Cross started baking bread in ovens that had been unused for forty years. Almost a year was spent in restoring the bakehouse and the original 'peel' ovens, a type of oven now a rarity for the majority have been demolished or converted to gas. They are fuelled with wood, consuming two tons of offcuts a week, for night-time baking only. Measuring seven feet wide and eight feet deep, the ovens are steel-lined with brick floors and cast iron doors. The baking capacity is 500 loaves daily. The name 'peel' derives from the implement used for inserting and extracting the loaves. The spatula-shaped end is made of beech, while the long handle is of ash for flexibility. Deliveries are made to Chichester and surrounding villages in two 1949 Morrison Electri-cars. One has seen service in Portsmouth as a bread van and a milk float. The body, which has been restored, is oak and canvas framed.

In 1998, baking ceased at The Old Bakery and deliveries are made no longer in the old Morrisons, and not to villages, but mainly to Farmers Markets in towns. It is hoped, however, that baking may sometime be resumed in Slindon and the fragrance of newly baked bread once more pervade Top Road.

Owned by the National Trust, The Old Bakery is a listed building, dated 18th century, built of flint and brick and lime-washed. The front door opens into the main room, once the shop, with a low oak-beamed ceiling and a large fireplace in one corner. There is evidence here of a bread oven. In the present kitchen is the site of another.

An inglenook fireplace occupying one wall in a tiny ' parlour' to the left appears out of proportion to the size of the room. When the kitchen floor was taken up during restoration of the building, heavy chains and hooks were found underneath, a relic of the days when sides of bacon were smoked in the wide chimney.

The original sliding shop window was replaced by a more modern casement during repairs but the shop bell remains over the door.

Records name the property as The Old Bakery back to 1840, when Charles Newland Esq was the owner and G.W. Cooper the occupier. It was then described as "house, shop, sheds, yard and garden."

Before the middle of the 19th century, all villagers baked their own bread and brewed their own ale and it is thought that the shop was then a pork butchers. The first baker was probably Henry Moses Oliver, known as 'Moses', who came to Slindon in 1863. He played for the village cricket team and for Slindon brass band. Weekly band practices were held at the bakery. Moses died in 1927 at the age of 83. When he retired, Bertram Clarke came from Petersfield and took over the bakery, followed by his son Hedley.

The oven used at that time was a single deck faggot oven in the bakehouse. Faggots were burned in the oven, the ash raked out and the loaves inserted. When faggots became difficult to obtain, green cordwood was used, but this was unsatisfactory and in 1937 the present ovens were installed by Lady Beaumont.

The introduction of the white sliced loaf after the war put many village bakers out of business and Hedley Clarke was one who gave up. After 1947 the shop became a tearoom and until the mid-1970s visitors could refresh themselves with Nan Clarke's excellent scones and cakes. It was patronised by the National Cycling Club and their badge adorned the exterior wall by the front door.

Further along Top Road, nurseryman and landscape gardener Ralph Upton cultivates the walled garden that once belonged to the Dower House.

All summer his produce is displayed for sale on the low stone wall in front of the lodge, but it is in late summer and autumn that this area becomes the most colourful and spectacular feature of the village. This is the pumpkin season, when not only the walls, but every available space round the lodge and nursery is stacked with pumpkins and squashes of all shapes and sizes and in every shade of orange, yellow and green. Among some fifty varieties are Atlantic Giants, Queensland Blues, Hungarian Mammoths and Turks Turbans.

After 29 years of growing pumpkins from seed imported from all over the world, the Uptons have achieved a wide reputation. Barbara Upton and her book of pumpkin recipes have appeared in newspapers, magazines and on television, and visitors come from far and wide to buy from 'the pumpkin lady.'

The farming industry has long been of prior importance in the parish. Up to fifty or so years ago the majority of working men in Slindon were employed on the estate or the farms. Today, with the advancement of mechanization and the decline of agriculture, the number is minimal.

Of the several farms in the Slindon Parish, mostly now owned by the National Trust, Court Hill Farm, north of the village, is the largest, comprising 986 acres, including woodland. This land embraces what was once three separate farms: Lees Farm, Court Hill and North Wood.

In the early 1900s it was farmed by the Bowley family. During World War I, Elwin and Prior ran a milk round from the dairies of Court Hill and Gaston farms under the name of 'Slindon Model Dairies'. Some fine red-brick buildings with tiled floors in Slindon Park were used at this time. Formerly the dairy for Slindon House in the time of the Leslies, they were sold with the estate to Mr Wooton Isaacson who leased them to Court Hill Farm with the surrounding fields. The dairy, with the fields, was later leased to Gaston Farm until it was burned down by vandals in the late 1950s.

At some time in the 1930s the whole farm was given over to sheep, tended by the owner of the flock, riding a stout cob and assisted by three dogs.

Over the years, Court Hill was leased from the estate then from the National Trust, to a succession of farmers until 1947, when it was taken over by Mr Leslie Langmead, a member of a well known West Sussex farming family, who farmed it until 1980. During this time, besides growing arable crops, the farm carried two herds of Friesian cows and followers, a large number of breeding sows and fattening pigs and, until 1963, five hundred head of sheep. There was also a 3,000 acre shoot.

Now entirely arable, with the exception of one dairy, the farm is carried on by a son, Mr James Langmead, as part of a syndicate.

Woodlands Farm, the fields and buildings of which lie on the south side of the A29, has been a dairy farm since 1920, when a Mr Cox bred Guernsey cows and retailed milk in the village.

The farm was taken over in 1948 by Mr Paul Wyatt who continued dairying with pedigree Guernseys, for some years exporting live cattle to Kenya. After the increased use of artificial insemination, he exported the semen to Australia, New Zealand and Africa.

At some time Biddleside Farm was added to Woodlands. The farm house and remains of former buildings are situated south of the A29, opposite the Greyhound Hotel, formerly The Spur. This farm is now part of Gastons.

A track leading from Copse Lane, Walberton, leads to other fields belonging to Woodlands Farm. The buildings which served this land are now under the A27. New buildings have since been erected Mill Road. A flint built house with buildings on the corner of Mill Road and the A29 is the home of Mr Philip Wyatt, who took over the farm on the retirement of his father. The land is now given over to arable and sheep grazing.

Gaston Farm, in the centre of the village, comprises 110 acres belonging to the National Trust, 12 acres of glebe land and 10 acres belonging to a local landowner. In 1959, Mr Gerald Sercombe took over the farm and started a herd of pedigree Friesians. This he gave up nine years later and the farm became arable, with a thriving potato business, mainly supplying fish and chip shops. Gaston farmhouse and buildings are situated on School Hill.

The fields of Mill Farm extend from Mill Road to Shellbridge Road and are used for sheep grazing. In the past it was farmed by the Bowley family, who kept milking cows and delivered milk in the village.

On the corner of Shellbridge Road and the A27, Stoneyfield Farm is a smallholding of 10 acres. The buildings have been used since 1970 for a variety of commercial purposes. Today there are plans for the use of the land and buildings but its future is still uncertain.

To return to the past and to Wellnap Corner, wheelwright William Graysmark lived in the one-storey, copyholder's thatched cottage by the pump. His wheelwright's shop was in the large garden, and there was a deep, saw-pit below the old malthouse. The cottage was later burnt to the ground and the present Pump Cottage built in its place.

William Graysmark would have taken his wheels for tyring down the hill to the forge in Reynolds Lane. The old tyring table can still be seen at the forge. The iron tyre was heated on the hearth and transferred with special tongs to the wheel on the table.

The earliest entry of a Graysmark was Thomas (b. 1768 m. Louise C, widow of one of Napoleon's generals). There was a Graysmark born about 1850, a carter on the Slindon estate. In 1921 the wheelwright was George Griggs and the wheelwright's shop was in Top Road, later the estate carpenter's shop, now the pottery.

In the 1841 Census the name is recorded as Gracemark. 'Francis Fleet, gardener' is listed next to 'William Gracemark, a wheelwright' and in 1850 at 36, School Hill a John Gracemark.

Except for a recession in the mid-1950s when it closed down, Slindon forge has been a busy place since it was built in the mid-19th century to replace an older one in Dyers Lane (the building is not marked on the Tithe Map of 1839 but appears on the Ordnance Map of 1875). Built in typical 19th century brickwork, the interior construction of pre-used timbers, it is in two sections connected by a narrow doorway. The workshop at the north end contains the original brick hearth, behind which are the old double action bellows, last used in 1974 during electricity cuts. A second, later hearth necessitated a modern chimney at the rear of the building.

Attached to the walls and heavy roof beams is a fascinating miscellany of old horseshoes, hand-made tools and a conglomeration of work and trophies left by farriers and blacksmiths for over a hundred years.

In an old account book are some interesting entries for the year 1910. There were a number of small jobs, priced at a few pence, e.g. "1 slip bolt to plough 2d; solder trap lamp 3d; repair turnip knife 2d; fasten shoe mare 3d; remove dressing foot Boxer 6d." A set of four shoes for a hunter was 2s 2d and 2s 10d for a heavy horse. To frost-nail five horses cost 2s 6d.[31] The largest single entry for that year was '11 coulter blades [to a plough] with cheeks' 2s 10d each, totalling £1.14s.

The only evidence of the forge in Dyers Lane is the date 1728 over a window of Little Martins, where it once stood. There is a reference in the Court Rolls to the death in 1739 of Owen Bateman, *"one of the customary Tenants who holds to him and his heirs by copy of the Court Roll of the Lord of the Manor one cottage and a smith's shop."* He left the property to his son John. The cottage mentioned was situated next to the forge. It was burned down after 1900 and the house Martins was built on the site. Further references to various Batemans, blacksmiths, and the premises in Dyers Lane follow.

---

[31] When roads became slippery in winter, carters took their horses to the forge to have the usual smooth-headed nail removed and replaced by a frost nail with a pointed head.

In 1849, "William Bateman blacksmith and Edward Bateman gardener surrendered to Thomas Bateman and John Willshear the yearly rent of one shilling and ninepence" and in 1888, James Sturt and Maria Bateman, widow of the last William Bateman and his sister Maria Jane, sold the property to William Twigger.

The building is marked as a smithy on the ordnance map of 1875, so it would appear that both this and the 'new' forge were in use for a while, perhaps one for farriery, the other for repairs and ironwork.

One of the first blacksmiths at the present forge was a Mr McCarthy, who lived at The Cottage, Slindon. In the early 1900s, Charles Hotston took over the forge, after qualifying in decorative ironwork, and employed two farriers – the trade then included heavy horses – he was followed by Fred Holmes, a veritable Longfellow's blacksmith in appearance, whose redoubtable bass voice swelled the choir at St Mary's every Sunday.

In 1912, Gilbert Bleathman came to live in Mill Road and took the forge. He shod heavy horses and racehorses. An example of his work in wrought iron is the pair of gates at the main entrance to Slindon House. He did work for Lady Beaumont and shod horses at the stables behind the Newburgh Arms. One of his sons, Clifford, was apprenticed to him but left soon after his father's retirement.

In 1958, after the closure, Jack E. James came to Sussex from Nottinghamshire, and rented the forge from the National Trust. Although an expert farrier, Mr James' main work was in wrought iron, which brought him acclaim not only in Sussex and the Midlands but also as far afield as America and South Africa.

When in 1970 he gave up shoeing to concentrate on this work, Peter Fenton, who served his apprenticeship at the Duke of

Norfolk's stables at Arundel, took over this part of the business. Sadly, Mr James died that year. Mr. Fenton carried on, making all his own horseshoes for the steadily increasing number of horses on his books, mainly middleweight horses and children's ponies, more than half of them shod cold on the owner's premises over a four to twenty mile radius of the forge.

Two years later, Jock Taylor, who had spent all his working life in iron, training as a fitter-welder in Dundee from the age of sixteen, went into partnership with Peter Fenton, who now shod horses full-time, while Jock Taylor made the horseshoes, did electrical and acetylene welding and all types of blacksmithing, including decorative ironwork, mostly gates and balustrades.

The partnership has continued until today, except for a few years in the 1970s when Mr Fenton took a forge in Scotland. During that time, the farriers at Slindon were Philip Mays, who was apprenticed to Peter Fenton, followed by John Reid, who trained at Young's Brewery Stables at Wandsworth.

A pleasing link with the past, Jock Taylor's wife Stella, nee Hotston, is a great-niece of Charles Hotston, who worked the forge in the early 1900s. Jock retired in 1989.

In 1972 the National Trust reroofed the forge, red tiles and a trim outline replacing the undulating lines of the old slate roof.

In the 19th century there were many industries on Slindon Common. Wedgemaking (the wedges being used in shipbuilding) was one of the timber crafts at their peak in the 1890s and early 1900s. Beech was the only wood suitable for making these wedges and only a few men in Slindon, nearly all members of one family, were experienced in making them. They were Harry Miles and his two sons Jack and Charlie and Harry's father-in-law Charles Jackson. The younger men rode to and from work on penny-farthing bicycles.

The wedges were made mostly in Northwood, the trees being cut down, drawn to the camp and cut to the required length. They were then split into the maximum number of wedges with the minimum blows from the axe. Each was about a foot long, three to four inches wide and three inches at the thick end. A onesided axe was used, different from the one used for felling, sharpened from one side, like a plane blade. The finished wedges were stacked in thousands to tens of thousands, identical in appearance.

Much of the beech that was useless for wedges was sawn into blocks and sent to the fishing ports for use as floats for trawl nets.

Charles Jackson was also a pale-cleaver. His workshops on the Common, just off Park Lane, were big sheds with a ridge of posts and poles, against which were set more poles on one side only. These were crossed with rafters and thatched to the ground. One was a workshop while the others were used for storing fencing pales and the oak for making them.

When Mr Wootton Isaacson bought the estate, a number of discarded posts and raids were bought by Alfred Day and put up round Fontwell Racecourse.

Another woodland industry was shaving ash for various purposes, including the making of tennis rackets. George Budgin and George Finch ('Budgie' and 'Finchie') worked at this. The wood was split and trimmed, then steamed in a wooden trough through which steam was passed from a huge covered copper. After steaming, the pieces of wood were put into clamps and left to dry and set, then sent to the makers 'in the rough'. The end of this industry came when the large thatched workshops full of shaving chips caught fire and were burnt out.

Arch Palmer, horse-trader of Slindon who died in 1972, recalled that George Bulbeck of Arundel was the timber merchant in those days. "A fine old gentleman," Mr Palmer remembered. "I used to drive with him when he went to the woods to inspect the work and pay the men. He was full of country lore and knew the woods better than anyone I have met. One bit of advice he often gave: *measure twice, cut once.* I have often thought," said Arch Palmer, a man of philosophy himself, "that this applies to many things besides cutting wood."

A book of recollections entitled "More About Slindon in the Old Days" compiled by Maurice Burn, states that George Bulbeck set up a timber yard near the Dog and Partridge on Slindon Common, "with steam saws, hoops, shavers and wedge-makers sheds. Suddenly, in 1902, the business folded up, there was a sale and everything was cleared off the Common."

Another Slindonian tells of a cooper who worked in a small, thatched, flint building on the site of the present C-of-E School. Arthur Dean, eldest son of Jimmy Dean, was apprenticed to him on leaving school at the age of 12, in 1896. The association was short, for two years later it is recorded that Arthur went to work in George Bulbeck's sawmills.

The cooper, whose name is not remembered, made tubs of all shapes and sizes. Water tubs or butts were bound with hazel, which he cut from Parson's Copse, behind his workshop. Others were bound with iron bands. These were made at the forge opposite and were tapered by making red hot, then hammering down over an iron cone or mandrel. One of these mandrels can be seen standing outside the forge today. There is another, larger one at the back of the building.

A dominant feature on the common was the white post mill, believed to be the one that once stood at the top of Mill Lane, Slindon, but then the Avisford Mill, and just over the border of what was then the Walberton Parish. Before the turn of the century the mill had a fair trade, supplying gentry and tradespeople, all of whom kept horses. Charles Carter, the noted millwright of West Tarring, came out regularly to keep the vanes in good repair.

The post mill is the smallest of three types of windmill and built entirely of wood, the whole structure being poised on a vertical post and usually turned into the wind by hand. "If the wind was not in the right direction," says Arch Palmer, "it took two men to swing the mill round on its main post by means of a projecting beam, fastened to a wheel."

The other types of mill are the Smock Mill (as at Shipley) built of wood except for the bottom two floors, which are within a roundel of brick, and the Tower Mill (as at Halnaker), built all of brick except for the revolving cap at the top.

Eventually, trade at the mill, which had dwindled to mostly ground barley meal and pig food, fell off completely and the mill was in need of repair. The owners, not wanting the expense of this, had it demolished, much to the dismay of Slindon people, who had a great affection for the 'their' mill, which was possibly one of the best examples of its type in the neighbourhood.

A brickyard is marked on a map near the junction of Mill Road and the A27. In the 19th century many villages had their own brickyards. In a wall of a house in Church Hill a few bricks bear the signatures of local brickmakers. According to Jimmy Dean, there was a bricklayers shop on the site of the present Club House.

There were gravel pits at Slindon Bottom, Slindon Common and the Rewell. Alfred Burch, who lived at Pine View, Sunnybox Lane, worked in the Rewell gravel pits for forty years and his father before him. In those days the gravel was hewn out with a pick. It was sieved twice by hand to take out the large then medium stones, leaving the gravel. It was then taken away to be washed, until a washing plant was installed at the Rewell pits in 1938. All the workings were closed by mid 1970s.

Although Slindon china cannot strictly be termed a village industry, it should be mentioned here. About the turn of the last century, a collection of china was manufactured for the village and a number of pieces still survive in the possession of local residents and in secondhand shops in various parts of West Sussex. Of a finer quality are a number of white plates with a blue ribbon border and a view of Slindon put on by a transfer taken from a photograph. These plates are of hard paste porcelain and bear the mark of a crown above an S, indicating that they were made in Germany at Tiefenhurt (Silesia) by a potter named Donath who opened a factory there in 1808. The china would have been made between 1897 and 1901 and sent in bulk, possibly to Staffordshire, where transfers were put on then glazed and fired.

A Bognor potter, Sam Masters, who had his shop and kiln in Lyon Street or Sudley Road just after World War I, made other china, also white with a slanted fluting and bearing a picture of Slindon with the words *A Present from Slindon*; this included teapots, milk jugs and sugar basins, candlesticks and other useful objects. They were sold in Slindon at Miss Bateman's shop on School Hill. Sam Masters also made china for Lady Beaumont, bearing a picture of Slindon House, to give to her guests.

About 1977 a Slindon resident, Mrs Bonnie Beere, rented from the National Trust, the little flint building formerly the workshop of the estate carpenters in Top Road and transformed it into an attractive and efficient workshop, with potter's wheel and a large kiln. Virtually self-taught, she created a wide range of ceramics with skill and originality. Mrs Jo Hyde followed her.

During these years another potter, Mrs Janet Upton, worked in her cottage at No.2 Slindon. Her kiln was in the greenhouse in the garden. Janet studied ceramics at Bishop Otter College, Chichester and worked in earthenware at Horsham School of Art, where she was a technical advisor. 'Coil pots', 'slab pots' and 'thumb pots', all requiring a different techniques, together with a variety of small ceramic animals, were displayed in the windows and shelves of her cottage. She also made corn dollies in traditional designs.

Slindon Pottery.

In 1992 she took over the Pottery, now producing a varied range of ceramics and also sells the work of other craftsmen, making the shop a fascinating place to browse.

Keen archaeologists, both Janet and her husband Robin have worked on Roman excavations in Chichester and Robin is well known for his extensive collection of prehistoric artefacts.

Living at The Old Post, Church Hill, Denis McQuoid was initially a silver engraver, known for his work in many parts of the world. He now works entirely with abstract, surrealist paintings which he has exhibited in Brighton, and water colours, exhibited in France and Germany.

X. Transport, Water & Amenities

Sussex was notorious for the bad state of its roads and far behind much of the country in making improvements; but by the end of the 18th century, traffic here, as elsewhere, was on the increase and stagecoach travel was popular. England and especially Sussex needed better roads. They were built by private companies who charged a toll, collected at tollhouses or turnpikes.

A turnpike road ran from Storrington via Parham, Amberley, Houghton, Madehurst and Slindon to the Ball's Hut public house (demolished in the 1990s).

A toll house then stood at the bend of the road at the south end of Fairmile Bottom, on the site of the present Chichester Lodge at the south entrance of Dale Park, according to the following notice outside the old Toll House by Houghton Bridge:

> "This Toll House, and the one at Hebenden Lane, Slindon, were built in 1813."

The Turnpike beyond Whiteways was a new road down Fairmile Bottom to the foot of the Downs near Slindon, to Ball's Hut on the Arundel-Chichester road.[32] This means that the Turnpike road entered the Slindon parish near the Toll House and continued down past the Sir George Thomas Arms to Slindon Common before it entered the Parish of Walberton (during the reign of George III).

---

[32] According to *Sussex Notes and Queries*, Vol. 14. No. 5

Slindon was on the route of the new stagecoach lines, brought about by the improved road, stopping places being at the Ball's Hut and the Royal Oak on the boundaries of the parish. A coach and four stopped at the Dog and Partridge.

The railway line from Brighton to Chichester started before the London-to-Brighton, and Shoreham was reached in 1840. In 1846 the line was extended to serve Arundel and Littlehampton.

Despite coach and rail services, many country people were still obliged to travel on foot. Slindonians walked to and from Arundel and Chichester for shopping or to visit relatives in hospital. When a young girl left home to go into service, her father would walk miles after work, perhaps as far as Brighton, wheeling her box.

The first local transport in Slindon was provided by Jackson, coachman to Colonel Leslie, who lived at Bleak House Farm stables. He made two journeys a week to Bognor with a four-horse waggonette, starting at the Newburgh Arms, while old James Bateman, born 1844, made a daily trip to Bognor in a donkey cart, selling greenhouse produce and giving lifts to children of the village.

The village carrier took passengers to Chichester. Little is remembered about the very early days of the carrier service; but at the beginning of the century, George Hotston, landlord of the Newburgh Arms, made journeys to and from Chichester with a single-horse covered waggon, carrying goods and passengers. After his death, his brother Charlie continued the service. On Bank Holidays he took passengers to Bognor in a two-horse brake.

One of Mr Hotston's drivers, Ernie (Mut) Mills of Vine cottage, took over the business but was so late on his rounds that he was nicknamed "the midnight carrier."

In 1923, Lady Beaumont offered Dairy Cottage in Slindon to Alfred Hunt and his son Cyril (Bert) Hunt, carriers of Walberton, if they would undertake her personal carrying. They agreed, and eventually took over the service for the village.

Their multifarious chores included fetching the newspapers from Barnham Station and all goods for Channer's Stores until the coming of the South Coast Carriers in 1930; bringing flour from Sadler's Mills to Slindon Bakery, and, when the Newburgh Arms ran short of beer, barrels from Henty and Constable's brewery. Incidental journeys tooks hens to Barnham Station, coffins to the mortuary at the Royal West Sussex Hospital and the Rector's nanny goat to the billy!

In the days when women with large families seldom ventured beyond the village boundaries, shopping futher afield was undertaken for them by the carrier, who would, for instace, bring out parcels of clothing on approval. Villagers requiring this service would put an H in their window, or in outlying districts, put up a flag or a bunch of newspapers on a stick.

The Hunts' first mechanised transport was a splendid Hotchkiss motor converted into a van. It had shining brass headlamps and was capable of a speed of fifty miles an hour. In this they took passengers to the dances held weekly in winter at Eartham Village Hall. The fare was 1/6 return. They went to the rescue when Bill's Bus, a conveyance owned by Billy Lucas of Fontwell Post Office, broke down. Billy took villagers to Bognor, via Tangmere and Colworth on Bank Holidays.

After the death of his father in 1941, Bert Hunt continued the service but gave up general carrying in 1959 for furniture removing, until his retirement ten years later. The business was carried on for four years by Andrew Upton of Slindon, then, the need having diminished, the service came to an end.

At the turn of the century, members of the Palmer family ran a two-horse bus daily, to and from Barnham Station. This service was taken over by Colonel Leslie, who increased it to three journeys a day, but this did not pay and the Palmers took over again.

After the first world war, Mr Cecil Walling, the third son of the marriage between Richard Walling, the Sussex diarist and Adelaide Maria Hervey, schoolmistress, ran a converted field ambulance, accommodating twelve passengers, daily to Bognor. This was so well patronised that Mr. Walling purchased what then seemed an enormous single decker bus; Slindon's first 'Silver Queen'. Later, he bought two more and ran an hourly service every day to Bognor and once a week on Wednesday, market day, to Chichester. The Silver Queen was regarded with great affection by Slindonians, for it would stop where and when they they wished; it would collect shopping and take letters for the late post in Bognor. When the Southdown Bus Company tried to take over the route, local people boycotted the Southdown bus. After a period of running empty buses, while passengers crowded onto the Silver Queen, the Southdown withdrew its competition.

After World War II however, Mr Walling sold out to Southdown and the village sadly said farewell to 'the old bus'.

For many years, the Southdown Bus Company ran an hourly service from Chichester to Bognor, stopping at Slindon Common, where a connection took Slindon passengers to the bus stop at the Newburgh Arms. This latter was discontinued and eventually the service to the common was drastically reduced. A voluntary car service was then organised by Slindon residents, which took non-car owners to Chichester once a week.

In 1986 a village bus was mooted. This reached fruition in 1988, with the first run in May to coincide with the opening of Slindon Week. The cost of the sixteen-seater minibus was met by the Rural Transport Development Fund and West Sussex County Council. The vehicle is shared with Amberley and driven by volunteers from both villages.

When, in the days before easy transport, a visit to the doctor often incurred a long walk, most villagers relied on the ministrations of Rebekah Fleet, 'old Bek Fleet' as she was generally known, who would attend anything from a sprained ankle to a confinement. Later, Mrs Wilmer was midwife and general nurse for twenty-five years. The first registered nurse, Nurse Edwards, lived at the Club House, but from 1924 until the late 1950s, when Slindon ceased to have its own district nurse, her house was No. 48 in Reynolds Lane.

In 1948, doctors from Arundel, Eastergate and Yapton held surgeries in houses in Slindon or Slindon Common. Today an Arundel doctor has a twice-weekly surgery at Mill Cottage.

The parish of Slindon has seldom been short of water. At the same time it is well drained, since it consists mostly of porous chalk, through which water percolates, accumulating at the junction of the chalk and underlying clay to form a springline. The clay prevents further downward movement, so water is forced to surface; the resulting springs once formed the main water supply of the village.

Villagers dug land spring wells where there was a spring in their garden. Several feet deep and lined with bricks, these wells filled with water overnight, providing a supply for the following day. There is a story of one Slindonian who, after an evening at the Newburgh Arms, fell into his own spring well and was quickly sobered!

There were storage tanks in cottage roofs and under the floors, and barrels and containers for rainwater. All the larger houses had wells, which were ninety to three hundred feet deep. Below is a list of wells in use in 1860:

> *Slindon House; St Richard's School [St Richard's Cottage]; The Well House; The Newburgh Arms; Gumber; Wellnap Corner; Court Hill Farm; Three at the bottom of Bleak Meadow; Court Hill Farmhouse; Presbytery [St Richard's House]; Old Farm House [possibly Bleak House or Gaston Farm]; Slindon Cottage [Dower House]; Church House; Slindon Common; Rectory [Mulberry House]; Biddleside; Sir George Thomas Arms [The Spur]; two close to the pond; two in Park Lane; Slindon Park.*

These wells were covered over or filled in after mains water was brought to the village in 1902, with the exception of the one at Gumber, which was 300 feet deep and still in use up to the 1950s.

There is a story told of a 17-year-old girl, Caroline Binstead, at Gumber, who was lowered down the well to rescue her cat, which had fallen in. Sitting securely in a new "bushel basket" attached to the well chain, she reached the surface of the water and with a furze stick pulled out the cat, which unfortunately was already dead. Afterwards she described the "ghastly sight" as she looked up at the eerie light cast upon the chalk sides of the well.

During the laying of water mains, walls believed to be of Roman origin were discovered in the garden of No. 47 Park Lane (the corner cottage) and this has since been known as the Roman Garden. There is also an ancient well, but this is considered to be medieval rather than Roman.

In 1973 a well and the site of a pump were discovered in the garden of Flint Cottage. The type of brickwork indicates 18th or possibly 19th century construction. A newspaper of 1925 was found during excavation of the well, suggesting that it was filled in at this time.

Not all Slindonians welcomed the arrival of a mains water supply, however. Jimmy Dean declared that the water from his well under the Roman wall was "as pure as gin" and that "one might as well take water to the sea as to Park Lane." Some villagers objected to paying £2 a year rates for main water.

It seems, however, that in times of drought, in spite of efficient water storage, Slindon did get a little thirsty. In 1835, according to Jimmy Dean, the village had to get all its water from Arundel. That year, even the village pond dried up and cricketers played on the site. In 1893 there was a drought of 76 days, when many tanks and wells were exhausted. During another in 1898, some of the wells of over 200 feet were dry, although there was plenty of water in the pond for cattle and domestic use.

In November of that year, Jimmy Dean entered in his dairy what appears to be an excerpt from a local paper. Headed "Abundance of Water" it reads:

> *"Messrs. Duke and Ockenden, who are engaged upon the new waterworks at Slindon in the South Fields, have found a splendid supply of water and have succeeded in raising 600 gallons per hour. Mr Dawson, the estate carpenter, found the site with the aid of his divining-rod, the surveyor assisting in the operation. A difficulty is the unusual quantity of hard flint and limestone to overcome. It is expected that the operations when completed will enable 200,000 gallons of water to be obtained daily."*

The following week, November 16th, the following appeared:

> *"In reply to Mr W. Lewis, Mr Barrett of Bognor writes to say that in his selection of the site for water supply 'the divining rod had no more influence in determining my judgement than my*

own walking stick.' He selected the ground in which the water was found 'before I ever heard of all that was claimed for the little twig.'"

In 1905 the analysis report on Slindon's water supply read:

"...the water is of excellent quality, free from suspicion of organic pollution, and may be used for drinking purposes with safety. The hardness is much below that of chalk water generally. It is recommended for village supply."

Mains water was taken to Court Hill Farm in 1907. A pump was installed in a field near Slindon Bottom, which pumped water to the reservoir on Nore Hill. A new reservoir for Bognor was constructed between Rose Barn Farm and Nore Folly in 1932.

Slindon Pond, probably as old as the village itself, was originally man-made by the damming up of an existing stream or weir, hence its old name 'Weir Pond'.

It was once a watering place for cattle and horses, and a venue for all who came to draw water from the pump. A well on the other side of the road provided drinking water. This well can still be seen behind an iron grill in the garden wall of Pond House.

A stone inserted beside it – inscribed 'R.S. 1764' – does not apply to the well but was probably taken from Rose Cottage. Mr Rowland in his reminiscences writes:

"The domestic water supply came from 'the well in the wall' and it was one of my simple pleasures to accompany my uncle when he went to draw buckets of this clear, sparkling water. I hope it was as good as it looked and tasted."

The pond also provided all year round entertainment; fishing in summer, mainly by boys with rods of clothes props or similar makeshift tackle; bent pins for hooks, and bread or dough for bait.

In winter, skating was the sport. Jimmy Dean records that on New Years Day, 1904, sliding and skating went on merrily by moonlight. On December 22nd that year, a youthful adventurer sailed across the pond in a pig tub, with a stick for any oar. Today fishing, boating and bathing are prohibited.

He also tells of an accident in 1860, with a timber waggon and team of three horses. The carter had failed to put the skid pan under the wheels before coming down Church Hill, and the lead mare, unable to hold back the load, fell, breaking her back, while the other horses with the waggon crashed into the pond. It took two days, with the help of all available Slindon men, to get everything out.

Jimmy Dean reports that the pond was cleaned out every year.

Bernard Keeling, in his history of Slindon Parish Council, gives an account of continuing problems with the pond, registered as a public green in 1967, from as early as 1897 to 1981. Operations such as cleaning out, strengthening the bottom, ridding of weed etc, were carried out funded by rates, public subscription, and the County Council.

In 1980, when money was available from the Arun District Council Lotteries Fund, a small promontory in the style of the one that supported the old pump was constructed, with a seat and two trees adjacent to the road. The banks and surrounding area were restored and strengthened.

The following year, a further small grant from the Lotteries Fund was used to restock the pond with water plants, shrubs and livestock. A gift of white water lilies enhanced the centre of the pond. In 1975 a Pond Committee was formed to help with the maintenance.

Long ago kingfishers frequented the pond; today swallows swoop above the water, but the many mallard ducks and drakes that generations of children loved to feed have deserted it in recent years. Only four moorhens swim and nest there. In summer it is the habitat of dragon and damsel flies.

The water-table having dropped considerably in recent years, two other ponds in Slindon have dried up, one at Gaston Farm and the 'pond with the spring' mentioned in pre-history. The latter is reduced to a mere trickle of water, running parallel with Maoh Lane. Before 1871, according to Jimmy Dean, "this public road connected Slindon with Biddleside and passed unrestricted by stile or gate from Reynolds Lane to the Portsmouth and London Highway (A27) near the Sir George Thomas Arms." It now survives as a rough, marshy track.

Main gas was brought to Slindon at the end of the 1914-18 war. The new amenity was used to run a gas engine to generate the electric light for Slindon House, replacing the old paraffin engine. Gas was also used to run the dynamo for the saw bench in the Park.

Electric lighting for the village was installed in 1932 by the Bognor Electrical Company.

The first wireless set was probably at The White House in Slindon, where a large number of villagers gathered on 23rd April, 1924, to hear the broadcast by George V on the opening of the Wembley Exhibition.

Cables were laid for telephone installation in March 1927. A decision to install public lighting was taken by the Parish Council in 1938 and this was extended to roads in Slindon Common in 1957. Mains drainage was brought to the village in 1965.

XI. Slindon Cricketers

The greatest celebrity to be born and bred in Slindon was undoubtedly Richard Newland, whose fame and skill as the founder of cricket, as we know it today, is best described by John Marshall in *Sussex Cricket*:

> *"At Slindon lived and died the man who may truly be described as 'the father of cricket' – the greatest all-rounder of his day, the cricketer who taught his nephew Richard Nyren – 'the general' of Hambledon – a skill and knowledge of the game never before imparted."*

With Richard Newland and his two brothers John and Adam forming the backbone of the team, Slindon became one of the strongest in the country, challenging London and county sides.

In 1742 there was an account of a match between the 'famous Parish of Slindon and eleven picked gentlemen of London. The above Parish has played forty-three matches and lost one.'

In 1744 there was another match between Slindon and London in which, in addition to the Newland brothers, there were four other players from Slindon. Cuddy, the village tailor opened the innings.

The occurrence of three brothers playing in the same team for England was only once repeated, in 1880, when the Graces achieved that distinction.

> *"As captain of England against Kent in 1744" says John Marshall, "Richard Newland was top scorer in both innings and may well have taken wickets too – eight fell to a Newland but as*

> *no initials are recorded it is not know which of the brothers claimed them. The England team was virtually the Slindon team.*"

In the following year, Richard Newland hit up 88 for a victorious England against Kent. By the end of 1741 they could claim that only once in 43 matches had they been defeated and that they had beaten Surrey. "The second Duke of Richmond," Mr Marshall continues, "grandson of Charles II, wrote sardonically of this triumph. 'Poore little Slyndon against almost your whole county of Surrey – we have beat Surrey in one innings.'

The Duke had some right to crow, for he had a large responsibility for the establishment of organised cricket in Sussex; indeed it is very likely that after 1731, when the Duke of Richmond's team was last recorded, Slindon and the Duke's side were one and the same."

One reason that has been given why a tiny Sussex village could attain such heights was the fact that, playing on Slindon Common, they had a ground of solid clay upon gravel which provided a good, level, fast surface on which correct strokes could be played. Other teams played on the downs, where the sheep kept the turf short, but it was too springy for what became known as 'scientific batting'.

In Richard Newland's day, cricket bats were curved and umpires sat in chairs. One of the eleven paintings depicting scenes from Sussex history in Eastergate village hall shows the famous cricketer umpiring. Soft Jim Crow hats were worn at that time.

Matches were often played on the short turf of the Downs.

When Richard and his brothers ceased to play for Slindon, the team's glory waned, but cricketing enthusiasm in the village did not die, and from that day to the present, Slindon Cricket Team has challenged other village teams with considerable success.

That there was some connection between cricket and smuggling is shown in an article by Timothy J. McCann [33]

> *"In the 1740s the counties of Sussex, Kent and Hampshire were the scene of a bitter and bloodthirsty battle between civil authorities and organised bands of smugglers. The 2nd Duke of Richmond, well known to cricketing historians as 'the Duke who was Cricket' was the central figure in the government drive to stamp out smuggling in the area and the evidence he so painstakingly preserved of one particular family of smugglers enables us to identify members of the famous Slindon and Hambledon teams of the 18th.century and another link between them."*

Mr McCann goes on to tell the story of one Henry Aburrow, a local blacksmith (of Hambledon) who was tried and sentenced to death in June 1748, having been found guilty of 'outrages' on the property of Henry Foxcroft, a Hampshire landowner. Efforts by influential friends to have the sentence commuted to transportation failed, the Duke of Richmond maintaining that' the sentence should be carried out.

A letter from the Duke to this effect says that Aburrow was a villain and a smuggler and that one brother gave evidence against him to save himself and another brother, who was a famous bowler, who went by the name of Curry was committed to jail for smuggling with firearms.

Timothy McCann's study reveals that in 1745, among others found guilty of smuggling with firearms was 'Edward Abuurow alias Aubrow or Curry, tailor of Slyndon'; that the name Cuddy (see Pg.152) might have been a nickname of Edward Aburrow; that Edward Aburrow, presumably born in Hampshire, moved to Slindon to practice his trade and married a Slindon girl. They

---

[33] *Journal of the Cricket Society.* Vol. 10. No.2 (1981)

had a son, also Edward, who in 1772 became a member of the Hambledon team, but went by the name of Curry. He died in 1835 and was buried at Hambledon. According to Mr McCann the date on his tombstone fits exactly with the baptism of Edward Aburrow at Slindon.

Richard Nyren, unfortunately for Sussex, took the skill imparted to him by his uncle to Hambledon, which became as great in the 1750s and 60s as Slindon had been in the 1740s. "Richard Nyren re-enacted the earlier achievement of his uncle Richard Newland," says Edmund Esdaile.[34]

The Nyrens were an Eartham family. The Revd S. Bates, former Rector of Slindon and Eartham, proved by his research into the family history that there were Nyrens or Nierens in Eartham, gentlemen, yeoman and some clerics, from the 13th and 14th centuries. The first from whom a pedigree can be traced (which Mr Esdaile has done) was a Nieren, a cleric from Kent, alive in 1619. His son, the Revd Jasper Nieren, was Curate of Eartham and Vicar of Stoughton. Three successive generations married Slindon girls. A Jasper Nyren married Elizabeth Martin at Slindon 1706; their son Richard married Susannah Newland in 1733 and became the father of Richard Nyren the cricketer who, in 1758, married Frances Pennicud. "The marriage," says Mr Esdaile, "is merely entered according to Act of Parliament in the Eartham register (signed by the Vicar and the bridegroom's father as churchwarden) but must have been celebrated in the chapel in Slindon House, for Frances was a Catholic."

Their son John, 1764-1837, is still held in great esteem by the Cricket Society, and his book *Cricketers of my Time*, written with

---

[34] In an article on the Nyrens in the 1967 *Hampshire County Cricket Clubs' Handbook*.

the graphic aid of Cowden Clarke and first published 131 years ago, is regarded as a major cricket classic.

Edmund Esdaile, in his article, refutes finally and convincingly the Nyrens alleged descent from the Jacobite Lords Nairne. In a further article on the Newlands[35] he explodes another time-honoured belief, that Richard Newland, cricketer, was also a surgeon of Chichester. Mr Esdaile's diligent research into church registers discloses that there were two contemporary Richard Newlands of Slindon; one was the surgeon, the other the cricketer.

Two 'surgical' Newlands are commemorated by memorial tablets in St Marys Church: to Richard Newland, surgeon of Chichester 1688-1762 and to Jane, nee Riggs, his wife 1695-1795 erected by their son Richard, surgeon of Chichester 1718-1791, who is commemorated in another tablet. These display a coat of arms; Gules, a chevron flory at the top, between two crescents in chief, and a lion rampant in base argent. The crest, not found at Slindon, is 'a bear's head, erased, holding in the mouth a broken spear proper.' There is a story about the motto *'Les Armes, la Loyaute'*, that it commemorates the part played by a Newland of Hampshire in the unsuccessful attempt to rescue Charles I from Carisbrooke Castle.

The surgeons and their relatives were Catholics in the 18th Century but afterwards probably not. The family were landowners in the Slindon area, enjoying a 'secure prosperity'. Another surgeon, Thomas Newland, was married in Slindon 1623.

It is said that the Newlands came to Slindon in the service of the Kempes. This is partially substantiated by Mr Esdaile's reference to a John Newland (1645 & 1649) servant for 40 years of Sir Garrat Kempe 'receiving rents and paying taxes', Presumably

[35] In the *Journal of the Cricket Society*, Spring 1969.

servant, in this case, meant steward. This John Newland's wife was the daughter of the 'minister' of Slindon.

The cricketing Newlands were yeomen and Anglicans; their tombs are at Slindon but without heraldry and in the church-yard, not in the church. Mr Esdaile, although unable to trace the relationship, surmises that the two families 'derived more or less distantly from the same parent stock.' A Richard Newland (yeo-man) married 1703, Elizabeth Hammond of Eartham. Three of their sons were Richard (b. 1713) John and Adam, the cricketers; there were two other sons and five daughters, one of whom mar-ried in 1732, an elder Richard Nyren and became the mother of Richard Nyren, cricketer.

On 26th February 1744, Richard Newland, yeoman and crick-eter, married Mary Newland, sister of Richard Newland, the surgeon. On New Years Eve 1747, Mary died giving birth to their first child, a daughter, who also died three weeks later. A head-stone in St Mary's churchyard has this inscription:

'Here Lyeth the Body of Mary, the wife of Richard NEWLAND,
Junr. who departed this Life the 31st. Dec. 1747 aged 24 yrs.
Cut down as grass snatched just at her bloom.
Her morning sun alas went down at noon.
Also Lyeth Mary their dau. who died an infant.'

At 35 Richard was left a widower and childless. "Surely the boy, Richard Nyren," says Mr Esdaile, "in some sort took the place of the dead child. Richard never remarried, but he was not unre-warded. Living until 1778 he knew of his nephew's fame; nor did the nephew or greatnephew who, at the time of Richard's death was a boy of 14, ever forget him."

There were Newlands in Slindon, taking part in the life of the village and of the church, for over three hundred years. There is an entry in the church registers of a Joan Newland, buried in

1559; a John Newland died in 1588; several Newlands were churchwardens, among them a John, a Thomas and a Richard. The last, a Miss Newland, died at The Grange, formerly called Newlands, in 1870, but the last descendant of the family in Slindon, a Miss Fleet, died as recently as 1936. Newlands was the family home for those three centuries and the land around it is still referred to as 'Newlands' fields.

The perennial question of whether Slindon or Hambledon in Hampshire should rightfully claim the title "cradle of cricket" still gives rise to argument today. In a modern edition of *The Young Cricketers Tutor* by John Nyren, collected and edited by Charles Cowden Clarke, John Arlott says in his introduction:

> *"John Nyren's sketches gave them (the Hambledon Cricketers) and other clubs a knowledge unusual in any sport. The impact of his description led some subsequent writers to call Hambledon "the cradle of cricket" when, in fact it was neither. The game was earlier and more strongly established in Kent, Sussex, Surrey and London than in Hampshire. Such towns as Addington, Slindon, Henfield and Chertsey had flourishing teams before the Hambledon club was founded, at some time between 1750 and 1760. It did not at once become established – its major successes were between 1763 and 1787."*

And on page 56:

> *"John Nyren owed all the skill and judgement he possessed to an old uncle, Richard Newland of Slindon in Sussex."*

It does seem, however, that Hambledon may have been responsible for the rules of present-day cricket.

> **Hambledon:** *This isolated village… is renowned as the early home of cricket. The Hambledon Cricket Club, founded in 1760, played on Broadhalfpenny Down… and gradually devel-*

*oped the laws of modern cricket. An inn sign (the Bat and Ball)
at Hambledon marks the fact that cricket as played today
started there in 1774, when the local team invented many of its
laws.*[36]

Although no longer famous, Slindon maintained a strong and
enthusiastic cricket team. Among their opponents in the 1860s
were Petworth, Chichester, Bognor, Littlehampton, Arundel,
Burton Park and Duncton. Slindon rarely lost a match.

Sometime afterwards, however, the club got into debt. Then
Jimmy Dean organised a concert in the National School, the
Arundel String Band giving a performance. From then on an
annual concert was held for the Cricket Club, Jimmy Dean singing his popular songs. This was followed by the Club supper at
the Newburgh Arms.

In the *West Sussex Gazette* there appeared a verse by W.J.S.
which evokes the spirit of those old cricketing times.

I call to mind some Slindon men
Who could at cricket play.
For Jimmy Dean has told us how
They'd bat and bowl all day.
When old Tom Bateman, umpire, stood
Wearing his hat so tall.
No man knew more than old Tom did,
How bat should meet the ball.

In 1871, as a result of the enclosure of the common land, the
club lost their old ground at the south end of Park Lane. The
land was ploughed up and planted with fir trees. A new ground

---

[36] The AA *Illustrated Guide to Britain*, p.101.

was made, after the removal of the furze and bracken, on the site of the present one, on what is now the recreation ground.

Throughout the first three decades of the twentieth century, Jimmy Dean continued to record the successes of the Slindon Club. In 1905 "a one guinea bat given to a member made the highest score in a five club matches." In a match against Bognor: "the club ran up 125 runs in one innings." In the 1920s there was a particularly memorable match against Addington, which Jimmy Dean helped to organise but he does not record any details.

During World War II cricket ceased to be played in Slindon and its revival was due to the energy and enthusiasm of Arthur Chamberlain and the late Jack Anderson, who, in 1946 rallied members to form a new club and made a collection in the village to raise funds to buy equipment.

The headquarters of Slindon Cricket Club since its revival has been the Newburgh Arms.

Perhaps the most eventful decade in the history of the post-war club was from the early 1970s to 80s. From 1973 to 1977, annual charity matches were held, the Slindon team playing teams of celebrities captained by Michael Marshall, MP for Arundel, who organised the matches in aid of the Disabled Living Foundation, a charity with which he has had a long association. The draw prize each year was a cricket bat autographed by cricketing celebrities; in 1973 by members of the England and West Indian Test Teams. Alec and Eric Bedser and Leslie Crowther were among the visiting team that year and the event raised £800 for the Foundation.

In 1976 the visiting stars in a match in aid of the Disabled Living Foundation and the Sussex Friends of the Lord Taverners, included Jimmy Ellis and Doug Fielding (then appearing on TV in *Z Cars*) and Jeremy Kemp. Googie Withers and her husband, John McCallum, at that time appearing at Chichester Festival Theatre, were special guests.

1976 was also the year of Slindon Cricket Club's first tour, a weekend tour to Somerset. They beat Wincanton by 18 runs and although they lost to Tydford-on-Fosse and Mells, the tour from a social point of view was highly successful.

In 1981, Slindon Cricket Club celebrated its 250th anniversary. A booklet was produced, containing articles on Slindon and Sussex cricket and Slindon history, with a commemorative cover designed by Frank Sharman, a leading Sussex designer. The stamp selected for the cover was the 17½p commemorative sports stamp issued in October 1980.

On 3rd May an anniversary match was arranged between Slindon and the Sussex County Cricket Team, but the weather failed to co-operate. Rain fell just before the start of play and the match was abandoned without a ball being bowled.

A second match to celebrate the anniversary was fixed for Sunday 30th August, this time against a team of celebrities from Chichester Festival Theatre. The sun shone and Patricia Hodge, then appearing in *The Mitford Girls*, got Slindon off to a good start by bowling the first ball of their innings. The star player for the actors was Ossie Clark, a former cricket blue, also appearing in *The Mitford Girls*. Most of the actresses from the play came along to watch the match. Actor Christopher Timothy, at the time famous for his role on TV in *All Creatures Great & Small* and a local Sussex resident, drew a raffle after the match. The Harriers Free Fall Parachute team gave a display over the recreation ground.

On Wednesday 10th June 1981 Slindon played The Hague Cricket Club, which 46 times had gained Championships of the

Netherlands and represented the top league of the Royal Dutch Cricket Union. The match played during their tour of the South of England proved a memorable occasion for the local team.

The first Slindon player to represent England since the Newland brothers 250 years ago is John North. In 1987 he was chosen to play for England in the under 15 cricket team. During August of that year he played in matches against Scotland and Wales, clinching that team's defeat by taking six wickets for 46 in their second innings. By extraordinary coincidence John North's grandmother comes from Hambledon!

Slindon Cricket Team, 1869.

XII. More Sports, Organisations & Occasions

The early days of Slindon football are not so well recorded as those of cricket and it is uncertain when the game was first played in the village. As with cricket, the earliest matches probably took place on the Downs.

The first official football field was on the left of Reynolds Lane, between the present Primary School and what is now the A29. The game was afterwards played in Bow Meadow in Park Lane before moving to the recreation ground, where the team shared a ground with the Cricket Club.

This led to controversy between the two clubs because of the state of the pitch at the end of the football season and a separate ground was made for football on the old allotment land.

Jimmy Dean is not as informative about football as he is about cricket; the only match he records is undated. On this occasion he went with the Slindon Football Club to Graffham. Slindon beat the Graffham team but the score is not recorded. After the match both sides had tea at The Foresters Arms, followed at 8.30pm by a concert given by Graffham Brass Band. Dancing with Graffham villagers continued until 10 o'clock.

Football ceased in organised form during World War II and was not revived until 1961. In November 1960, at a meeting at the Coronation Hall, a committee was elected to carry out the business of forming a new club. A series of dances and whist drives were then held to raise funds for equipment and clothing and in March 1961 it was agreed that some friendly matches should be arranged. By August that year the club had been accepted into V Division of the West Sussex League and had entered for the Barnham Trophy.

On the front of a programme for a match between Slindon and the ex-Portsmouth Championship and Professional XI, on Sunday 11th September, 1970, the following short history of the present club appeared:

> *"Since the club was revived in 1961 it has had a record probably unique. It moved progressively from Division V of the West Sussex League to Division I.*
>
> *In 1961-2 the Club were champions in Division V, and in 1962-3 champions of Division IV. They were runners-up in Division III in 1963-64 and in Division II in 1964-65, in which season they won the Chichester Charity Cup.*
>
> *The high water mark was reached in 1965-66 when they were champions of Division I, at that time the Senior Division of the West Sussex League.*
>
> *After that fortune deserted the club and they slipped back to Division III in which they have played for two seasons.*
>
> *Last season things improved once more and the Club was third in Division III...*
>
> *In 1966 a second team was created which made it possible for many more members of the Club to enjoy a weekly game of football."*

The formation of the new club in 1961 was due largely to the efforts and enthusiasm of Mr William 'Bill' Blackman, who was secretary-treasurer from that time until shortly before his death in 1982.

In 1975, the Slindon Minor Football Team was formed. In December of that year the team in their new red kit, provided by

Slindon Pudding Club, the youngest member five years old, the eldest aged eight, played their first match against Walberton and Binstead School team at Walberton School. Unfortunately the team was disbanded after one or two seasons.

In the 1920s Slindon had a Ladies' Hockey Club. Jimmy Dean records that on 13th April 1922 Slindon's new Hockey Team played Petworth away. They were defeated 4-0.

The Sussex game of stoolball has been played in Slindon for almost sixty years; it was first started in the mid-1920s by Miss Jane Izard and Miss Dorothy Marriott. It may have lapsed during the war years but there was again a team in 1950.

The present one, the first mixed team, was formed in 1967. All home matches, both league and friendly, are played on Slindon recreation ground throughout the summer months. Slindon also takes part in tournaments, consisting of ten teams, at various venues in Sussex from the Hampshire to the Surrey borders.

In 1975 and 1980 the team were winners of the Coastal Stoolball League, a league in which they still play.

The recreation ground on which these sports take place lies adjacent to the A29 and Mill Road. Originally received from the Churchwardens and Overseers of the Poor, as their share of the Enclosure Act 1870/1, it was registered by the County Council as a public green in 1969, and is now the property of the Parish Council.

In 1898 Slindon Cricket Club erected a small pavilion by the A29. The present pavilion stands by the Mill Road entrance to the ground. The implement shed behind the pavilion has an interesting story. Originally an abandoned bathing hut near Climping, during World War II it was used by the Slindon Home Guard when on night duty near the coast. When their duties took them to the Downs the hut went too. Later it became the

ladies loo at the old pavilion, before fulfilling its present purpose.[37]

Slindon has seldom lacked social clubs and amenities. In the
late 1950s teenage girls formed a club which met at the Club
House, Top Road, Slindon every week. Classes in art, needlework and singing were given to members by local residents at
their own houses. The girls raised money by sales of work and
when they disbanded the residue of their fund was divided between Oxfam and the local scouts and also paid for the kit for the
new football team.

A Rock and Roll Club met at the Coronation Hall for dancing, table tennis and darts. From the group of boys who attended,
Bill Blackman formed his football team.

In 1967 the chairman of the Parish Council, the Rector, the
headmaster of Slindon School, with some of Slindon's senior
residents, met at the Coronation Hall with the purpose of forming a Youth Club in the village. Covering an age bracket from
thirteen to twenty-one, the club successfully fulfilled a need in
the village for some years.

The 1st Walberton and Slindon Scout Troop was registered
under that name when it moved to Slindon in October 1961.
Formerly the 1st Walberton, which met at Walberton Pavilion,
the five members took up their headquarters at Slindon Club
House. After that time their number rose to over thirty.

Under the expert leadership of John Pegler, assisted by his wife
June as Assistant Scout Leader, the boys raised funds for a number of projects and have interests in photography, fishing, the
flora and fauna and local history of the area, as well as learning
self-reliance and survival. An interest in geology prompted an

---

[37] A fully comprehensive account of the recreation ground appears in Bernard Keeling's History of *Slindon Parish Council.*

expedition to Andorra in 1986 for rock climbing and abseiling. In 1987 the Group was awarded the County Standard. Early in 1988 a Venture Scout Unit was formed.

For several years in the late 1970s successful gymkhanas were organized by local riding enthusiasts on the field below the Coronation Hall. These attracted young riders from a wide area.

For many years the Slindon branch of the Womens' Institute met every second Tuesday afternoon at the Coronation Hall, until its disbandment in 1986. For a short while during this time a second branch for younger members met in the evenings.

The WI is now replaced by the Afternoon Group for mainly senior members and the Village Link for the younger women, both organizations meeting at individual members' houses.

A Mothers, Toddlers and Babies Group meets weekly at the Coronation Hall. The village also has a Red Cross unit. (Welfare Group)

In 1971, the Pudding Club was formed by Mr H. Dymock, then Slindon's postmaster. The club originates in a centuries-old custom recorded in Warwickshire, Shropshire and Worcestershire, whereby the agricultural labourers saved from their meagre wages enough money to give a hearty meal to the old people of their village at Christmas, Easter and Harvest Thanksgiving. The meal consisted basically of a pudding, probably containing rabbit and salt pork, served with vegetables – very filling.

Slindon's Pudding Club, in the old tradition, provides accessories for the comfort and enjoyment of its senior citizens including an annual tea and entertainment. The twelve members meet once a month to "wine and dine and enjoy each others company, having always in mind the purpose of their membership." They pay a levy on the cost, which goes into their fund.

Slindon has always marked Royal occasions with forethought and enthusiasm. In earlier times such celebrations were usually held on the Downs.

Jimmy Dean reports that on Queen Victoria's Diamond Jubilee on June 22nd, 1897 there was a procession, headed by Slindon Brass Band to the Downs, where there was maypole and other dancing and singing. To feed the multitude, which sat at long trestle tables, 150lbs of roast beef, 70lbs of mutton, 2 large hams, 150 meat turnovers and 301 lbs of boiled potatoes were provided. After the feast, cricket and other sports were held.

On the occasion of the Diamond Jubilee and on the Golden Jubilee of 1887, Jimmy Dean was commissioned to see that the huge Union Jack which had belonged to the Newburghs was raised high above Slindon village. He was told to cut the longest straight ash pole and fasten it to the lime tree with the flag attached, so that it would wave fifteen feet above the top of the tree.

In 1911, to organise the preparations for George V's coronation celebrations, a special parish meeting was called for the first time, to appoint a working party to arrange the festivities. On that occasion, there was a dinner for the elderly and tea and sports for the children.

At the Silver Jubilee in 1935, in addition to the usual festivities, the planting of a lime tree took place on the recreation ground.

The Coronation of Elizabeth II in 1953 was celebrated by a fancy dress parade from the lime tree in Top Road to the recreation ground, where there were sports and tea, followed by a dance in Slindon House.

The Silver Jubilee in 1977 was marked in permanent form by the planting of a cedar tree in the upper playing area by Albert

Roberts, who at 84, was Slindon's oldest resident at that time. The day started with a peal of bells, followed by a thanksgiving service at St Mary's. After the treeplanting ceremony came the presentation of Jubilee plaques and mugs to all young people of 16 and under. Each plaque was handmade, inscribed with names of the recipient, and donated by Slindon potter, Mrs Bonnie Beere.

The Royal Wedding of 1981 was celebrated by a childrens' tea party, and a village barn-dance followed by a sheep roast, barbecue and disco dancing. A red chestnut tree was planted on the recreation ground, near the crossroads.

To commemorate the wedding of Prince Andrew, Duke of York to Miss Sarah Ferguson in July 1986, the Rector, the Revd John Cossar and Mrs Cossar planted a white chestnut tree to complement the red one.

A particularly pleasing feature of the proceedings was the arrival of the Mother and Toddler Club, who congregated on the upper playing field and marched down to the tree-planting on the recreation ground, waving Union Jack flags.

Over the years there have been other occasions for felicity, as recorded by Jimmy Dean.

In 1904, on 30th December, the scholars of Slindon School had their annual Christmas treat. Buns, apples and oranges were distributed and the 78 children each received three new pennies from Mr Coles. All received a useful garment, carols were sung and the young hand-bell ringers gave a selection. The Revd Arthur Izard showed views and sketches with his magic lantern.

On July 6th 1891 Jimmy reported:

"It is said that the Goodwood of 1891 broke all records as regards visitors to Slindon, and that not a spare bedroom or conveyance to the course could be had for 'love or money'. There

was a large party at Slindon House during the week and on Cup Day the band of the 3ʳᵈ Battalion of the Royal Sussex Regiment were engaged to play there."

Jimmy also describes a General Election Day at Walberton around 1900:

"All Slindon went to Walberton to vote for the Unionist candidate, Lord March of Goodwood. The Liberal candidate was Gibbs, who brought over a whole lot of Liberal supporters from Bognor, who filled all the front seats of the meeting hall.

Mrs Jane Leslie offered to take Jimmy Dean in the carriage and pair, but after thanking her, he said he would prefer to go with the Slindon Estate workmen in the large estate waggon pulled by its two rare fine horses and covered with gaily flying orange ribbons.

When Lord March addressed the crowd he was loudly heckled by the Bognor group. Attempts to oust the hecklers were resisted and the meeting continued in uproar.

It appears that the Slindon crowd considered the whole proceedings to be 'rare good fun,' to be followed by a drinking spree, for the rest of the day. They ignored the order to return to work after voting at the booth set up in the Walberton National School, and repaired to the Holly Tree where many pots of ale were enjoyed. Then homeward bound but not to work, but to Mrs App's Beer House, where they remained until 10pm. The horses and waggon, empty of estate workers, returned to the stables.

To celebrate the 21ˢᵗ birthday of Charles Radcliffe Aloysius Leslie in 1880, a huge bonfire blazed at Black Jack on Slindon Downs, lighting up the countryside for miles around. The refreshments consumed by the crowd included 18 gallons of beer.

The festivities lasted three days. On the first day the steward at Hassop attended with five tenant farmers from the Leslie estates in Aberdeen, with all the tenants and tradesmen from Slindon. Village workmen and their wives were entertained on the second day and the children were given a grand party at Slindon House on the third.

There were many choir outings; a memorable one was to the exhibition "Venice in London" Jimmy and a few friends missed the last train home and spent the night on Victoria station. On reaching home next morning he found that his wife had given birth to a daughter. He promptly named the child Venice.

He also recalls a choir festival Slindon attended with Boxgrove and other village choirs at Chichester Cathedral. All were afterwards given a dinner at the Waterbeach Hotel.

Slindon Flower Show was another popular annual event. A large tent, hired from Chichester, was pitched in the meadow at the top end of Dyers Lane, in front of Bleak House (except for one year when it was held at Slindon House). Slindon's Brass Band played throughout the day and in the evening provided music for dancing.

On 19th July 1988, Slindon, Eartham and Madehurst joined in the celebrations to mark the 400th anniversary of the defeat of the Spanish Armada. Two hundred people from the three villages gathered on Nore Hill to witness the lighting of their beacon, one of many across Sussex. While the bonfire was blazing, hot dogs and drinks were served to the spectators.

Life in Slindon has rarely been dull!

XIII. Writers & Personalities

Hilaire Belloc, although he was born in France and spent much of his life in London, is nevertheless remembered as a "Sussex man" and Slindon can lay considerable claim to this gifted man of letters. His association with the village began in 1878, when his widowed mother, Madame Bessie Parkes Belloc, concerned for the health of her only son, left her London house in Wimpole Street and moved with him, his sister Marie, a nurse and governess to Slindon Cottage (now the Dower House). In a letter to a friend she expressed the hope that the pure, sweet air of the Downs would keep her son free from the sicknesses and epidemics of the city. She was not disappointed, for by the time he was eleven years old he had climbed the Wrekin with her and soon afterward walked the Downs from Petersfield to Beachy Head, sleeping outdoors en route.

In these formative years he developed the love of Sussex expressed in many of his poems. Nostalgia for its countryside oppressed him when he was away. He writes of a time when sailing in the Channel of being possessed with the memory of home and the Downs; with the scent of the first flowers in North Wood and at Gumber Corner.

These sentiments were not shared by his sister, however, who wrote of being "selfishly glad to leave Slindon" – she could not adapt herself to the English countryside, which was so different from the France she loved. She found English girls poor company, devoting too much time and thought to hunting. Happily for Marie, the family spent an annual summer holiday at La

Celle St Cloud, Hilaire's birthplace, with the children's French paternal grandmother.

Hilaire Belloc. A portrait by David Goodman.

When Madame Belloc moved to Newlands, which she re-named The Grange, Hilaire found a playmate in the Rector's nephew Bertie Izard. The boys must have been a lively pair: the young Izard who later, at Oxford, was a triple blue, and went on to become an Archdeacon and Bishop of Singapore, and Belloc, whose active mind was ever bent on some new enterprise – one, it is told, ended with a ducking in the village pond.

Marie disliked the change from the roomy Slindon Cottage to Newlands, which was older and smaller, possessing a dark sitting room on the ground floor and a drawing room on the first "although it had a pleasant kitchen." Madame Belloc, however, found a certain charm in her new home and wrote of "the great screen of rose bushes and laurustinus which divides the lawn from the vegetables in this small domain".

While at The Grange, Madame Belloc wrote a collection of essays entitled *In a Walled Garden*, one of several books, which were very well received; she also wrote articles on literary subjects, verse and childrens' books.

Her daughter, later Marie Belloc Lowndes, wrote many thrillers, the best known of which is *The Lodger*, and several autobiographical works. Her second novel *Barbara Rebell* was set in Slindon House, Slindon Cottage and Newlands, with fictitious characters.

It was to Newlands or The Grange that Belloc brought his young bride-to-be, the lovely Elodie Hogan.

During the latter part of her life Madame Belloc lived at Gaston Cottage at the top of the village. French windows opened onto the lawn where she would have tea and watch the "silver line of the sea". In old age she dressed always in "ample, black, silk clothing," wrote her grand-daughter, Mrs Eleanor Jebb, "white lace over her silver hair which in youth was auburn. She wrote with a quill at her little bureau in Slindon."

It was here that Daisy Hersee went to live with her as her personal maid and companion.

Gaston Cottage was but a short distance from Mill Lane House, the home of Mr and Mrs Rowland Wedgwood, and thus the grandchildren of two famous men came to live in close proximity; Mr Wedgwood was a grandson of Josiah Wedgwood the

Staffordshire pottery tycoon, and Madame Belloc was a grand-daughter of Dr Joseph Priestley, discoverer of oxygen. They became great friends.

When Madame Belloc died in 1925, the following passage appeared in a local newspaper:

> *"The wonderful lady who, at 95 years of age has just passed away, was marvellous in eyesight and hearing until after 90. I spent an afternoon, writes a correspondent, with Madame Belloc and was amazed at her clear recollection. She talked of George Eliot, of whom she was probably the last surviving very intimate friend. She recalled her Manchester days and her first years in France. In the room were her gifted son, Hilaire Belloc and her daughter Marie Belloc Lowndes. She had a lively wit and could sketch a portrait of a contemporary with a skill that made it memorable. For many years Madame Belloc lived beneath the shadow of Westminster Abbey but she had lived in Sussex in later years, and it was in that favourite county, praised by her son in prose and verse, that she died."*

There is a belief that Hilaire Belloc, with Elodie and their four children, lived at Bleak House from 1903-1905. A plaque commemorating this occupation was placed on the north side of the house in March 1996. A short ceremony of dedication performed by Bishop Cormac Murphy-O'Connor, Roman Catholic Bishop of Arundel & Brighton, preceded a buffet lunch in Slindon College, attended by celebrities, including Patrick Garland, Director of Chichester Festival Theatre, Sussex folk singer Bob Copper, members of the Belloc family and local residents. However, Eleanor Jebb, the elder of Belloc's two daughters in her book Testimony to Hilaire Belloc, written in cooperation with her husband Reginald Jebb writes:

"For a few weeks in the late summer of 1903 Mamma and Papa rented Bleak House at Slindon and we all moved down (from 104 Cheyne Walk) in a body by train to Barnham Junction and thence by hired trap to Slindon."

She recalls that Frances and Gilbert Chesterton stayed nearby for a few days and called at Bleak House; that her father did a great deal of writing that summer and sailed his boat from Little-hampton; and visits to their grandmother who lived "a little way down the village street."

They returned to 104 Cheyne Walk where the youngest son, Peter, was born, until it was sold in the autumn of 1904.

In February 1905 the family again moved to Slindon, this time to Court Hill Farmhouse, where they lived until the summer of 1906, when they found "the house of their dreams" at Kings Land, Shipley.

The move to Slindon was prompted by financial rather than nostalgic reasons. "My going out of London in 1905 and keeping no house or flat there was disastrous," he wrote to Mrs Raymond Asquith in 1920, "but I was driven by real, even dangerous pov-erty."

Elodie, however, welcomed the retreat to the country. She en-joyed the fresh vegetables and fruit from the large, flint-walled garden at the farmhouse and driving her children in a pony-cart to Arundel or to Ford to see the Balfours and for picnics beyond Dale Park. The children often played with their two cousins, the daughters of Mrs Belloc Lowndes, when they stayed with Ma-dame Belloc.

Belloc too was happy to be in Sussex again. In Hills and the Sea he describes this return to the haunts of his boyhood and his pleasure in finding them not less but more delightful than his memory recorded. He refers to familiar places: Baycombe, the

Fairmile, Gumber, the Nore and the stretch called No Man's Land.

On occasions when the farmhouse was let separately from the land a piece of meadow continuing from the front garden to the bend of the road went with the house. It is the scything of this piece that Belloc describes in his essay *The Mowing of a Field*.

Soon after his arrival he bought a steady chestnut cob called 'Monster' to ride across the Downs. In *Hills and the Sea* he tells how he had been riding his "kind and honourable horse" for two hours when he took a path that made for the High Wood between Gumber and No Man's Land. There he met a tramp, albeit a cultured tramp, and shared with him some stimulating conversation and half a raw onion.

Hills and the Sea was one of several of Belloc's books published in 1906, and it is very probable that he wrote it, or some of it, at Court Hill. His study was "in an excellent attic at the top of the house approached by a little winding stairway" wrote Eleanor Jebb.

His sister tells how, living at the foot of the hill on which stands St Richard's Church, he was happy to be near mass again. No doubt he would have walked to church up the steep road or the path between the trees and the field, but he owned a Model T Ford car, in which he would dash off to Maurice Baring at Rottingdean or the Duff Coopers at Bognor or H.V. Morton at Henfield. While at Court Hill he often entertained his great friends and contemporaries G.K. Chesterton and E.V. Lucas.

Lucas wrote of Slindon:

"... *this Sussex backwater; it has no road that anyone travels, except for the purpose of going to Sussex or coming from it, and those who perform either of these acts are few – yet all who have not seen Slindon are so much the poorer, for Slindon House is nobly Elizabethan and Slindon beeches are among the aristoc-racy of trees."*[38]

~ ~ ~ ~ ~

A poet, who had associations with Slindon a century earlier, was William Hayley. He lived at Eartham; but with many celebrated friends whom he entertained at Eartham House – Cowper, Gibbon, Warton, Blake and Flaxman – he loved to walk in Slindon Woods.

At Slindon Cottage, before Madame Belloc, lived Lady Georgiana Fullerton, a writer of historical romances, but remembered in Slindon not so much for her writing as for the goodness and simplicity of her life and for her great generosity. Madame Belloc told her story in one chapter of *In a Walled Garden*. Lady Georgiana Leveson Gower was the daughter of the 1st Earl Granville, for many years British Ambassador to France. She was named after her lovely grandmother, the Duchess of Devonshire, who was painted by Gainsborough and Sir Joshua Reynolds.

Lady Georgiana married, when very young, an untitled gentleman, Captain Fullerton. Her son and only child was born when she was twenty one. Ten years later Lady Georgiana began her career as an authoress and her first books received great acclaim. Although her son's health had sometimes caused anxiety, he prepared for a military career, but at the outbreak of the Crimean War was considered unfit for active service. He was killed shortly afterwards in an accident, at the age of 21.

After the death of her son, Lady Georgiana took upon herself a vow of poverty. "She, who must have worn the finest dresses at the house of an ambassador of the first rank," writes Madame Belloc, "now dressed habitually in a black dress and shawl, and

---

[38] *Highways and Byways of West Sussex*, Macmillan 1937.

plain cap; even dispensing with gloves that she might give their value to the poor." She continued writing, though doubtful at first whether it was right to spend so much time in writing romances, but deciding that in this way she could earn more money for the needy. Very beautiful were her many historical novels. Madame Belloc does not say in what year of her life Lady Fullerton came to Slindon Cottage, but with her husband she attended the ceremony, in 1864, of laying the foundation stone of St Richard's Church. She died in 1885. During the time she lived there, the village benefited by the many charities of this kind and industrious woman. Lady Fullerton is buried in the graveyard of St Richard's Church.

~ ~ ~ ~ ~

Few villages can have so many associations with writers past and present. Two authoresses, Agnes and Rose Weeks, lived at Gasson Cottage (now part of Gassons), They wrote many novels set in Majorca and the Spanish mainland. Their work was published in America under the *nom de plume* 'Anthony Pride'. After the death of her sister, Rose ceased writing and devoted her tireless energies to the comfort and help of those in need. When she died at the age of 86 she was mourned by many friends.

~ ~ ~ ~ ~

The widely acclaimed book *Night Fighter* was written by Slindon resident Squadron Leader Cecil Rawnsley in conjunction with Robert Wright, who as a member of 604 Squadron and afterwards 85 Squadron flew, first as air gunner, later as navigator, with John 'Cat's Eyes' Cunningham, the celebrated night-fighter ace of World War II. He had first crewed up with the then very young but brilliant pilot in 1937; it was the beginning of a wonderful partnership that continued for nearly seven years. During this time 'Jimmy' Rawnsley was one of the first to use the highly secret Radar system and in 1942 was given the job of Navigation Leader of the Squadron. He was awarded the DSO and DFM.

He died in 1965 at the age of 60. His ashes were scattered from a Trident aircraft over Coltishall, site of his former RAF base, by Sir John Cunningham. Along with his father-in-law and friend John Burley, he is remembered by a headstone in the churchyard of St Mary's, Slindon.

~ ~ ~ ~ ~

After the death of Miss Jane Izard in 1970, a first cousin of the Izard family and her husband Brigadier H.A.F. Crewdson came to live at Church House. The Brigadier was the author of a history of the Worshipful Company of Musicians, of which he was Master from 1962-63 and clerk from 1930-67. In his later years he wrote and published a delightful little book, richly illustrated, about his ancestors *George Fox of Tredrea and his Three Daughters: A Century of Family History*. His wife Edith (nee Churton) was an accomplished cellist.

~ ~ ~ ~ ~

In the autumn of 1970, Dr David A. Bannerman OBE, MA, ScD (Cantab), Hon LLD (Glasgow), FRSE, FZS, the famous ornithologist and his wife W. Mary (Jane) Bannerman OBE came from Scotland to make their home in Slindon.

While on the supernumerary staff of the British Museum in the early 1900s and travelling for them on various zoological and ornithological surveys to many parts of the world, he wrote *The Canary Islands, their History, Natural History and Scenery* and (by order of the Secretary of State for the Colonies) *The Birds of Tropical West Africa*. This latter work, in eight volumes, which describes 1,500 different birds, took 22 years to complete.

In retirement, he completed twelve volumes of *The Birds of the British Isles*, magnificently illustrated by George Lodge (these and his books on West Africa are regarded as major classics) and *Birds of the Atlantic Islands* in four volumes. Three of these were written in conjunction with his wife. In 1958 they completed *The Birds of Cyprus* to be followed in 1970 by a handbook of the birds of that island, the first to be published from Slindon: and finally *History of the Birds of the Balearic Islands*, which Jane Bannerman completed after the death of Dr Bannerman in 1979. She died in 1984.

~ ~ ~ ~ ~

At Old Inn House, Sir Michael Marshall, former MP for Arundel, lives with his wife Caroline. He entered politics in 1974, retiring in 1997. He was knighted in 1990.

Throughout the latter part of his career and since, he has followed a second career as an industrious and versatile writer. His first book, a biography of the great musical comedy actor-manager Jack Buchanan, entitled *Top Hat and Tails* was published in 1978. Research took him to America where he met many stars of stage and screen including Fred Astaire, who wrote a foreword to the book. This was followed by two books about Stanley Holloway, based on the actor's monologues. On an entirely different theme, *The Timetable of Information and Technology* came shortly afterward then, *Gentlemen and Players* which, as the title suggests, is about cricket. Further cricket books followed including *Cricket at the Castle*, the *Centenary History of Cricket at Arundel Castle*. His latest contribution has been for *Sussex Scenes Too*, a millennium compilation of travel writing on Sussex.

~ ~ ~ ~ ~

Maurice J. Burn, MA, LLB, came to Flint Cottage, Slindon, in 1953. Since retiring from law practice some twenty years ago he has written many historical articles for local newspapers and history magazines. He has done a great deal of research into the history of Slindon House and its owners, particularly of the 19th century, and has collected and edited much of the writings of local diarist, Jimmy Dean. He was instrumental in depositing the original Jimmy Dean's Diaries with the West Sussex Record Office at Chichester. At 80 he collected his own verse, much of which had appeared in the Parish Magazine.

~ ~ ~ ~ ~

At Beechcroft, Bridle Lane, Arthur Russell, a former editor and producer in the BBC's External Services, has produced in retirement two volumes of verse with the support of the Southern Arts Association, adding to earlier publications. With his wife Anne he has also published several one-act plays.

~ ~ ~ ~ ~

Ray Cottage, Bridle Lane was for ten years from 1969, the home of Molly Corbally. During this time she wrote articles and poems, one of which was published in War Poems '39, and a later, a biblical novel *The Cave*, which received much acclaim, as did her later autobiographical book *Just Visiting*, an entertaining account of her many years as a District Health Visitor in the West Midlands.[39]

~ ~ ~ ~ ~

Oxford MA, psychologist, World War II pilot, BOAC Captain, best selling author and the man who brought greater insight into

---

[39] *Just Visiting*, is also published by Woodfield Publishing *see page 237.*

the field of aircraft safety, David Beaty, MBE, DFC and bar, MA, MPhil, MRAeS, came to live at Manchester House in 1986 with his wife Betty, also a writer, whom he met when she was an officer in the WAAF. David Beaty's writing was inspired by his years of flying, both as an RAF pilot, from June 1940, and later with BOAC as a senior captain. During the latter time he wrote his first full length novel, *The Take Off*, followed by *The Heart of the Storm*, which became an international best-seller, translated into 14 languages, after which he was persuaded by his American publisher to relinquish flying for full time writing.

It was at this time that Betty Beaty began her own writing career. She also achieved great success, writing many novels under the names Catherine Ross, Karen Campbell and Betty Beaty, drawing on her life in the WAAF and as an almoner and an air hostess with BEA.

Besides many novels, two of which were filmed, David Beaty wrote two non-fiction works on history and psychology. Having taken a degree in psychology at London University he wrote, in 1969 *Human Factors in Aircraft Accidents* and continued to write and lecture on this theory, being awarded the MBE for services to aviation.

A labour of love was the publication in 1995 of Light Perpetual, an illustrated history of aviators' memorial windows in churches throughout the UK, all profits going to the RAF Benevolent Fund.

David died on 4th December 1999 and is buried at St Mary's, Slindon. The church was full for the thanksgiving service for his life. His former squadron, No. 206, had planned a flypast but the aircraft were diverted at the last minute to an urgent operation.

~ ~ ~ ~ ~

Although artists have not been as numerous as writers in Slindon, a series of art classes held in the 1970s by well-known local painter Cilla Ritchie, then living in the village, discovered a lot of local talent. The art classes continue today, weekly at the Coronation Hall, under different tutelage.

For twenty years Lady Beaumont employed a butler, William (Jimmy) Pearse, who achieved a reputation as an artist. Many of his watercolours of local scenes and buildings adorn the homes of older residents in Slindon and neighbouring villages today. An energetic man, he would sometimes set off, always at a brisk pace, a canvas stool and a bag of painting utensils over his shoulder, to more distance locations that took his artistic fancy, such as Amberley and Boxgrove.

He lived at No.11, Slindon with his wife who became part-time needlewoman at Slindon House and their daughter, Dolly. Jimmy Pearse regularly attended St. Mary's Church where he sang in the choir and often read the lesson. This he used to practice in the cellar of Slindon House, unaware that his voice carried along an underground passage fro the cellar to a point near North Lodge, so relaying the Scriptures to passers by.

When Lady Beaumont and her brother moved to Somerset in 1941, he bought a bungalow on Slindon Common. During retirement he continued his hobby of painting, leaving a pictorial record of Slindon between the two wars.

Since 1983, artist John Stephen has made his home in Bridle Lane, and his landscape and wildlife paintings became increasingly popular at art exhibitions in Sussex until his death in 1996.

~ ~ ~ ~ ~

In the early part of the last century some of Slindon's colourful characters followed a walk of life so different from any we know today that their stories have almost a Dickensian flavour. So it was with Charles Palmer, who as a young boy rode postilion on the Brighton to Chichester coach. It was a rough ride from Arundel; the coach took the road at the ravine at Avisford Hill, descended the dip and crossed a deep stream, then came up the opposite slope to the Royal Oak. All trace of this old route has been erased by the present A27. Often all the payment young Charles received for the difficult job of controlling the horses on such a route was a meal of bread and cheese.

Some years later, Charles Palmer came to Slindon collecting rabbit skins and selling oranges and nuts, first with a hand basket, finally graduating to a horse and cart. He then sold mostly fish and eggs. To special customers, one of whom was the Countess of Newburgh, he took only the biggest and best, having candled them carefully. This was done by looking at each egg in the light of a candle through a small hole in a piece of paper to see if it was clear.

Prosperity came when, with a partner Robert Sadler, Charles Palmer began to trade horses from fairs all over England, from Horsham to Huntingdonshire, often walking their horses back to Sussex, stopping at other markets and fairs on the way and putting up at inns where stabling was available. Each man led three horses, others being tied on to the tails.

Later they went to the French fairs, of which Caen was a popular one. His fortune made, Charles Palmer bought property in Slindon, living at Flint Cottage with his wife and three sons. The eldest, William, he educated well so that he might learn French, for all the sons continued trading across the channel, until one disastrous voyage, when all but two horse died, brought an end to the French trading.

William Palmer returned to Slindon and rented Gaston Farm, but farming conditions in 1879 were bad and he moved away.

The other two sons remained in the village with their wives and families.

Arch Palmer, grandson of Charles, rented farms at Slindon and several neighbouring villages where there was good accommodation and stabling for horses. During the 1914-18 war, Arch Palmer and his sons, now the fourth generation of horse traders, supplied horses to the army. After the war they supplied the Territorials with twenty to thirty horses at a time for their training camps held in Arundel Park.

Arch Palmer died in 1972 in his 91st year. His sons, in keeping with the times, turned to mechanisation but still recall the slower but more peaceful days of the horse.

From the earliest times there have been outstanding families who for many generations have woven strong and colourful threads in the tapestry of Slindon's history. The Refoys, Hersees, Fleets, Batemans, Bowleys and Saxbys were such families. Some of them can be traced back to the Norman Conquest.

The Pendrells came to Slindon in the 17th century from Boschobel, Shropshire, where they had allegedly assisted Charles II when he hid in the oak tree. The King later bequeathed an annuity to all those who had assisted him in his flight after the battle of Worcester. The bequest has never been rescinded and more than two centuries later one of the Pendrell daughters made several claims to this annuity but without success.

The first of the Smart family came to Slindon more by accident than intention when he was rumrunning, so goes the story, along the Sussex coast. His ship left hurriedly, leaving him stranded at Littlehampton. He walked to Slindon and got work, eventually managing the Eartham Estate for Admiral Milbanke. A later generation rented Court Hill Farmhouse and farmed the glebe land toward North Wood.

The writings of Jimmy Dean recall some long-forgotten characters. Every Sunday morning from the age of eight, when he went to church with his grandfather (the old man wearing that good Sussex garment, the round frock, a large collar and silken handkerchief for his neck, and a broad soft hat) Jimmy saw old Seamore Gout, who lived in one of the three cottages that stood, facing downhill, close to the church gates. He stood by his door, passing the time of day to all as they went into church.

> *"Through summer and winter, Sundays and workdays, his clothes never varied... consisting of strong heavy boots well made at Slindon, strong corded trousers with a broad leather strap round his middle, stockings and a white shirt, no collar or hat, his shirt wide open from neck to bosom; always as brown as an oak and his hair snow white. He was 6 foot in height and as hard as iron."*

Arch Palmer remembered old Blucher Fleet, who lived on the common. A notorious poacher, though never caught at the game, his method was to lie in the undergrowth with raisins on a fish-hook and grab the birds as they were hooked, carrying them home down his trouser legs, never in his pockets. Passing Mr Charles Palmer's house, where the housekeeper would be looking out of the window, he would hold up his fingers to show the number of his catch. No doubt some birds found their way onto the old man's table.

Burly Mark Luxford was a popular miller on Slindon Common. He farmed fifty acres owned by Colonel Fletcher of Dale Park, where he kept a herd of cows, supplying local houses with milk and butter and keeping pigs on the skim milk.

David Voller followed him, until the milling trade was nearly finished, when he went to Angmering Mill; his place was taken by William Luxford, who taught young Hilaire Belloc to ride a penny-farthing bicycle. His wife and three daughters were musical, playing the violin and organ at church and concerts. The eldest daughter, Nora, married Arch Palmer and the pair settled down at Mill Farm, where Mr Palmer worked the mill for a time after the early death of his fatherin-law.

Although Alfred Hunt had come from Wimbledon to Walberton before becoming Slindon's carrier, he was no stranger to the village. A native of Kirdford, he settled in Slindon as a young man, working at Gumber Farm. A man of very great strength, he was said to be able to lift 3-cwt sacks of linseed when, for a period, he was engaged at Billingshurst corn mill.

He was a well known singer of Sussex songs and when in Wimbledon came to the notice of Ralph Vaughan Williams, who was collecting folksongs for the English Folksong Revival of 1904. He included several of Mr Hunt's songs in his collection.

Alfred Hunt was also one of five singers who contributed to the now famous *Sussex Carol* published by Miss Lucie Broadwood two years later.

Moving to more modern times, in 1968 Slindon could boast the oldest working postmaster in Britain, William Cole, who at that time was ninety-three. The fact was brought to light by a visit from Independent Television. At the same time, local papers announced Mr Cole's retirement, not from the Post Office, but from local government in which he had taken part since 1900, first as a member of Westhampnett Union (now Chichester Rural Council) then as clerk to Eastergate Parish Council.

William Cole was educated at the first Secondary School in Brighton. In 1890 he joined the staff of the Board of Guardians at Lewes as assistant clerk, in which capacity he had ample opportunity of observing life in the workhouses of Chailey and Uckfield. Chailey, he said, was a clean, bright and happy place, but Uckfield was cold, and bleak and cheerless. He recalled seeing in the stores the corsets that were worn by the women, with inch-wide laths of wood in place of whalebone.

A talented entertainer, he helped form Chichester Operatic Society in 1910. He also sang Gilbert & Sullivan at Chichester and Bognor's Theatre Royal and later joined the Bognor and Slindon Operatic Society. He was a life member of this and the Chichester Society. Mr Cole had come to Slindon Post Office from Mayfield in 1939. Unhappily he was not long to enjoy his semi-retirement. He died suddenly in March 1969.

At the beginning of the century, new houses were built on the plots of estate land sold by Colonel Leslie. One, the White House, built by a Refoy, was bought by William Bramson, who settled there with his three daughters. Mr Bramson had an arch enemy on the Stock Exchange, a certain Mr Simpson, and to his chagrin he found that the next property, Millstones, had been acquired by his old foe. He was further incensed when Mrs Simpson, who was a keen horsewoman, built some tall stables between the two houses, obstructing the view over his neighbour's premises.

If he could not overlook the Simpsons, he declared, then he would look over them, and he proceeded to build another storey to his house without first inquiring whether the foundations would stand the addition. Very soon cracks appeared in the walls and ceilings. An architect hastily summoned, looked, and left as hastily, refusing an invitation to lunch, in case the house collapsed during the meal. Some sturdy buttresses were erected to support the house, and the crisis was solved, but it is doubtful whether the relationship of the Bramsons and the Simpsons was ever mended.

Mr Bramson was the owner of a penny-farthing bicycle and of the first motor-car in Slindon in 1901.

In 1969 Mrs Elsie Simpson died at the age of 96, at Millstones, Slindon, which had been her home since it was built in 1909. Its name derives from a probably unique collection of millstones, the work of Mrs Simpson after a spinal injury, following a riding accident, prevented her from riding to hounds, which had hitherto been her greatest enthusiasm. When Lord Leconfield heard of her new hobby, he immediately offered all the old millstones on his estate, whereupon Earl Winterton offered those from the Shillinglee Estate.

Very soon the horsetrailer was put to a new use, transporting millstones, one at a time, from these estate farms and later from many parts of Sussex, some as far as Uckfield. Help had to be hired from the farms to remove and load the stones, those from watermills giving the most trouble, as they had to be brought up from a depth.

Today there are forty-eight complete millstones, a half stone and one incomplete, forming steps and paths in the beautiful garden of Millstones House. They are of two types. Those worn thin over the years are of the softer Derby Peak stone and cast in one piece. The others are of the more durable French Burr stone, which are cut in triangular sections, backed with plaster of equal thickness and bound with iron bands. Both types are approximately 3ft 6in to 4ft in diameter. Mrs Simpson was one of the few women to balloon over London in 1909.

Henry Izard, JP, a son of the Revd Arthur Izard, was by inheritance and in his own right an integral part of Slindon, but his career often took him from the village and indeed from this country.

He was appointed Assistant District Commissioner in the East African Protectorate in 1914, resigning shortly afterward to join H.M. Forces. Besides active service in Mesopotamia and Persia, he flew singleseater scout biplanes in the Royal Flying Corps, and became instructor in the Royal Air Force in Egypt. After many post-war appointments in Kenya he was promoted to Provincial Commissioner. He continued to be an Honorary Director of the International Tea Market Expansion Board and a member of the London Tea Trade Committee until his death in 1968.

In 1967 he retired from Arundel Magistrates' Court after serving as a magistrate since 1953 and as Vice Chairman of the Bench; but he continued to take an active part in public affairs on Councils and Committees in West Sussex, in positions he had held since his return from East Africa in 1948. He served on the Slindon Parish Council and Parochial Church Council, as a governor of the local Secondary Modern School and as manager of the Church of England School in Slindon founded by his grandfather.

Henry Izard's brother, Edward Whitaker Izard, was a campanologist for most of his life, having learned to ring the bells of St Mary's Church, Slindon, as a small boy.

Edward, known to his family as 'Wick', went to Canada in the early 1900s to establish a branch of a large shipbuilding firm. He was general manager of the Canadian firm, which made important contributions to the allied cause in two world wars, until his retirement in 1957, after half-a-century in shipbuilding.

Throughout this time and after, campanology continued to be his absorbing hobby. In 1936 he was responsible for the installation of the ring of eight bells in Christ Church Cathedral Victoria, British Colombia. From this time until his death he held the title "Master Ringer of the Cathedral Bells" and trained a great many ringers. A brass plaque acknowledging his service was unveiled in 1972.

He was again honoured, five years after his death in 1978 at the age of 90, by the inscription of a bell to his memory in Christ Church Cathedral. The bell was one of two cast at the White-chapel Bell Foundry, London. The other is inscribed to Prince William. They were dedicated at a special service in the cathedral in the presence of the Queen and Prince Philip.

The eight original bells, also cast at Whitechapel, in 1935 - replicas of those in Westminster Abbey, bear the names of generations of the Royal Family.

Wick Izard loved Slindon and made frequent visits to the village until he was over 80 years of age.

In 1914, two young maiden ladies, Dorothy Marriott and Hilda Gray, came to live at The Hermitage. They very soon joined the nursing staff of Lady Beaumont's hospital, but later Miss Marriott left to drive ambulances in France as a member of FANY. The two friends worked equally hard in the second World War, Miss Marriott on committees of various organisations (for which she was awarded the MBE) and Miss Gray, in a more manual way by digging for victory in garden and allotment.

One day, as she pushed her wheelbarrow nonchalantly across the road, she failed to see an approaching car or the coat of arms it bore. Only when the car was forced to stop did she observe the Duke of Gloucester on his way to inspect the troops at Slindon House.

In 1928 Miss Gray specifically commissioned from the manu-facturers, a Star motor car. Her instructions were meticulous even to the exact colour of the sidescreen fabric and the dimen-sions and lettering of her initials on the door. It was a sporty model, in black, with a dicky seat, wire wheels, 'knock on' hub-caps and a 12 horsepower engine.

An excellent and enthusiastic driver, Miss Gray owned a succession of open sports-type cars, which suited her personality and dress. She used the Star until just before the war, when she sold it to a Walberton garage proprietor. After being laid up during the war years, and many vicissitudes of fortune, it was rebuilt in 1978 by a vintage enthusiast near Manchester and restored to its former glory, one of only two Star motor-cars of that model in the country.

After Miss Gray died in 1949 at the age of 68, Miss Marriott continued to live at The Hermitage. A leader in every aspect of social life; church, school, politics and welfare; she commanded with her kindness, humour and force of personality, the respect and affection of all who knew her. She died suddenly in 1965.

Slindon not only once had the oldest working postmaster, but also, during the 1970s the youngest church organist in the country. Nicholas J. Luff of Eastergate received his first lessons at the organ at the age of 11 years from Miss Kathleen Bryant, teacher of music and for many years organist at St Mary's Slindon. A year later he took over from Miss Bryant as regular organist at Slindon. This youthful musician was the subject of a feature on BBC TV's *Nationwide* programme in 1970. At 17 he studied the organ at Chichester College of Further Education, passing from there to Trinty College of Music, London, where he passed, with great success, the licentiate examination, the only candidate out of 40 to do so. The move to London brought an end to Nicholas's seven years of service as Slindon's organist.

Today he is deputy organist at Southwark Cathedral. He gives many recitals, some of which are broadcast, and teaches the organ in Battersea.

Vice-Admiral John HughesHallett, CB, DSO, has been associated with Slindon since he came as a boy with his mother and brothers to The Little House in 1918, the year in which he went to sea to begin what was to become a very distinguished career.

In 1940, while still a Captain, he joined Admiral Mountbatten, the Chief of Combined Operations, as Naval Advisor, and in this capacity, he planned a number of raids and commanded the raid on Dieppe in August 1942. In 1943, as commander of the Naval Assault Force, he was responsible for the outline plan of the main invasion force, Overlord, and also planned the Mulberry Harbour project at the end of that year.

Afterward he went to sea as Captain of HMS *Jamaica*, which was credited with the final sinking of the German battleship *Scharnhorst*. After the war he captained HMS *Vernon*, at Portsmouth, the Headquarters of the Anti-Submarine Branch. His last command as a Captain and one of which he has the happiest memories was of HMS *Illustrious*.

His first appointment after his promotion to Vice-Admiral in January 1950 was vice-controller of the Navy. Then, in June 1952, he took up the command of the Heavy Squadron, which involved the position of second-in-command of the Anglo-American Striking Fleet – the NATO Force. During this time, he flew his flag in *Eagle*, a 50,000-ton aircraft carrier.

In 1954 Vice-Admiral Hughes-Hallett retired and entered Parliament as Conservative Member for Croydon. He continued to represent this constituency until he gave up politics in 1964.

During his political career Vice-Admiral Hughes-Hallett served for four years as British delegate on the Council of Europe. From April 1961 to October 1964 he was appointed Minister with Responsibility for Shipbuilding and Harbours, in which capacity he acted as Junior Minister to Ernest Marples. He was for a short while Governor of the Westminster Hospital.

Of his two highly successful careers it was the latter one, in Parliament, that gave him the greater satisfaction, for in this he earned the distinction of being the only person of high rank in the services to reach the front benches. He died on 5th April 1972 at the age of 70 and is remembered with his mother in a memorial tablet in St Mary's Church, Slindon.

Cottages in Slindon – by Nicholas Duggan Rees.

XIV. Woods, Downs & Wildlife

For all its charm, Slindon is not, perhaps, more beautiful than several other West Sussex villages, Graffham, Amberley, Thakeham or picturesque Burpham, but in its surroundings it is unsurpassed. Its views and the loveliness of its woods and Downs which are its pride and glory, earn it a mention even in Camden's *Britannia*, although his account of the whole of Sussex is brief. He writes of:

> *"a Faire wood belonging to the Bishop of Canterbuyni, and a park and an ancient place in it caulled Slydon."*

The beeches in this park were described by Arch Palmer centuries later as "rearing straight up, not a branch for thirty or forty feet and roofed by the interwoven branches; not an interloper of an inferior breed; the trunks of silver and shining like polished plate; a carpet of leaves, thick with the fall of many years."

Sadly, since the hurricane of October 1987 most of these fine trees are standing no more.

Twenty-five years ago, primroses bloomed in great profusion in all Slindon woods in spring. They can still be found with violets, the blue purple common violet and the white sweet violet, wood anemones and the dainty moschatel, but they are no longer plentiful.

There are still places where the woodland floor in May is a haze of bluebells. A very few cowslips bloom on the edge of a wood and there is one place where an oxslip has been found.

In April and May, the local species of Cuckoo-Pint or Arum Lily (Arum Italicum) grows in the woods on the chalk. With orange spadix and unspotted leaf it is quite distinct from the common variety (*Arum maculatum*).

By this time the beeches are past their translucent green and the white beam its silvery buds; the oak, the ash, the sweet chestnut and the dainty silver birch are all in full leaf and the woods are cool and dense.

All the woods are named: Baycombe, The Dencher Wood, Dale Park, Great Bottom Wood and Black Jack, once a rendezvous of smugglers and named after a great beech that stood there, the diameter of its branches assessed at 100 feet. It was black-hearted and many generations of children played in its hollow trunk. Few flowers grow in this wood in summer, save the modest cranesbill and herb robert, the stitchworts and the occasional coltsfoot dandelion, but it is pink-hemmed with rose-bay willow herb and hemp agrimony.

There are Rough Wood and Hooks Wood, Eartham Wood, West Slindon and Nore Wood, on the edge of which the great mullein stands tall, with yellow toadflax, centaury and marjoram, while below the Folly is spread a carpet of yellow rock rose and yellow-flowered silverweed. Rare species of fungi also grow there.

Adding to the rich colour of the beech woods in autumn are clusters of crimson hawthorn berries, the scarlet hips of the sweet briar, the dog rose and the white flowered trailing rose, holly berries, orange skeins of the white bryony and the pink and orange lanterns of the spindle-tree. There are the glossy black berries of the dogwood and the wayfaring trees, while over hedgerows and bushes is softly laid the white, downy coverlet of wild clematis, or old man's beard.

There is another little wood, known as Parson's Copse, at the top of Mash Lane. The primroses, oaks and butcher's broom found there are evidence of its great age. The copse, which once belonged to the Rector of the parish remains private property.

The National Trust owns the 750 acres of woodland which tops the hills, covers the side slopes, and fills the valleys from Fontwell to Bignor. Gradually small areas of woodland are felled and replanted, thus achieving a forest rotation. The trees planted have been mainly beech, with nurse conifers such as larch, spruce, pine and cypress. In more recent years the beech have been interspersed with lime trees, cherry and oak.

The woods are fringed with wild flowers, the foxglove, meadowsweet, the nettle-leaved bell-flower, red campion and knotted figwort, wall lettuce - their skeletons attractive for winter flower arrangements; the modest flowers too of germander speedwell, selfheal, ground ivy and the scarlet pimpernel. The yellow pimpernel and the dainty wood-sorrel grows within the wood.

Of the orchids, only the Twayblade, Early Purple and Common Spotted are common, although the Butterfly, Bird's Nest, Pyramidal and Bee orchids do occur. Small colonies of Autumn Ladies' Tresses are found in lawns on Slindon Common.

Wild raspberries grow on the downs and the tiny, sweet wild strawberries are plentiful upon the chalk, together with a variety of tiny creeping plants, the milkworts, ranging from pale blue to purple; the yellow creeping cinquefoil, heartease, the crimson saxifrage and the little kneeling eyebright.

On the top downs the fragile harebell still grows, though in lesser numbers, with the round-headed rampion, the field scabious, red bartsia, lesser knapweed and birdsfoot trefoil. Even today the species of flora of the woods and Downs is too varied to enumerate here; the pungent-smelling wild parsley grows with the sweet scented creeping thistle; the scotch thistle grows on the Downs, the spear thistle and the burdock, with vervain, St. John's wort, yellow Archangel, betony and woundwort: many members of the compositae family and the rubiaceae - e.g. lady's bedstraw and crosswort; and the umbelliferae, while fragrant honeysuckle intertwines in bush and hedgerow.

Other species of botanical life are found in the old sand workings on the north-west fringe of the Rewell Woods. The horsetail grass grows there in profusion; the wood sage, teasles, blue fleabane (erigon acer), common fleabane, the carline thistle, ploughman's spikenard, golden rod and devil's bit scabious, with a variety of mosses and lichens.

The practice of coppicing the hazel and chestnut plantations, together with the growth of birch trees and budleias on the sand workings, attract many moths and butterflies to the area, including the silverwashed fritillary, the ringlet and the white admiral. It is a favourite haunt of the common wave and the white wave moths, the colourful cinnibar, the orange underwing and the speckled yellow.

Professor G.A. Gaydon, FRS, who is well known for his photography and illustrated talks on butterflies, also identifies the moths that frequent his garden in Shellbridge Road, which backs onto the Rewell Woods. They include many types of hawk moths; the Privet Hawk, Lime Hawk, Poplar Hawk, Hummingbird Hawk, Elephant Hawk, Small Elephant Hawk and Pine Hawk.[40]

Foxgloves grow in abundance in clearings in these woods as they do in felled areas in woods on either side of the A29, where

---

[40] For more comprehensive reading about the wildlife of this area there is a WSWRC report *The Rewell Woods*, published by M. Edwards of Midhurst.

there are many species of fungi including the fly agaric and the parasol.

In a Slindon Common garden where plants are especially grown to attract butterflies and a record of them is kept, about seventeen species are seen throughout the spring and summer.

First to appear in March and April are the four which hibernate, the small tortoiseshell, the brimstone, the comma and the peacock, followed by the orange-tip which feeds on the honesty and garlic mustard, and the green veined white. In 1979 forty-six butterflies were counted on a lavender hedge, mostly large and small whites with gatekeepers and small skippers; in 1987 thirty-five small tortoiseshell were seen feeding on ice plant (*sedum spectabile*). In 1983, the year of the clouded yellow, several of this species were seen in the garden. The painted lady, the silver-washed fritillary, the speckled wood, the meadow brown and the common blue also visit, while the red admirals feed on rotting apples late into the autumn.

All these species also occur in the woods or on the Downs with the addition of the small heath, the large skipper, the chalkhill blue and the pearl-bordered fritillary.

In 1986 there were also several sightings of the hummingbird hawk moth in this garden.

The most frequent visitor to the garden's peanut containers in winter are those chimpanzees of the bird world, the blue tits, which perform their acrobatics in the branches of an old apple tree, with their relatives the great tits. Nuthatches, coaltits and marsh tits come singly or in pairs. Greenfinches are numerous; the great spotted woodpecker pays an occasional visit and in a nearby garden the lesser spotted has been seen.

Of the ground birds blackbirds, chaffinches and dunnocks are resident; the wren, and the mistle thrush, who throws his melodious voice from the top-most branch of a tall Norwegian Spruce. The crow family are much in evidence, the rook, jackdaw, magpie and jay; also, of course, the ubiquitous starling.

In 1986, flocks of redwings appeared in mid-November in Slindon gardens where there were fallen apples; and in lesser numbers, fieldfares and bramblings. Sadly many of them perished in the bitter winter that followed.

Occasional visitors are the goldcrest, siskin, pied wagtail and green woodpecker. In summer an occasional redstart, garden warbler and blackcap are seen; small flocks of long-tailed tits and a family of spotted flycatchers. A pair of goldfinches come frequently; a charm of over a hundred of these colourful little birds has been seen feeding on thistles on the Downs. Bullfinches raid the buds of flowering trees in spring; chiffchaffs dart in shrubbery and border. Song thrushes appear on the lawn.

The Rewell Woods and North Wood are the habitat of nightingales; linnets and yellowhammers add their song to that of the larks on the Downs; swallows and housemartins nest in the eaves of houses and farm buildings; grey herons often rob the village fish-ponds.

Although its numbers were devastated by trapping by downland shepherds from the 18th to early 20th century, the wheatear can still be seen on the Downs and occasionally in gardens. (The first one at Court Hill in 1988 appeared on March 29th). Thousands were caught annually between June and September and sold to nearby towns, where they were a great delicacy, the shepherds supplementing their meagre wages with the annual wheatear harvest.

Lapwings, although to be seen in flocks of several hundred in other parts of West Sussex, are no longer numerous in the Slindon area. They lay their eggs in a scrape on the bare arable land

and tractor drivers move them from the path of their machines as they work the fields. Perhaps twenty years ago, about a dozen nests a year were saved on Court Hill Farm. In 1987 there were none, but one pair of birds was seen on March 13th 1988.

In the spring of 1988, yellowhammers were more numerous than for many years. The cuckoo was first heard on 18th April.

Of the birds of prey the kestrel is the most common, while buzzards and sparrowhawks are sometimes seen. In 1987 a hen harrier was a rare visitor. Little owls and tawny owls are fairly common; but the barn owl, as in many parts of the country, has disappeared. In 1969 a female long-eared owl was found dead in Slindon Woods. Wild game birds include the woodcock and the french partridge.

Jimmy Dean made many notes on the wildlife of the area.

1896: "a flycatcher built its nest in a hat hanging in a plum tree."

1902: "the wryneck was heard, his voice delightfully sweet"

1903: "the lark and the nightingale were heard in April, singing beautifully in the ashbed on Sunday morning."

1905: "the nightjar was heard on Saturday evening, arriving unusually early in April – he usually comes when the ferns are growing without a nest."

The wryneck, like the stone curlew has vanished from the woods and Downs, but the soft, churring note of the nightjar can still be heard in the gravel pits of the Rewell on summer nights.

Jimmy Dean also recorded various other phemonena in his notes for the *West Sussex Gazette*.

1892: "a rabbit's nest was found containing two black, one blue and two of the usual colour with a white shirt."

1893: "a fight was witnessed between a hive of bees and a strong contingent of wasps. The fight lasted some time and many were killed on each side. 135 [wasps] nests were destroyed that year in Slindon and the neighbouring villages."

1901: "On Boxing Day Colonel Leslie while out shooting gathered some ripe blackberries and in spite of sharp frosts and snow on Bignor Hill, primroses were gathered the following Sunday."

At certain times of the year adders were to be seen in great numbers on Slindon Common and Slindon Bottom, and today they still inhabit the woods of the Rewell and the forestry areas, though seldom as large as those recorded in old press cuttings. Vipers of 2ft 10ins and 3ft in length were killed by the 'riners' who dislodged them while stripping bark off trees, and by other workers in the woods.

Albinos occur in various species. A white roedeer doe and a white buck were seen for many seasons in Black Jack and the woods at Court Hill; a white blackbird had its territory in The Stanes at Court Hill, flying in the clearing like a small white dove; and Jimmy Dean records a pure white sparrow in 1903.

The collared dove, which first reached Britain in 1952, soon afterward appeared in large flocks on Slindon fields and Downs and even in large gardens. This corn-eating bird became as much a menace to the farmer as the wood pigeon, but the delightful pair of turtle-doves, which for many years had their territory at Court Hill Farm, have disappeared.

In 1977 many wrens built their nests at Court Hill: over the porch of the farmhouse; in a pile of fencing stakes in the yard; in a dog-kennel regularly used by a pair of lively retrievers and in a coil of rope in the stable, the top of the coil forming the 'roof' of the nest which the wren usually builds.

In the late summer of 1979, walkers on the Downs were surprised by the clear bubbling notes of the curlew. Throughout the autumn, a colony of 17 birds flew daily from their usual feeding ground, probably in Chichester Harbour, to feed on the Downs, returning at a regular time of 4.30pm to the coast.

Mammals and reptiles that frequent the gardens of Slindon Common include frogs and newts in the ponds; toads; slow-worms in rough ground and compost heaps; field mice, yellow-necked mice and short-tailed voles; hedgehogs and the occasional fox. In the Shellbridge Road area, roedeer and rabbits raid the vegetables and the herbaceous borders.

Deer are numerous in Slindon woods, fallow in the higher woodland, roe in the lower covers. There has been evidence of muntjac but these small shy creatures are rarely seen; there are still a few badger setts in certain parts of the woods.

Beech leaves upon chalk form a favourite habitat for snails. About 1948, Mr A.G. Davies, FGS, palaeontologist and later President of the Conchological society, made a study of the Slindon area and found several rare and interesting species. A local species, the lapidary snail, inhabited the crevices in the bark of the beech trees in Bay Coombe Wood. (The majority of these trees have since been felled for replanting). The Stag Beetle can also be found in wooded areas.

Much of the North Wood was cleared in the first World War, and Canadian lumberjacks built a camp there. Every tree in over 1000 acres was cut, mainly for pit props or possibly for trench supports. Beside the Canadian Camp Forestry Corps were the camp of the Naval Cadets, and the Airship Station. A quarter of a mile away in Eartham Wood was a German POW camp.

The Airship Station first consisted of six bell tents and three marquees. There were three airships moored in L-shaped bays cut into the wood off the main drive. This gave shelter from the winds. The 'Folly' was used as a wireless station and messages came through in morse. The Camp's carpenter, who also assisted when necessary in the landing and launching of the airships, spent most of his time roaming North Wood in search of straight young trees to fell for the building of huts, which were covered with airship fabric. The largest project was a camp cinema, which was nearing completion at the time of the Armistice.

During the summer of 1918, the airships made a continuous patrol over the Solent, looking for submarines. This meant that every day at 10am and 6pm, one airship came in and another went out. The crew was made up of a commissioned pilot, an NCO wireless operator or gunner and an engineer. A 90hp Rolls-Royce engine drove a push propeller and the armament consisted of two 50lb bombs and a Lewis gun.

Landing and launching the airships took twenty-five men in calm weather, but in rough the whole station of about 100 men was called out.

On Sundays, a morning service was conducted by the Revd Arthur Izard, Miss Jane Izard providing the music on an accordion or violin. All the camps in North Wood came under the care of the Revd Izard, and the Christmas the war ended there was a service in St Mary's Church followed by a social for the members of the Forces in the School.

After the war North Wood was replanted, but as late as thirty years ago, signs of the old tent sites and of the incinerator remained.

During World War II, a dummy airfield was situated at Gumber. On the left of the farm buildings are two grass meadows, crossed at the top by Stane Street. A dummy hanger and two model Spitfires were positioned here, looked after by a 6-man

RAF crew. It was bombed one night, without damage, and was moved away soon afterwards.

Three members of the Home Guard, Joe Chamberlain, his son Arthur and Bert Roberts recalled being on guard duty by the Folly.

Above and beyond North Wood, the Downs stretch as far as the eye can see. "Behind my house, behind my little farm," wrote Hilaire Belloc at Court Hill, "are as many miles of turf as one cares to count." Today most of that turf is ploughed and sown to cereal crops. Those who remembered the open Downs, and found themselves confined to a little path between a strip of woodland and the field fence, had no joy in the acres of golden brown wheat and waving purple shaded barley. In the 1950s they were partially placated by the opening of a bridle-path, with hunting gates, across the corn from Slindon Down to Bignor. But to those who did not know the country in the past, the Downs, as they are today, present a pretty enough picture.

From Downes Barn piggeries at the commencement of the Downs, one can see Halnaker Mill of Belloc's poem, and to the left, the spire of Chichester Cathedral. Downes Barn was first mentioned in 1397 as 'Downesgarden'.

A four mile walk from this point, along tracks between a belt of trees and arable land, through Black Jack Wood, brings the walker to open down rich in gorse and wild flowers, called Bignor Hill. Here stands the Roman signpost made now of stout new wood but retaining the old names, *Noviomagus* (Chichester) and *Londinium*, of Roman times.

About a mile to the east at an elevation that commands views of the Arun Valley and Chanctonbury Ring is the solitary monument, in the form of a mounting block, of James Wentworth-Fitzwilliam 'Toby' 1888–1955, former owner of Burton

Park at the foot of Duncton and brother of Baroness Wentworth, who was the world's leading authority on Shetland Ponies. He was a field sports enthusiast, secretary of the Cowdray Hunt (1922-1930), Member of the British Field Sports Society (1930-1953) and Master of Foxhounds Association (1945-1955).

His epitaph reads; *'Here he lies where he longed to be'*. At his request his ashes were scattered at the place where the monument now stands, on a windswept piece of down surrounded by a panorama of the Sussex countryside. On the reverse side is an epitaph to his wife, movingly worded: *"You shall wake grown young with perfect sleep."*[41] Sadly, Toby's Stone has since been completely demolished by vandals.

On the left of the signpost are the radar pylons on the highest point of the Downs, which commands a view of the coast from the Isle of Wight to Brighton. On the Isle of Wight, above a little place called Bonchurch, near Ventnor, is another such hill with pylons atop and from this one sees the opposite view, looking across the Solent to the pylons at Bignor.

From the signpost one can walk across the Downs to Sutton or Madehurst; to Petworth or Fittleworth; or retrace one's steps to Slindon.

Slindon Down was first cultivated during the First World War, when it was liberally dotted with corn stacks. Between the two wars the land reverted to turf and furze, but at one time during this period, Alfred Day, who had stables at Fontwell, turned this stretch of turf into gallops and kept a three mile strip beautifully mown, from Downes Barn, where there was a walking ring, to the signpost. Colonel Fletcher of Madehurst also had gallops on the lower stretches of the Downs.

---

[41] 'Toby's stone' has since been completely vandalised, presumably by those who disapprove of fox hunting.

Children of Slindon Church of England School, who at that time had no playing field, used the mown strip by Downes Barn for their sports and games. They had their annual treat on the Downs when long tables were laid end to end to seat a hundred.

One owner of Court Hill, George Coote of Tortington, Arundel, one of the founders of the Cattle Herd Book Society, kept great flocks of Southdown sheep on the Downs. When a flock was taken to Chichester market it was moved very early in the morning so that the villagers perhaps heard, but rarely saw, the sheep as they were driven through Slindon.

Sheep-shearers travelled from farm to farm. Then Henry Hersee, father of Daisy, who worked the rest of the year on the land and in the woods, was captain of the band of shearers. He was responsible for organising the work and attending to any correspondence connected with it, even though his schooling had been of only three years duration, he having left at the age of eight to mind sheep. The men started at 4.30 in the morning, covering on foot the many miles to their work.

Once a year the band would meet for their 'ram supper', at which every shearer provided a share. During the season, for every twenty sheep sheared, so much was put by for this event. The suppers were usually held at the Sir George Thomas Arms or the Newburgh Arms, but the last was at Mr Hersee's cottage where his wife gave them a good meal.

Sheep had to be counted into the pens by twos. They were counted in different ways in different parts of the country.

George Bowley, shepherd for Henry Halstead at Court Hill, remembered counting sheep the Slindon way, which went like this; from two to twenty;

One the rum, two the rum, cocker rum, shutter rum, shether rum, shather rum, wim berry, wig tail, darry diddle dess.

214

From a shepherd boy earning four pence a day, George Bowley became a prosperous farmer, owning 2,000 acres and in 1896 founded a flock of Southdowns by the purchase of some of the best blood in the breed.

On Findon Fair Day, 1965, the last sheep went from Court Hill and from Gumber a little later. Now, perhaps for the first time in over one hundred years there are no sheep on this part of the Downs, and the old sheep-dip by Court Hill dairy is used no more.

Another owner of Court Hill Farm laid tracks and rails across the Downs, and trucks loaded with flints ran busily to and fro, leaving great piles ready for road making. The flints were trodden in by the users of the road. 'The largest stones,' said Jimmy Dean, 'were knocked with a hammer'. These methods must have done much to keep the shoemakers of Slindon in business! The trucks also carried fleeces and hides.

Perhaps the most beautiful stretch of woods and downs is at Gumber, where the primroses bloom even more profusely, forming great footstools among the briars, and where numerous varieties of wild flowers grow.

Gumber, when an extra-parochial district of Slindon, was owned by the Duke of Norfolk, but in 1797 was exchanged with the Kempes for South Stoke.

Gumber Corner, mentioned on the tithe map as West Gumber Gate, where the enclosure joins that of Dale Park, is the highest point of Stane Street, 700 feet high, and almost certainly was one of the sighting points of the Romans when they planned the road.

Gumber is first mentioned as Gumworth in the Assize Rolls for 1261. In 1274 in a Survey of the County of Sussex it is spelt Gumworth. Guma was an old English name. In the marriage

Registers of the Archdeaconry the place is first called Gumber in 1690.

An article in S.A.C. XXXI records:

"In 1712 a John Sefton, a church minister of Chichester, did stay for a considerable time in a lodge or watch-house belonging to the warren called Gumber in Slindon Parish, which I supposed was not inhabited. But upon further enquiry into that affair I find that the lodge was inhabited, and that he only resorted thither as he did to other friends' houses and did not suffer so much hardship as was at first represented. This indicates the sufferings of the clergy in the West part of Sussex at that time."

Many families have lived at Gumber in the past (its three cottages flanked by farm buildings are now made into two) and generations of children have walked the four-mile-long rough road to Slindon School. The road today is just as long and rough and few follow it on foot, but fifty years ago a bride walked to her wedding in her bridal gown, from Gumber Farm to St Mary's Church, and no doubt many an anxious father trudged weary miles to summon the nearest doctor, who lived in Yapton. When Henry Hunt was due to arrive in this world, his father, living in one of Gumber cottages, walked to Yapton to fetch Dr Collins, who was out, so the unlucky parent walked on to Arundel to find another doctor, then all the way home, to be greeted by the news of the happy event.

To the south east of Gumber are 'the beautifully rounded knolls and deep glens' of Dale Park. Dale Park House, demolished in recent years, was a beautiful mansion, built by Sir George Thomas, Bart at immense expense, from a design from Bonomi, the Italian architect. Begun in 1784 it took four years to complete. The windows of its numerous and spacious rooms commanded extensive views of sea and land. It was probably built on the site of an earlier house, for according to *The Place Names of Sussex*, Dale Park was the home of William de la Dale and later John Dale. A modern house now stands on this same site at the head of a valley.

Dale Park is part of the Parish of Madehurst, which with its manor and estate consisting of 200 acres formed part of the domain of Richard, Earl of Arundel. It subsequently passed to Sir Garrett Kempe of Slindon and was sold to Sir George Thomas by the last Earl of Newburgh.

~ ~ ~ ~ ~

The description of the woods and Downs in this chapter applied before the 'great storm' of October 1987. The following is part of an account of the storm written for the Slindon Parish Magazine by John Apps of Slindon Common, a scion of one of Slindon's oldest families:

"On the afternoon of 15th October 1987, a small low pressure area (depression) over the Bay of Biscay began to move north-east, towards north west France and the English Channel, following a track that was in no way unusual. Later that day it moved into the English Channel and we all experienced a dark, wet, gloomy day with periods of rain.

Weather forecasters were accurate thus far, and continued to predict that rain would continue and that strong winds would develop overnight. It seemed clear to them, however, that this 'low' would be very intense and would cause very strong winds, but with the worst weather likely to be confined to the Channel and in particular the coast of north-east France.

During the late evening of 15th October, however, this weather system began to track towards the south coast of England, defy-

ing the weathermen's predictions and at the same time intensifying in strength from a deep low with severe gale (Force 9 winds) into a 'storm' (Force 10 winds).

With the winds now strengthening further, the 'low' had moved close to the coast by midnight, and winds quickly increased over Sussex to Force 9, then 10, still not that unusual. This 'low' was different, however, and grew stronger, and soon gusts of Force 11 were being experienced. The first signs of damage were becoming evident by 1.00 a.m. on 16th October.

Then from about 2 to 4 a.m. the storm achieved a ferocity unparalleled in recent years, with winds constant at Force 10-11 and gusting to Hurricane Force 12, with records subsequently showing that wind speeds reached 106mph in the Slindon area.

At these speeds the wind force is unbelievably powerful and the noise created was enough to wake most villagers, who then spent the remaining hours of darkness unable to sleep, and like my family in a downstairs room fearing that roof damage or falling chimneys and trees were now a real threat to life and limb.

Throughout the early hours, those of us on Slindon Common could hear constant tearing crashes above the noise of the wind, as trees that had stood for over 150 years were torn apart, or felled completely. In addition to this frightening experience, the power-lines brought down near Mill Road flashed and sparked, with temporary fires glowing in the shattered woods. At times it was easy to mistake the flashes for lightning, but lack of static on the longwave radio frequency eliminated the latter cause.

Around the village, similar destruction was taking place, and almost every household experienced some damage to buildings, trees and gardens. When daylight came, the scene was almost unbelievable, with the skyline across Slindon Common completely changed. It soon became clear that every road out of the village was blocked, not by one, but by dozens of fallen trees.

At the back of the recreation fields the 'Soldiers' woods had been ravaged right through to Mill Road, and across to Shellbridge Road, almost every tree having either been flattened or seriously damaged, and both power and telephone line systems had been wrecked.

Large trees lay in the recreation fields and the A29 to Fontwell was literally full of fallen trees. Around the village, people began to emerge and walk about, trying to take in the damage. Trees and branches lay everywhere, lead piping on roofs had been curled back by the wind, and tiles, slates and masonry ripped out. Slindon College lost two of its tower domes; and walls, fences and hedges looked as though they had been battered by a giant's club.

During the day I ventured down Park Lane to see what had happened to Slindon Park, and the scene was almost impossible to believe. From the Park entrance to the A29 the lane was completely blocked and the woods either side of the lane devastated, a tangle of dozens of fallen tree branches and their huge upturned roots having changed the aspect of the whole area. With some difficulty I found the Park entrance and car park, again a jumble of fallen giants, and it was impossible to find and follow any of the known paths. I was determined, however, to find out what had happened to our famous beech trees in the Park and with great difficulty I finally managed to get through to the central fields, enabling me to by-pass the blocked paths.

I almost wished I had not bothered as, although I was beginning to appreciate the magnitude of the destruction, I was not prepared for the shock awaiting me.

Looking across the field to what should have been a magnificent vista of giant beech trees, I was appalled to see them gone, except for a few survivors, most of which were broken or damaged in some way. Many of them had fallen into the fields, and when I reached the area I could see that what had been a glorious woodland of tall straight beeches, famous throughout Britain, had been virtually destroyed.

The giants lay everywhere, mostly lying south to north, signifying the direction from whence the most powerful gusts had come. It was quite impossible for a while, after entering the area I knew so well, to get my bearings and exact location. I could not find the paths or tracks; the popular glade with the two seats was gone, buried amongst piles of trunks and branches; and movement was major effort, as to get anywhere trees had to be passed – almost impossible – or climbed over.

Shocked and saddened I left, retracing my steps, trying to take in the unfamiliar skyline, and to absorb the fact that trees over 200 years old and 100 feet high had been lost overnight.

During that day, when it was impossible to travel out of the village until Mill Road was opened later in the afternoon, I visited some other woods; but several days elapsed before the complete picture could be appreciated. As well as the Park, woods either side of the A29 were smashed, and many of the large trees behind 'The Folly' on Nore Hill were down, although the building suffered only minor damage. The Coronation Trees on the Downs were badly mauled, and Black Jack Woods near Gumber virtually destroyed. Many large trees were down in and around the village, whilst hedgerows and isolated woods were also hit.

When the roads were finally opened we were all able to see some of the damage, and a drive or walk down the A29, Mill Road,

Shellbridge Road and particularly Park Lane brings home the spectacular consequences of this storm."

After the storm the village was without electricity for two days, and Slindon Common for five – the unfortunate residents of Shellbridge Road for three weeks – although telephones, except in the Shellbridge Road area were working again quite quickly.

The sense of hardship was greatly relieved by the helpfulness and neighbourliness among the community that was reminiscent of the spirit that prevailed after the air raids of World War II.

There were grave fears for the wildlife, much of which must have been killed by falling trees, but throughout the winter the garden birds maintained their number; the tits, nuthatches and greater spotted woodpecker were present; only jackdaws were missed from the scene until the spring. The rooks built in the few standing trees in Mill Road. Birds are back in the 'Soldiers' wood – a belt of woodland parallel with Sunnybox Lane – so named because soldiers bivouaced there in World War II prior to D-Day; and there are deer and foxes in Court Hill woods. In the spring the fallow deer moved down from the higher woods and nineteen were seen at one time.

Happily, much wildlife has survived, but the sense of shock among the community remains at the scene of devastation. Although much clearing has been done by the National Trust, the Forestry Commission, Councils, farmers and volunteers, there are still vast areas that are impassable and will be for an unforseeable length of time.

"No Slindoner will forget the storm in the early hours of 16th October 1987," writes John Apps, "which will go on record with the snowy winter of 1962/3 as the most impressive weather phenomena to affect Slindon in recent memory."

XV. Smugglers & Ghosts

During the 18th and early 19th centuries, the woods and Downs of Slindon were favourite haunts of smugglers.

The land smugglers, whose job was to ensure the disposal and distribution of contraband, often ran greater and more prolonged risk than the sea smugglers, and they had their own secret sunken ways through the woods, so that even in broad daylight horses and men could not be discovered. The Downs provided a signalling base and signs were flashed to the bold coastwise sailor who, with lights dimmed, slipped in to deliver his contraband cargo of lace, wine, tobacco and perfume.

The excisemen were frequently at a disadvantage; the smuggler knew the roads better and was often better mounted; he had many confederates to warn him and aid him in outwitting King George's men.

"Slindon was once the home of poachers and smugglers", writes Jimmy Dean, "and a very noted place for gypsies who camped in lanes and byroads and on Slindon Common and at Slindon Bottom. Some villagers were afraid to go out after dark because of the gypsies roaming about after rabbits, hares and pheasants, sometimes poultry; they also took vegetables from gardens."

People were afraid of the smugglers too, and some dared not look out of their windows when they heard the ponies go by.

"In the dykes which surrounded the orchards in Park Lane," said Jimmy Dean, "were hidden many tubs of gin and brandy, brought up from the coast by night by the smugglers and covered over until a suitable time came to remove them. Slindon smugglers went to sea in couples. The poachers also had their mates. Two of a party would engage the keeper, one kept watch, while the others went setting wires in another direction, returning with a sackload of rabbits in the morning".

The old Dog and Partridge Inn on Slindon Common was a regular rendezvous of the smugglers. A capacious cellar was excavated in the garden much larger than a small country inn could require for business purposes. It was known as 'the smugglers' cellar' and extended under the A29 into the field opposite. It was filled in during the 1950s, and all that remains of the old inn is a portion of walling in the present house on the site.

Many of the local people took part in smuggling, and the houses and cottages had hiding-places in cellars, under the roofs, and behind the hearths where there was always a good fire burning when the Excise man called.

Biddleside Cottage had a large hiding place under the roof: Bleak House was a stopping place for the smugglers before they set out over the Downs to London.

The Pendrells of Slindon brought their contraband up from Climping. One dark moonless night, so the story goes, Bill Bateman the blacksmith received a hasty summons to come to the Sir George Thomas Arms, where Smuggler Jack was stranded with a lame horse. For some years afterward, on Christmas Day, a mysterious keg of brandy was found on the Bateman doorstep.

Another story is told about the Excisemens' visit to an old lady who lived alone in a cottage at Well Nap Corner. She invited them to search as much as they wished while she sat placidly in her chair by the fire, washing her feet. They found nothing however, for the kegs of brandy were concealed in cavities under the flagstones on which the old lady's chair was placed. These cavities were rediscovered when the cottage was refloored many years later.

These stories sound lighthearted enough and maybe give a false impression of the smugglers. But connected with the business of Free Trading were many murderers and desperadoes and some of the worst scoundrels in the land, as other stories in a grimmer vein will prove.

In 1749 Richard Hawkins, a farm worker, was whipped and kicked to death in the cellar of the Dog and Partridge on Slindon Common by two smugglers, Mills and Curtis. John Mills was the son of Richard Mills, member of the notorious Hawkhurst gang, whose heinous murders of Customs Officer William Galley and shoemaker Daniel Chater have been given in many accounts. The brutal attack on Hawkins by John Mills took place soon after his father's execution.

The trouble with Richard Hawkins arose over some tea, which had been landed at Poole and brought by a band of smugglers through the New Forest. Mills and Curtis had hidden their share under some straw in a barn at Yapton, where Hawkins was working, threshing wheat with a flail. As he worked, he inadvertently covered the tea with a greater load of straw until, when the smugglers came to look for it, they could not find it, and accused Hawkins of having taken it. They took him to the Dog and Partridge where they tied him to a chair and brutally beat and kicked him, questioning him further about the tea, but he, poor fellow, knowing nothing about it, could not tell them. Finally he said that some cousins of his, the Quellens at Yapton, had the tea. Mills and Curtis left for Yapton. When they returned, having got nothing out of the Quellens, Reynolds the landlord told them that Hawkins had died of his injuries. Reynolds, who had taken no part in the murder was now very frightened, but the smugglers told him that the crime would not be discovered. They put Hawkins' body on a horse and rode ten miles to Parham Pond into which they threw the dead man. But three months later the body was discovered. Curtis escaped, but Mills was captured at the house of an outlawed smuggler at Beckenham. He was tried and convicted at the assizes at East Grinstead and hanged there; after execution he was hung in chains on Slindon Common.

Although an Act of Parliament in 1823 forbade the practice of gibbeting, the old gibbet from which smugglers were hung still stood at the crossroads on Slindon Common (not the crossroads of the present day) until the beginning of the 20th century.

From the time of George III's reign comes the tale of Slindon's 'Godiva', Betsy Thorpe, a simple village lass who loved a preventive officer, Will Garland. Will was captured by a band of ruthless smugglers, who announced their intention of stripping him and whipping him across the common.

Betsy went to their leader, Ben Tapner, and offered herself in Will's place. The ruffian laughed and consented. That night, Betsy, clothed only by her long hair, was tied to a horse, which was sent galloping across the common, one smuggler following lashing both horse and girl.

Betsy did not survive the ordeal but died before the ghastly ride came to an end. Her lover was later shot by the smugglers.[42]

Perhaps these nefarious and spine-chilling deeds account for some of the ghosts reported to have been seen or heard in various houses and cottages and on the Downs of Slindon.

Several stories are told of a white ghost horse on the Downs. One writer to a local paper declares that she was walking on Slindon Down and was about to enter the wood leading to Mill

---

[42] from *The Spirit of the Downs* by Arthur Beckett.

Lane, when she looked back, to see a riderless white horse gal-loping up the hill toward Bignor, until half way up the slope it vanished in the midst of open country.

This story has been confirmed by another who saw the ghost horse while riding. Her horse on subsequent occasions refused to pass the spot where the white horse had appeared. This lady also claims that ghost horses have galloped past her, on several occasions, in Mill Lane. Were they perhaps the ghosts of smugglers' ponies two hundred years before, or the mounts of a fugitive monarch and his followers?

The occupiers of Club Cottage claim a ghost – one who smokes a pipe, for there is often a strong smell of pipe tobacco in the front porch when there are no pipe smokers in the house. Chairs are moved, usually the one on the left of the inglenook. All the family have had the sensation of glimpsing a figure, but on the second glance there is no one there.

A previous tenant also sometimes felt that she 'was being watched' and heard 'strange bangings'. A medium visited the house and claimed to have seen a tall figure in 15th century cos-tume sitting and walking in the front room. He seemed particularly interested in books.

Another ghost with a penchant for bookshelves haunts Old Inn House. He wears the uniform of an Admiral of the Fleet and usually makes his appearance via the bookcase. He is a benign figure who appears chiefly to children of the household.

The Old Bakery is said to be haunted by the ghost of Moses Oliver. The present baker has heard weird noises and observed strange occurrences outside the bakehouse when he has been working in the small hours, but he has yet to see Moses standing under the old birch tree, as one story goes, crying "tuppence a loaf!"

Court Hill Farmhouse is said to have once been haunted by the ghosts of smugglers, but Mrs Eleanor Jebb has less sinister recollections. She remembers asking her mother, "Who is the little lady with the red shawl who goes through doors without opening them?" and once her sister Elizabeth saw a large phantom dog sitting on the end of her little bed.

Many ghostly noises can be explained by the presence of rats, mice or birds in the houses, as in the case of Jimmy Dean's mother's ghostly night visitor at Biddleside Cottage. Every night Mrs Dean was kept awake by the sound of heavy breathing between the ceiling and the thatch above her head, as she lay in bed. She declared that the place was haunted. At last Jimmy was persuaded to investigate this heavily breathing 'ghost'. With the local bricklayer and his mate he borrowed a long ladder from Anthony Refoy and climbed to the top of the bedroom side of the kitchen chimney, searching between the chimney and the thatch with a lighted candle, when to his amazement he saw two huge owls perched, fast asleep. The owls were removed and perhaps returned to their normal habitat for Mrs Dean's rest was disturbed no more.

~ ~ ~ ~ ~

In the year 2002 Slindon is still a happy, flourishing village and a good place to live. A number of projects marked the new millennium. St Mary's, in line with churches throughout the land, planted a new yew tree in the churchyard. In the village a Millennium Doomsday Book was compiled, containing the reminisces of many residents. A sundial was made for St Mary's memorial garden and the National Trust planted a long length hedge in Mid (or Mud) Lane. An illustrated Millennium Map of the village was compiled by Slindon artists.

A New Years Eve party for the whole village to welcome in the new century and preceded by a church service was held at Slindon College, ending with fireworks at midnight.

A millennium party was held on the recreation ground on 29th May.

Thus Slindon, whilst fondly remembering its past, goes forward-looking into the new century.

End

Cattle watering at the Pond, Slindon, c.1890s

BIBLIOGRAPHY

Geology of Sussex, F. Dixon, W.J. Smith, Brighton, 1878.

Archaeology of Sussex, The Sussex Archaeological Collection, Vol. 44.

The Life of St. Richard, E. Cecil Curwen. Methuen.

Costumals of the Sussex Manors of the Archbishops of Canterbury, Sussex Record Society.

English Poor Law, S. & B. Webb. Longman, 1910.

Burke's Peerage & Landed Gentry.

Sussex Poor Law Records, Jane M. Coleman BA. WSCC Chichester.

Sussex Notes and Queries, Vol. 14.

The County of Sussex, Hilaire Belloc. Cassell & Co.

The Victoria History of the County of Sussex, Vol. IV, 1953.

The History of Sussex, James Dallaway. Sussex Press, Lewes, 1815.

The Manors and Churches of West Sussex, Horsfield. Oxford University Press, 1835.

Records of Chichester, T.G. Willis, 1928.

The Castle, Mansions and Manors of West Sussex, Elwes & Robinson, Longmans.

Place Names of Sussex Vol. VI, A. Mawer & F. Stenton. English Place Name Society.

Monumental Effigies of Sussex, H.R. Mosse. Cambridge, Hove.

In a Walled Garden, Madame Belloc. Ward & Downey Ltd, London 1895.

The Young Hilaire Belloc, Mrs Belloc, Lowndes. P.J. Kennedy & Sons, New York.

Sussex Cricket, John Marshall. Heinemann.

The History of St. Richards, Father Michael Costello.

The History of Pagham Vol. I & II, Lindsay Fleming. Ditchling Press 1949.

'John Nyren' and 'The Nyrens' by Edmund Esdaile in *The Hampshire Handbooks*, 1966/67.

'Their Chivalry was Cricket' by Edmund Esdaile in *Journal of the Cricket Society*, 1969.

Archbishop Peckham, Decima Doucie. Oxford, 1928.

Testimony to Hilaire Belloc, Eleanor and Reginald Jebb. Methuen, 1956.

Hills and the Sea, Hilaire Belloc. Charles Scribner's Sons, New York 1906.

The Life of Hilaire Belloc, Robert Speaight. Hollis & Carter, 1957.

Sussex, Nairn & Pevsner. Penguin.

Prophesying Peace, James Lees-Milne. Chatto & Windus.

Slindon Parish Council 1894-1984, Bernard Keeling.

The Countess of Newburgh's Diaries 1842 and 1847, MSS.

Slindon Post Office – drawn by Lou Friend

INDEX

Aburrow, Edward, 160, 161
Adam's Field, 119
Aethelwalh, King of the South Saxons, 10
Airship Station, 210
Anderson, Jack, 166
Anselm, Archbishop, 13
Apps family, 112
Archbishop Theodore, 82
Archbishop Winchelsey, 20
Avisford Mill, 144
Ayling, Roy - builder, 35
Bandini family, 64
Bannerman, Dr David A. OBE, MA, ScD, 186
Bannerman, Mary (Jane) OBE, 186
Barkhale Camp, 8
Bartholomew, James 4th Earl of Newburgh, 29
Bateman, Edward, 141
Bateman, James, 149
Bateman, Thomas, 141
Bateman, William, 39, 141
Beaty, Betty, 189
Beaty, David, MBE, DFC and bar, MA, 189
Beauty Tree, the, 76
beech woods, 202
Beere, Bonnie, potter, 146, 175
Beerhouse Act of 1830, 112
Bellamy, Dr David, 81
Belloc, Madame Bessie Parkes, v, vi, 59, 97, 104, 179, 180, 181, 182, 184, 185, 229
bell-ringers, 50
Biddleside Farm, 138
Bignor Hill, 8, 209, 212
Binstead, Caroline, 153
Bircher, Ann, 133
Bishop Seffrid, 82
Bleak House, 111, 124, 149, 153, 177, 181, 182, 223

Bleathman, Gilbert, 141
bootmaker, 132
Bourchier, Thomas, Archbishop of Canterbury (1454-1486), 16
Bowley family, 137
Bowley, George, 214, 215
Bowley, Linda, 61
Bramson, William, 195
brass band, 52, 135
Bridle Lane, 61, 71, 127, 132, 188, 190
Bronze Age, 7
Bryant, Kathleen, 199
Budgin, George, 143
Bulbeck, George, 143, 144
Burch, Alfred, 145
Burn, Maurice, v, 144
Burn, Maurice J. MA LLB, 188
Burne-Jones, Edward, 101
buses, 150
Caedwalla, of the West Saxons, 10
Catholics in Slindon, 101, 105
Cave, Gladwin Cloves, 65
Chalk, Harriet, married Jimmy Dean, 46
Challen, Eric, 121
Challen, Sidney, 120
Challoner, Bishop Richard, 102
Chamberlain, Arthur, 166
Chamberlain, Joe, 212
Channer, John, 130, 131
charity, 91
Charles II, 29, 31, 76, 79, 159, 192
Charlotte Maria, Countess of Newburgh, 29
Chater, Daniel, 224
Chesterton, GK, 182
Chicheley, Archbishop, 14
Church Cottage, 116
Church House, 96, 116, 126, 153, 186
Church of St Mary Magdalene, Madehurst, 100
church organ, 93

Clarke, Bertram, 135
Clarke, Hedley, 136
Clarke, Nan, 136
Club Cottage, 113
Cole, William, 194
Cooper, GW, 135
Corbally, Molly, 188
Coronation Hall, 121, 122, 169, 172,
    173, 190
Cossar, Andrew, 87
Cossar, Revd John, 87
Cosy Cottage, 120
Countess of Newburgh, i, vi, 32, 33, 34,
    38, 39, 45, 62, 63, 64, 65, 67, 74,
    103, 104, 105, 191, 230
Court Hill Farm, iii, 4, 9, 35, 46, 80,
    107, 137, 153, 155, 208, 209, 215
Court Hill Farmhouse, 125, 182
Courts, 23
Cranmer, Thomas - Archbishop, 11, 19,
    25
Crewdson, Brigadier HAF, 186
cricket, 47, 50, 52, 59, 97, 107, 134,
    135, 158, 159, 160, 162, 164, 165,
    166, 167, 168, 169, 174, 187
cricket team, 135, 165, 168
Dairy Cottage, 71, 121, 150
Davidson, Pauline, 132
Day, Alfred, 143, 213
de Carleton, John, 12
de Clifford, Richard, 91
de Clifforde, Richarde, Rector of
    Slindon, 17
de la Haye, Robert, 15
de Montgomery, Roger, 12
de Spyney, Roger, 20
Dean, Jimmy, iii, iv, vi, 45, 46, 47, 48,
    49, 51, 55, 56, 57, 58, 59, 68, 70, 74,
    76, 92, 93, 107, 129, 132, 144, 145,
    154, 156, 157, 165, 166, 169, 171,
    174, 175, 176, 188, 193, 208, 209,
    215, 222, 227
Dog and Partridge Inn, 51, 132, 144,
    149, 223, 224
Domesday, 11, 12, 13, 82

Dower House, 41, 44, 69, 74, 80, 125,
    136, 153, 178
Drummond , Katharine Georgina, 68
Dyer, Charlotte, 117
Dyer's Lane, 116
Dyers Lane, 45, 50, 105, 139, 140, 177
Dymock, Mr & Mrs HM, 133
Earl of Newburgh, 114
earthquakes, 57
Edward I, 20
effigy of Anthony St Leger, 85
Elm Cottage, vi, 118, 129
Eyre, Dorothy, 63
Eyre, Francis, 62
Eyre, Venerable R.M.S., 88
Fenton, Peter, blacksmith, 141, 142
Ferdinand, Roque, 101
Finch, George, 143
Firgrove, 127
Fleet, John, 54, 133
Fleet, Rebekah, 152
Fletcher, J.C. of Dale Park, 107
Flint Cottage, 120, 121, 153, 188, 191
flora & fauna, 205
Football Club, 169
Forden, Minnie, 60, 61
Foreshew, Joseph, 130
Foreshew, Walter, 130
Forge, the, 139
Fullerton, Lady Georgiana, 104
Fullerton, Lady Georgiana, 125, 184,
    185
Galley, William, 224
Gammons, Mrs Florence, 99
Garland Day, 37
Garland, Will, 225
Gassons, 123
Gaston Cottage, 60, 123, 180
Gaston Farm, 123, 137, 138, 153, 157,
    191
General Enclosure Act of 1845, 72
George IV, 36
George V, 78
ghost stories, 225
Giustiniani family, 64
Gladwin, Elizabeth, 65

glebe land, 94
Golcot, Polycarpus - a beggar, 90
Gray, Hilda, 198
Gray, Revd H.R., 109
Graysmark, Thomas, 139
Graysmark, William, 139
Great Storm of October 1987, 76, 217
Green, E.J.F., Chairman, West Sussex
    County Council, 109
Grevett, Frederick, 130
Grey, Lady Jane, 27
Greyhound, public house, 126
Griggs, George, 139
Gumber, 8, 58, 107, 134, 153, 178, 183,
    194, 211, 215, 216, 220
Halstead, Henry, 106, 214
Hawkins, Richard, 224
Hayley, William, 99, 184
Henry I, 13, 19
Henry II, 23
Henry III, 17
Henry VIII, 11, 25, 27, 101, 127
Hersee, Charlotte, Daisy, 97, 180
Hersee, Henry, 214
Hervey, Adelaide Maria, 151
Hilaire Belloc, v, 4, 31, 86, 97, 178, 179,
    181, 193, 212, 229, 230
Hockey Club, 171
hogs, slaughter of, 48
Holmes, Fred, 141
Holmes, Richard, 107
home-brewed beer, 48
Hotham, Sir Richard, 36
Hotston, Charles, 97, 141, 142
Hotston, George, 97, 126, 149
Huberden, Robert, 20
Hughes-Hallett, Vice-Admiral John,
    CB, DSO, 200
Hundred of Pagham, 11, 12, 25, 26
Hunt, Alfred, 150, 194
Huskisson, Rt Hon William, MP for
    Chichester, 99
Hyde, Jo, potter, 146
Iron Age, 8
Islep, Archbishop Simon, 12
Izard, Edward Whitaker, 197

Izard, Henry, JP, 196
Izard, Jane, 90, 96, 186
Izard, Mary, 108
Izard, Revd Arthur, 61, 94, 95, 175, 196,
    211
Izard, Revd William Chantler, Rector of
    Slindon, 19, 71, 84, 85, 87, 92, 93,
    106, 108, 116
James, Jack, 122
James, Jack, blacksmith, 141
Jebb, Eleanor, 180, 181, 183, 227
John Peckham, 14
Keeling, Bernard, 70, 133, 156, 172, 230
Kempe, Anthony, 25, 27, 28, 73, 91, 104
Kempe, Barbara, 29, 31
Kempe, Cardinal John, 27
Kempe, Francis Boniface OSB, 104
Kempe, Sir Garrett, 25, 28, 31, 101, 217
King John, 17
Lady Beaumont, 3, 73, 74, 78, 80, 90,
    91, 97, 122, 136, 141, 146, 150, 190,
    198
Langmead, James, 137
Langmead, Leslie, 137
Langton, Archbishop Stephen, 14
Langton, Steven, 15, 25, 87
Launce, Rev Robert Stiles, 100
Leslie, Allan Charles Malcolm, 68
Leslie, Charles Radcliffe Aloysius, 67,
    68, 69, 119, 176
Leslie, Charles Stephen, 67, 123
Leslie, Col Charles, 61, 63, 65, 66, 67,
    70, 103, 133, 149, 151, 195, 209
Leslie, Colonel Charles, 19
Leslie, Sylvia Mary, 69
Levingstone, Sir James, 29
Lime Tree House, 39, 110
Lindfield School for Boys, 80
Long, Commander John S.L., RN, 127
Long, Dora, 128
Long, Victor, 127
Luden, Thomas, Abbott of Battle, 17
Ludlowe, Thomas, 14
Luff, Nicholas J, 199
Luxford, Mark, 193
Macauley Cottage, 129

Magna Carta, 14, 87, 100
Manchester House, 129, 130, 189
Marriott, Dorothy, 198
Marriott, Dorothy Frances MBE, 98
Marshall, Michael MP, 81, 166, 187
Martin, Mary, 88
Mary Tudor, 31, 101
McCorquodale, Hugh, 131
McQuoid, Denis, 147
Mellie, Johannes, Rector of Slindon, 90
Mew, Sarah, epitaph, 97
Milbanke, Sir Peniston, Bart, JP of
    Eartham House, 107
Miles, Harry, 142
Mill Cottage, 1
Mills, Ernie, 149
Mills, John, 224
Millstones, 119, 128, 195, 196
Millstones House, 119
More, Sir Thomas, 14
Morton, John, Cardinal, Archbishop of
    Canterbury, 14
National Cycling Club, 136
National Trust, iv, 1, 2, 3, 35, 39, 74, 77,
    79, 80, 81, 110, 135, 137, 138, 141,
    142, 146, 204, 221, 227
Neolithic Age, 6
Newburgh Arms, 38, 45, 49, 53, 56, 58,
    59, 69, 106, 116, 126, 131, 132, 133,
    141, 149, 150, 151, 152, 153, 165,
    166, 214
Newland family, 117, 163
Newland, Anne, 91
Newland, Charles, 135
Newland, Richard, 97, 158, 159, 161,
    162, 163, 164
No.2 Church Hill, 111
No.2 Slindon, 110, 147
No.33 Slindon, 110
North, John, 168
Nyren family, 161
Nyren, Richard, 158, 161, 163
Old Inn House, 115
Old Post, 111, 115, 133, 147
Oliver, Henry Moses, 135
Palaeolithic camp, 6

Palmer family, 151
Palmer, Arch, 143, 144, 145, 192, 193,
    194, 202
Palmer, Charles, 120, 191, 193
Palmer, Sir Thomas, 27
Park View, 120
Parson's Copse, 144
Pearse, William (Jimmy), 190
Peel, Father
    RC priest, 122
Pegler, John, 172
Pendrell family, 192
Penicott, George, 112
Petworth House, 36
Pine Trees, 128
Pine View, 126
plague, 89
Poland, Ann, 134
Pond House, 130, 155
Pond, the, 155
Poole, Sir Geoffrey, 27
Pope Gregory IV, 17
pottery and china, 146
Prince Giustiniani, 62, 64
Princess Charlotte, 36
Pudding Club, 173
Pump Cottage, 139
pumpkins, 136
Purdeux, William, 21
Purdy, Jack, 45
Pym, Francis - architect, 35
Queen Mary, 78
Radcliffe, James Bartholomew, 4ᵗʰ Earl
    of Newburgh, 29
railway carriage, 116
Ratcliffe, Charles, 62
Ratcliffe, Mary, 63
Rawnsley, Sq/Ldr Cecil, 185
Ray Cottage, 132
recreation ground, 171
Rectors of Slindon, 92
Rectory
    new, 117
Rectory Cottage, 45
Refoy family, 35
Refoy, Samuel, 33

Reid, John, blacksmith, 142
Reliance Garage, 121
Reliance Mews, 120
Rewell woods and gravel pits, 3, 145, 146, 205, 207, 208, 209
Richard of Wyke, 17
Ritchie, Cilla, 190
Roman Catholic School in Slindon, 105
Rose Cottage, 129, 130, 155
Rowland, AWG, 130
Russell, Arthur, 188
Salvin, Anne, 111
School Hill, 1, 60, 106, 120, 121, 123, 132, 138, 139, 146
Scouts
    1ˢᵗ Walberton and Slindon Scout Troop, 113
secret passage, 102
See of Canterbury, 11, 12, 13, 15, 25, 101
Sellinger's Hole, 27
Sercombe, Gerald, 138
Silveira, Rev. Joseph, 102
Silver Queen, vi, 151
Simpson, Elsie, 196
Sir George Thomas Arms, 126, 148, 153, 157, 214, 223
Slindon Band, 106
Slindon Bottom, 4, 69, 70, 145, 155, 209, 222
Slindon Brass Band, 174
Slindon CE School
    new building, 109
    opening of, 106
Slindon Choral Society, 46, 95
Slindon College, 80, 181, 219, 228
Slindon Common, 1, 2, 6, 37, 51, 52, 69, 70, 71, 90, 120, 126, 128, 132, 142, 144, 145, 148, 151, 152, 153, 157, 159, 190, 193, 204, 206, 209, 210, 217, 218, 221, 222, 223, 224, 225
Slindon Cottage, 125
Slindon Court Rolls, 114
Slindon Cricket Club, 52, 113, 166, 167, 171

Slindon Fair, 52
Slindon Flower Show, 177
Slindon Folly, 34
Slindon Football Club, 169
Slindon House, i, 3, 4, 13, 14, 15, 19, 27, 29, 33, 35, 36, 37, 42, 46, 49, 52, 58, 60, 64, 67, 68, 69, 70, 72, 73, 74, 75, 78, 79, 80, 81, 87, 95, 100, 101, 102, 104, 121, 137, 141, 146, 153, 157, 161, 174, 176, 177, 180, 183, 188, 190, 198
Slindon Parish Register, earliest records, 89
Slindon Park, vi, 4, 5, 6, 9, 18, 19, 81, 137, 153, 219
Slindon Pond, 155
Slindon Post Office, vi, 38, 78, 115, 121, 129, 130, 133, 134, 150, 194, 195
Slindon Pottery, 147
Smart family, 192
Smelt, Fanny Elizabeth, 98
Smelt, Margaret Jessy Hertzel, 98
Smelt, Revd John, 90, 105
Smelt, Revd Maurice, 45, 94, 98, 100
Smelt, William Anthony Casterton, 98
smugglers, 222
Southdown Bus Company, 151
Spinaway Cottage, 129
St Edmund Rich, 14
St John, William & Roger, 15
St Leger, Sir Anthony, 27
St Mary's, 9, 13, 14, 26, 46, 81, 85, 88, 97, 100, 108, 114, 117, 122, 128, 133, 141, 163, 175, 186, 189, 197, 199, 201, 211, 216, 227
St Mary's Chapel, 88
St Mary's, 82
St Richard's Church, 14, 70, 101, 103, 183, 185
St Richard's Cottage, 111, 153
St Richard's House, 3, 113
St Wilfrid, 10
Stane Street, 8, 70, 211, 215
Stephen, John, 190
stoolball, 171
Sunnybox, 126

Sunnybox Lane, 126
Tapner, Ben, 225
Taylor, Jock, blacksmith, 109, 142
Terry, Ellen
    visit to school, 108
The Grange, vi, 31, 117, 164, 179, 180
The Hermitage, 198
The Little House, 115
The Old Bakery, 110, 134, 135, 226
The Presbytery, 114
The White House, 157
Thomas, Sir George of Dale Park, 101
Thomas, Sir George, Bart., 216
Thorpe, Betsy, 225
Tithe Apportionment Book of 1839, 131
Toby's Stone, 213
Toll House, 148
Toogood, Clara, 90
Top Road, 1, 3, 39, 105, 106, 111, 125,
    130, 132, 134, 136, 139, 146, 172,
    174
Turner-Cross, Andrew & Anne, 134
Twigger, William, 141
Upton, Andrew, 150
Upton, Janet, potter, 147
Upton, Ralph & Barbara, 136
Van Davies, Mrs, 72
Venables, Mr E.M., 6
Victorian postbox, 131
village pond, 155
Viscount Kinnaird Garron Levingstone,
    29
Voller, David, 193
Voysey, C.F.A., 128
Wades Cottage, 120
Walling, Cecil, 151
Walling, Richard, 151
Walmsley, Daisy & Anne, 119
War Memorial, 99

water supply, 152
Watkins (cottage), 129
Watkins, John, 129, 130
Webb, Anne, later Countess of
    Newburgh, 33
Webb, Sir Thomas, Baronet, 33
Wedgemaking, 142
Wedgwood, Rowland, 104, 124, 180
Weeks, Agnes & Rose Weeks, 185
Well House, 123, 124
Wellesley, Lady Victoria
    visit to school, 108
Wellnap Corner, 118, 123, 129, 131,
    132, 139, 153
Wellnap Cottage, 129
Wentworth-Fitzwilliam, James (Toby),
    212
West Sussex Gazette, iii, v, 45, 46, 56,
    59, 62, 67, 72, 95, 106, 165, 208
Wethershed, Archbishop Richard, 17
White, George, 99
White, Mr & Mrs Charles, 99
William Rufus, 13
Willshear family, 129
Willshear, John, 129, 130, 141
Wilmer, Mrs - midwife, 152
Wilson, Ronald Patterson, 128
Womens' Institute, 173
woodlands, 203
Woodlands Farm, 69, 138
Wootton Isaacson, Mr F., 3, 72, 73, 78,
    88, 93, 120, 121, 143
Wootton Isaacson, Mr F., death of, 80
Wyatt, Father Richard, 101
Wyatt, Paul, 138
Wyatt, Philip, 138
Ye Olde Butcher's Shop, 130
Yew Tree Cottage, 116

More books of local interest from Woodfield Publishing

Corduroy Days by Josephine Duggan Rees
The author recalls her younger days as a teenage volunteer in the Women's Land Army during World War II in a succession of warm-hearted and gently humorous stories which follow her progress from clueless city-girl to proficient countrywoman, on the way meeting up with a host of colourful rural characters and Duggan, her husband to be. Her delightful depiction of their less-than-romantic courtship is one of the book's many highlights.

ISBN 1 873203 48 9 | 226 pp with photos | softback £9.95

Boys & Other Animals by Josephine Duggan Rees
This fine collection of stories, first published to national acclaim in magazines in the 1960s, tell, in an engaging and lighthearted way of the trials and tribulations of the author's young married life, trying, and often failing, to juggle the daily duties of a farmer's wife with the demands of looking after a boisterous all-male family. Very entertaining, and, of course, set in Slindon.

ISBN 1 903953 27 8 | 200 pp | softback £9.95

20th Century Farmer's Boy by Nick Adames
Nick Adames' unravels the fascinating history of his family, who have farmed in Sussex for over 400 years and still own farms at both Flansham and Madehurst. He entertainingly recounts their fortunes and misfortunes during the last century and recalls the many local people and events they have been involved with over the years. Older Slindonians will doubtless remember 'Buckle' Adames, Nick's uncle, a well-known local character, whose eecentric antics are among the many tales of local interest to be found in this highly enjoyable book.

ISBN 1-903953-01-4 | 388 pp with photos | softback £12.00

Just Visiting by Molly Corbally
Molly Corbally, who was a well-known resident of Slindon for many years, tells of her former life as a District Health Visitor in the early years of that profession, the 1950s & 60s, when the villages around Kenilworth in the Midlands comprised her 'district'. In a series of funny, warm and insightful stories, set in a postwar England now vanished, she describes the many wierd and wonderful personalities her professional life bought her into contact with and how she dealt with their many eccentricities and predicaments.

ISBN 1-903953-06-5 | 300 pp | softback £9.95

A Little School on the Downs by Mary Bowmaker

In 1897, the village school at Sompting on the South Downs above Worthing became the focus of national and international interest due to the revolutionary teaching methods of its headmistress, Harriet Finlay Johnson who invented what she called 'the dramatic method of teaching'. The results she achieved with the village children were outstanding, and soon eductionalists from far and wide were making their way to Sompting to see for themselves the benefits of this new way of teaching. Many of Harriet's ideas would later become part of the 'progressive movement' in eduction. They have been used by teachers all over the United Kingdom and abroad ever since. That such a movement could have its roots in a little Sussex school is truly remarkable, as is the rest of Harriet's story, told here for the first time.

ISBN 1-903953-26-X | 136 pp | softback £9.95

The South Coast Beat Scene of the 1960s by Mike Read

In this very large and meticulously researched book, nationally-known broadcaster Mike Read, originally from Worthing, tells the story of the South Coast's booming popular music scene in the 1960s, with particular reference to the Shoreline, Bognor Regis, the Top Hat, Littlehampton and the Mexican Hat, Worthing, where many local and nationally-known groups played to packed audiences.

Mike's many tales of the optimism, frustration and dedication of the South Coast's budding musicians are illustrated by hundreds of atmospheric photographs, posters and cuttings. They are all here ... from the Aardvarks to the Zabres via The Untamed, Mike Stuart Span, the Beat Merchants, the Detours, the Diamonds, The Pathfinders, Deke Arlon and the Tremors, the Giants, the Chimes, the T-Bones, Mickey and the Sapphires, Steamhammer, the Southbeats, the Web and dozens more... From their ranks emerged Mike Read (ex-Amber), Sir Tim Rice (ex-Aardvarks), Keith Emerson (ex-John Brown's Bodies), Sir Christopher Meyer (now HM Ambassador in Washington DC but a former Shoreline regular) and many more.

The book also features the history of the unique Shoreline Club and 'Teenotel' in Bognor Regis, run by and for teenagers, that for a brief time in the early 60s played host to emerging stars such as Sir Elton John (then Reg Dwight); David Bowie (David Jones), The Who, Brian Auger's Trinity, Jeff Beck, Rod Stewart, Procul Harum, Pink Floyd and many others.

ISBN 1 903953-14-6 | 400+pp | many photos, some in colour | softback £25.00

All books available direct from the publishers
Woodfield Publishing, Babsham Lane, Bognor Regis PO21 5EL
Buy online at www.woodfieldpublishing.com
Or telephone 01243 821234